AF510682

Thermal Analysis with SolidWorks Simulation 2012

***Paul M. Kurowski**, Ph.D., P.Eng.*

ISBN: 978-1-58503-765-0

SolidWorks

SDC PUBLICATIONS

Schroff Development Corporation

Design Generator, Inc.

Schroff Development Corporation
P.O. Box 1334
Mission KS 66222
(913) 262-2664
www.SDCpublications.com
Publisher: Stephen Schroff

Trademarks and Disclaimer

SolidWorks® is a registered trademark of Dassault Systémes SolidWorks Corp.

Microsoft Windows® and its family products are registered trademarks of the Microsoft Corporation.

Every effort has been made to provide an accurate text. The author and the manufacturers shall not be held liable for any parts or products developed with this book or held responsible for any inaccuracies or errors that appear in the book.

Copyright © 2012 by Paul M. Kurowski

All rights reserved. This document may not be copied, photocopied, reproduced, transmitted, or translated in any form or for any purpose without the express written consent of the publisher, Schroff Development Corporation.

IT IS A VIOLATION OF UNITED STATES COPYRIGHT LAWS TO MAKE COPIES IN ANY FORM OR MEDIA OF THE CONTENTS OF THIS BOOK FOR EITHER COMMERCIAL OR EDUCATIONAL PURPOSES WITHOUT EXPRESS WRITTEN PERMISSION.

Examination Copies:

Books received as examination copies are for review purposes only and may not be made available for student use. Resale of examination copies is prohibited.

Electronic Files:

Any electronic files associated with this book are licensed to the original user only. These files may not be transferred to any other party.

About the Author

Dr. Paul Kurowski obtained his M.Sc. and Ph.D. in Applied Mechanics from Warsaw Technical University. He completed postdoctoral work at Kyoto University. Dr. Kurowski is an Assistant Professor in the Department of Mechanical and Materials Engineering, at the University of Western Ontario. His teaching includes Finite Element Analysis, Product Design, Kinematics and Dynamics of Machines and Mechanical Vibrations. His interests focus on Computer Aided Engineering methods used as tools of product design.

Dr. Kurowski is also the President of Design Generator Inc., a consulting firm with expertise in Product Development, Design Analysis, and training in Computer Aided Engineering.

Dr. Kurowski has published many technical papers and taught professional development seminars for SAE International, the American Society of Mechanical Engineers (ASME), the Association of Professional Engineers of Ontario (PEO), the Parametric Technology Corporation (PTC), Rand Worldwide, SolidWorks Corporation and others.

Dr. Kurowski is a member of the Association of Professional Engineers of Ontario and SAE International. He can be contacted at www.designgenerator.com

Acknowledgements

I would like to thank the students attending my various courses for their valuable comments and questions. I would like to thank Tom Kurowski for editing and proof reading the text and the exercises. I thank my wife Elżbieta for her technical support and encouragement that made it possible to write this book.

Paul Kurowski

Table of contents

Notes:

Before You Start

Notes on hands-on exercises and functionality of Simulation

This book goes beyond a standard software manual. It takes a unique approach by bridging the theory of heat transfer with examples showing the practical implementation of thermal analysis. This book builds on material covered in "**Engineering Analysis with SolidWorks Simulation 2012**".

We recommend that you study the exercises in the order presented in the book. As you go through the exercises, you will notice that explanations and steps described in detail in earlier exercises are not repeated in later chapters. Each subsequent exercise assumes familiarity with software functions discussed in previous exercises and builds on the skills, experience, and understanding gained from previously presented problems.

The functionality of **SolidWorks Simulation** depends on which software **Simulation** product is used. The functionality of different products is explained in the following **Simulation** Product Matrix:

	SOLIDWORKS PREMIUM	SOLIDWORKS SIMULATION PROFESSIONAL	SOLIDWORKS SIMULATION PREMIUM	SOLIDWORKS FLOW SIMULATION
Tolerance Stack-Up Analysis	■	■	■	
Assembly Simulation	■	■	■	
Mechanism Analysis		■	■	
Event-Based Motion		■	■	
Compare and Optimize Design		■	■	■
Simulate Natural Frequencies		■	■	
Predict Buckling or Collapse		■	■	
Simulate Heating or Cooling		■	■	■
Simulate Drop Test		■	■	
Simulate Fatigue		■	■	
Simulate Plastic and Rubber Components			■	
Simulate Composites			■	
Simulate Forced Vibrations			■	
Nonlinear Dynamics			■	
Fluid Flow Simulation			■	■

Information on **SolidWorks** and **Simulation** bundles is available at: www.solidworks.com/sw/products/10169_ENU_HTML.htm

Exercises presented in this book require **SolidWorks Simulation Professional.** All exercises in this book use **SolidWorks** models, which can be downloaded from www.SDCpublications.com. These exercises do not contain any **Simulation** studies; you are expected to create all studies, results plots, and graphs yourself. All problems presented here have been solved with **SolidWorks Simulation Premium** running on Windows 7 in a 64 bit operating environment.

We encourage you to explore each exercise beyond its description by investigating other options, other menu choices, and other ways to present results. You will soon discover that the same simple logic applies to all functions in **SolidWorks Simulation**, be it structural or thermal analysis.

This book is not intended to replace software manuals. Therefore, not all Thermal Analysis capabilities with **Simulation** are covered. The knowledge acquired by the reader will not be strictly software specifics. The same concepts, tools and methods apply to any FEA software.

Prerequisites

"**Thermal Analysis with SolidWorks 2012**" is not an introductory text to **SolidWorks Simulation**. Rather, it picks up Thermal Analysis from where it was left in the pre-requisite textbook "**Engineering Analysis with SolidWorks 2012**". If you are new to **SolidWorks Simulation** we recommend to use "**Engineering Analysis with SolidWorks 2012**" to gain essential familiarity with Finite Element Analysis at the very least go through chapters 1, 2, 3, 7, 8, 11 of that pre-requisite textbook.

The following prerequisites are recommended:

- An understanding of Heat Transfer analysis
- An understanding of Structural analysis
- An understanding of Solid Mechanics
- Familiarity with **SolidWorks Simulation** to the extend covered in "**Engineering Analysis with SolidWorks 2012**" or equivalent experience
- Familiarity with the Windows Operating System

Selected terminology

The mouse pointer plays a very important role in executing various commands and providing user feedback. The mouse pointer is used to execute commands, select geometry, and invoke pop-up menus. We use Windows terminology when referring to mouse-pointer actions.

Item	Description
Click	Self-explanatory
Double-click	Self-explanatory
Click-inside	Click the left mouse button. Wait a second, and then click the left mouse button inside the pop-up menu or text box. Use this technique to modify the names of folders and icons in **SolidWorks Simulation** Manager.
Drag and drop	Use the mouse to point to an object. Press and hold the left mouse button down. Move the mouse pointer to a new location. Release the left mouse button.
Right-click	Click the right mouse button. A pop-up menu is displayed. Use the left mouse button to select a desired menu command.

All **SolidWorks** file names appear in CAPITAL letters, even though the actual file names may use a combination of capital and small letters. Selected menu items and **SolidWorks Simulation** commands appear in **bold**, **SolidWorks** configurations**, SolidWorks Simulation** folders, icon names and study names appear in *italics* except in captions and comments to illustrations. **SolidWorks** and **Simulation** also appear in bold font. Bold font may also be used to draw reader's attention to a particular term.

Notes:

1: Introduction

Topics covered

- Heat transfer by conduction
- Heat transfer by convection
- Heat transfer by radiation
- Thermal boundary conditions
- Analogies between thermal and structural analysis
- Thermal elements: solids and shells
- Scalar and vector entities, presenting results
- Steady state thermal analysis
- Transient thermal analysis
- Linear thermal analysis
- Nonlinear thermal analysis

What is Thermal Analysis?

Thermal analysis deals with heat transfer in solid bodies. We approach thermal analysis from the perspective of a user experienced in structural analysis such as static, modal, buckling etc. as implemented in **SolidWorks Simulation**. You will soon notice that experience in structural analysis is directly transferable to thermal analysis because of the close analogies between structural and thermal analyses. The temperature is analogous to displacement in structural analysis, strain to temperature gradient, and stress to heat flux. Selected analogies are summarized in Figure 1-1.

Structural Analysis	**Thermal Analysis**
Displacement [m]	Temperature [K]
Strain [1]	Temperature gradient [K/m]
Stress [N/m^2]	Heat flux [W/m^2]
Load [N] [N/m] [N/m^2] [N/m^3]	Heat source [W] [W/m] [W/m^2] [W/m^3]
Prescribed displacement [m]	Prescribed temperature [K]
Pressure [N/m^2]	Prescribed heat flux [W/m^2]
Hook's law: $\sigma = E\frac{du}{dx}$	Fourier's law: $q = -k\frac{dT}{dx}$
Stiffness matrix	Conductivity matrix

Figure 1-1: Analogies between structural and thermal analyses with units in SI system.

Different system of units may be used except of radiation problems where temperature is absolute and must be expressed in Kelvins.

The primary unknown in structural analysis is displacement; the primary unknown in thermal analysis is temperature. This leads to an important difference between structural and thermal analysis performed with the finite element method. Displacement, which is a vector and includes both translation and rotation requires up to six degrees of freedom per node. The number of degrees of freedom in structural analysis depends on the type of elements, for example solid elements have three degrees of freedom and shell elements have six degrees of freedom per node. Two dimensional structural elements have two degrees of freedom per node. Temperature is a scalar and requires only one degree of freedom per node, regardless of element type. This makes thermal problems much easier to solve because thermal models typically have fewer degrees of freedom as compared to structural models.

Another, conceptual difference is that thermal analysis is never a "static" analysis. If heat flow does not change, then the problem is "steady state analysis" and not static because heat flow never stops. If heat flow changes with time, then problem is called transient.

Mechanisms of heat transfer

Conduction

In a solid body, the energy is transferred from a high temperature region to a low temperature region. The rate of heat transfer per unit area is proportional to the material thermal conductivity, cross sectional area and temperature gradient in the normal direction; it is inversely proportional to the distance (Figure 1-2). This mode of heat transfer is referred to as conduction:

$$Q_{COND} = kA(T_{HOT} - T_{COLD})/L$$

Where:

Q_{COND} – Heat transferred by conduction [W]

k – Thermal conductivity [W/m/K]

A – Cross sectional area [m^2]

T_{HOT} – Temperature on the hot side [K]

T_{COLD} – Temperature on the cold side [K]

L – Distance of heat travel [m]

Conduction is responsible for heat transfer inside a solid body.

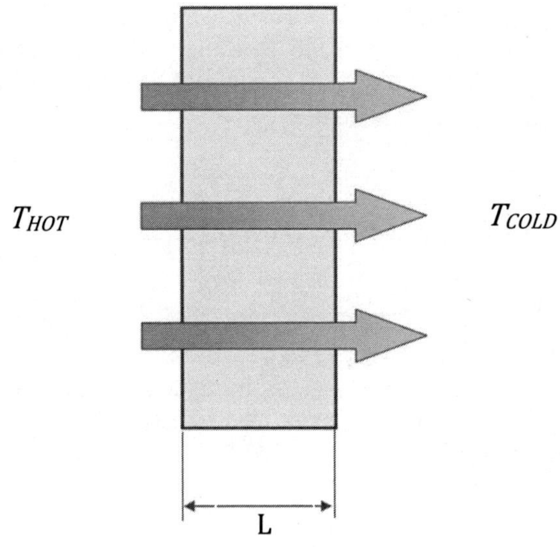

Figure 1-2: Heat transfer by conduction.

Conduction is responsible for heat transfer inside a solid body.

Thermal conductivity is vastly different for different materials as shown in Figure 1-3.

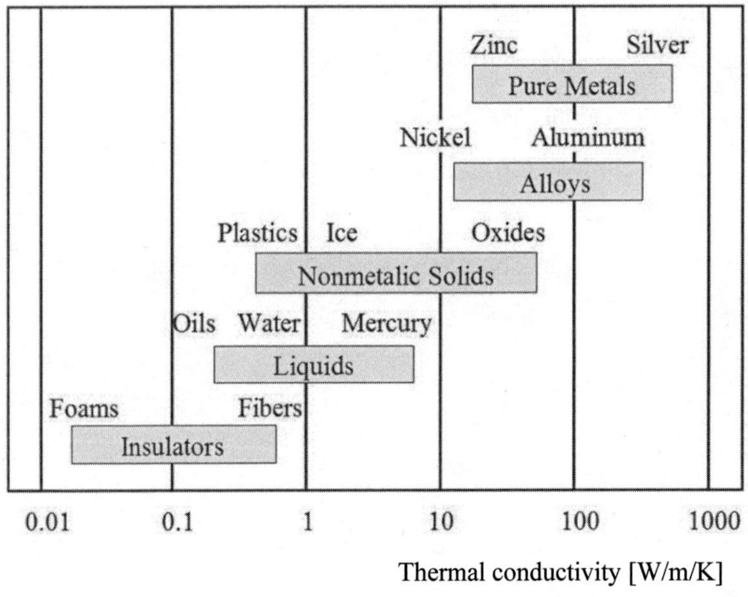

Figure 1-3: Thermal conductivity for different materials.

There are five orders of magnitude difference in thermal conductivity between the best conductors and best insulators.

Convection

Convective heat transfer is the heat flow between a solid body and the surrounding fluid (either liquid or gas). Convective heat transfer can be either natural convection where the fluid flow is due to the variation in specific weight of a hot and cold fluid, or forced convection where the fluid is forced to flow past the solid body. Therefore, natural convection requires gravity (Figure 1-4), and forced convection does not require gravity (Figure 1-5). Since fluid (air, water, steam, oil etc.) is required for heat transfer by convection, this type of heat transfer cannot happen in vacuum. Heat exchanged by convection is expressed as:

$$Q_{CONV} = hA(T_S - T_F)$$

Where:

Q_{CONV} – Heat transferred by convection [W]

h – Convection coefficient [W/m^2/K]

A – Surface area [m^2]

T_S – Surface temperature [K]

T_F - Fluid bulk temperature [K]

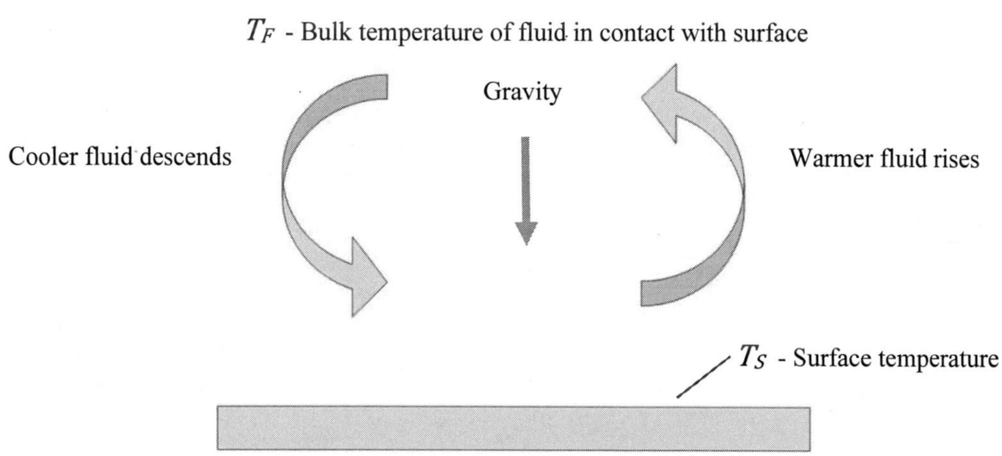

Figure 1-4: Heat transfer by natural convection.

Convective heat transfer can take place only in the presence of fluid and gravity.

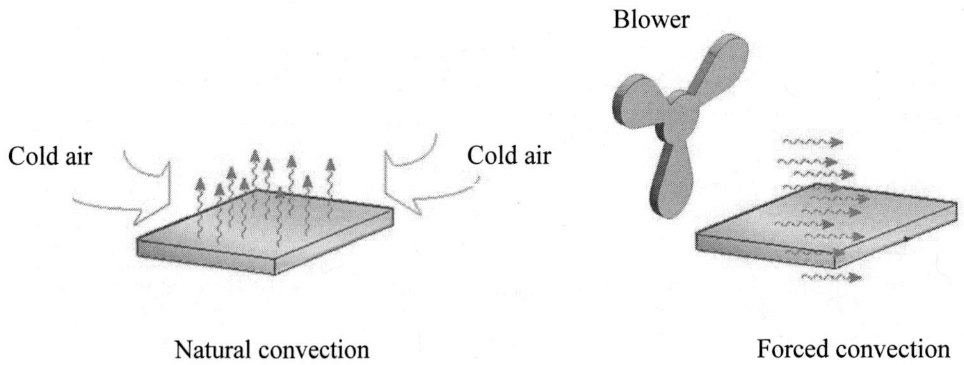

Figure 1-5: Natural and forced convection.

Forced convection doesn't require gravity

The magnitude of the convection coefficient strongly depends on the medium (fluid) surrounding a solid body (Figure1-6).

Medium	Convection coefficient $W/m^2/K$
Air (natural convection)	5-25
Air/superheated steam	20-300
Oil (forced convection)	60-1800
Water (forced convection)	300-6000
Water (boiling)	3000-60000
Steam (condensing)	6000-120000

Figure 1-6: Convection coefficient for different media.

There are five orders of difference in convection coefficients between different media and type of convection.

Radiation

Radiation heat transfer occurs between a solid body and the ambient or between two solid bodies without presence of any medium (fluid). This is the only type of heat transfer that occurs in a vacuum. Heat flows by electromagnetic radiation. The upper limit to the emissive power is a back body radiating heat and is prescribed by the Stefan-Boltzmann law:

$$q = \sigma T_S^4$$

Where:

q – Heat flux (heat emitted by radiation per unit of area) [W/m^2]

σ – Stefan-Boltzmann constant = 5.67x10^{-9} [W/m^2/K^4]

T_S – Surface temperature [K]

The heat flux emitted by a real surface is less than that of a black body at the same temperature. It is given as:

$$q = \varepsilon \sigma T_S^4,$$

where ε is a radiative property of a surface called emissivity. Values of ε are in the range of $0 \leq \varepsilon \leq 1$ and provide a measure of how well the surface emits radiative energy in comparison to a black body. It depends strongly on the surface material and finish. For example a polished aluminum surface has an emissivity of about 0.05; an oxidized aluminum surface has an emissivity of 0.25. The emissivity also depends on the temperature of the face emitting heat by radiation.

In heat transfer by radiation, heat may be radiated out to space by a single body; it may be exchanged between two bodies or it may be exchanged between two bodies as well as radiated out to space (Figure 1-7).

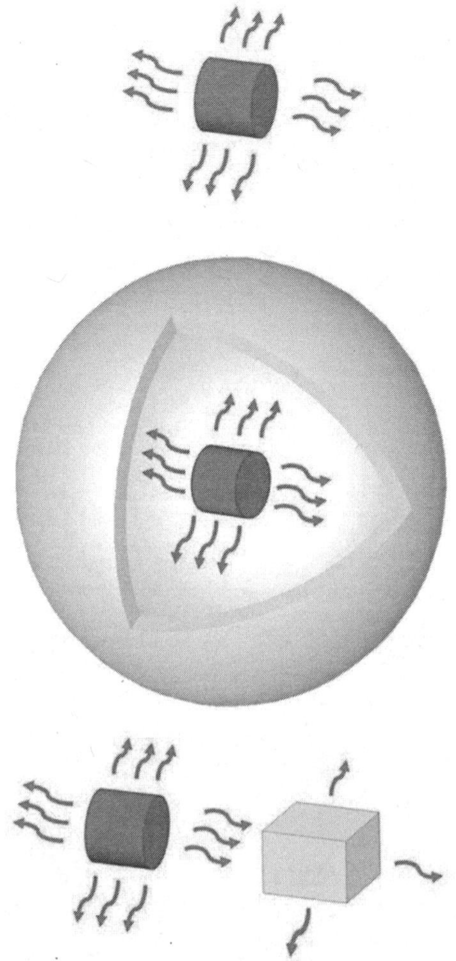

(1)
Heat radiated out to space

(2)
Heat radiated from one body to another body

(3)
Heat radiated from one body to another body and to space

Figure 1-7: Different cases of heat transfer by radiation.

If heat is exchanged between two bodies only and not radiated out to space, then one body must be fully enclosed by the other body (2). Heat gained by radiation may be radiated out again into space (3).

Having introduced three mechanisms of heat transfer we need to make a very important statement. With **SolidWorks Simulation** which uses finite element method, only heat transfer by conduction is modeled directly. Convection and radiation are modeled as boundary conditions. This is done by defining convection and/or radiation coefficients to faces that participate in heat exchange between the model and the environment.

The next two examples show how a prescribed temperature, convection and heat load work together to induce heat flow inside a solid body. These examples are not hands-on exercises. Hands-on exercises will start in chapter 2.

Heat Flow Induced By Prescribed Temperatures

Just like stresses may be caused by prescribed displacement, heat flow may be induced by temperature differences defined by prescribed temperatures. Consider the model BRACKET TH with different temperatures defined on two faces as shown in Figure 1-8. Note that the temperature field establishes itself in the model but heat flow continues due to temperature gradients. Also notice that no heat escapes from the model because we have not defined any mechanism to exchange heat through any surfaces other than the two faces with prescribed temperatures. This implies that model is perfectly insulated, except for two faces where prescribed temperatures are defined.

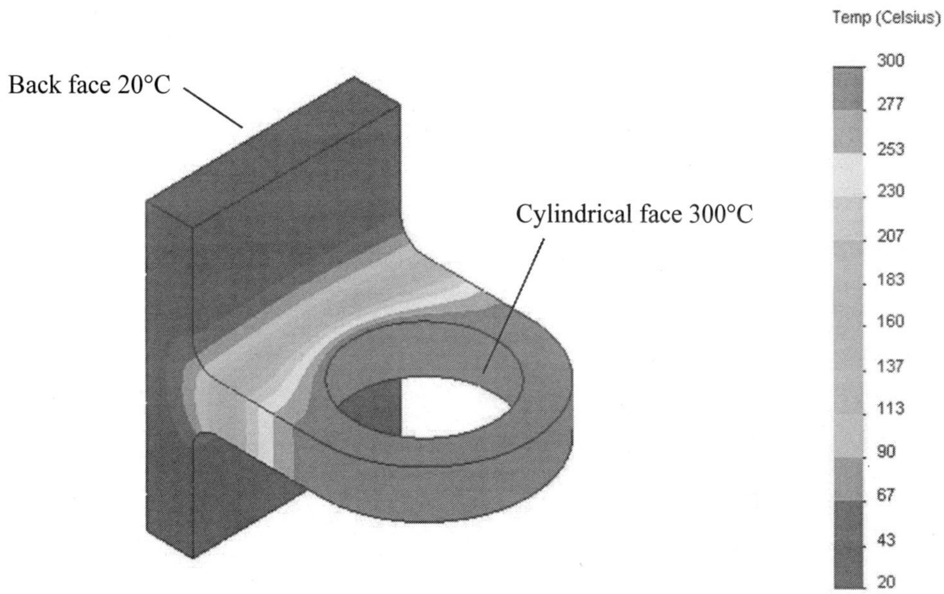

Figure 1-8: Temperature distribution in the model where heat flow is induced by prescribed temperatures.

A temperature of 300°C is applied to the cylindrical face, and a temperature of 20°C is applied to the back face.

This may correspond to a situation where the bracket holding a hot pipe is mounted on a cold surface and heat escaping through faces exposed to air is negligible.

Heat flow induced by heat load and convection

Heat flow can also be induced by the applied heat load. The unit of heat load applied to a surface is called heat flux; heat flowing through an imaginary cross-section is also called heat flux. Total heat applied to a volume or face is called heat power. Notice that since thermal analysis deals with heat flow, a mechanism for that heat flow to occur must be in place. In the heat sink problem HEAT SINK01 shown in Figure 1-9 heat enters the radiator model through the base, as defined by the applied heat power which is a close analogy to force load in structural analysis. Convection coefficients [W/m^2/K], also called film coefficients, are defined for all remaining surfaces and provide the way to remove heat from the model. Heat enters the model through the base where heat power is defined. Heat escapes the model through faces where convection coefficients are defined.

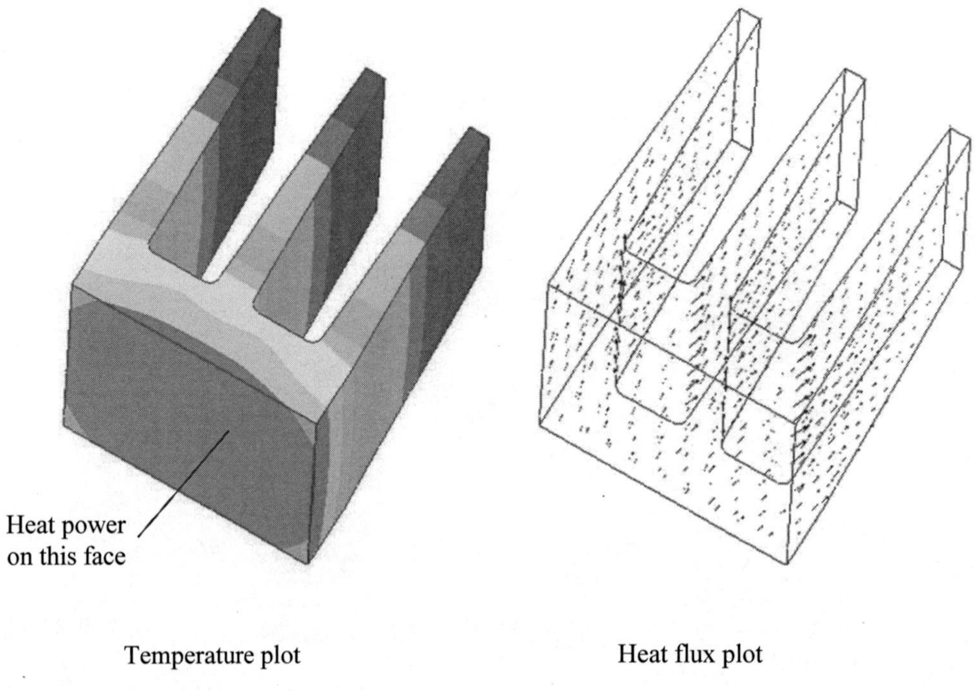

Figure 1-9: Temperature distribution and heat flux in a heat sink model.

A temperature plot being a scalar quantity can be only shown using a fringe display. Heat flux is a vector quantity and can be illustrated either by a fringe plot or vector plot. Notice that arrows "coming out" of the walls illustrate heat that escapes the model because of convection.

The structural analogy of convection coefficients is a bit less intuitive. Convection coefficients are analogous to elastic support offered by distributed springs. Just like supports and/or prescribed displacements are necessary to establish model equilibrium in structural analysis problem, convection coefficients and/or prescribed temperatures are necessary to establish heat flow in thermal analysis problem. Indeed, an attempt to run thermal analysis with heat loads but with no convection coefficients or prescribed temperatures results in an error similar to the one caused by the absence of supports in structural analysis.

Modeling considerations in thermal analysis

Symmetry boundary conditions can be used in thermal analysis based on the observation that if symmetry exists in both geometry and boundary conditions, then there is no heat flowing through a plane of symmetry. After simplifying the model to ½ in case of single symmetry or to ¼ in case of double symmetry (Figure 1-10), nothing needs to be done to surfaces exposed by cuts. No convection coefficients defined for those surfaces means that no heat flows across them.

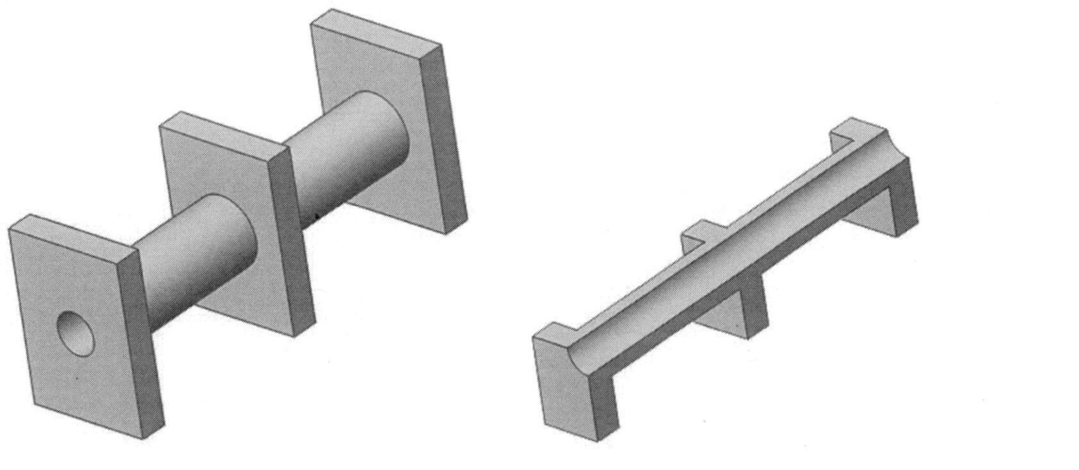

Full model ¼ model

Figure 1-10: Model DOUBLE SYM with double symmetry can be simplified to ¼ of its size.

No thermal boundary conditions are applied to faces in the place of symmetry.

Axisymmetric problems may be represented by 2D models as shown in Figure 1-11.

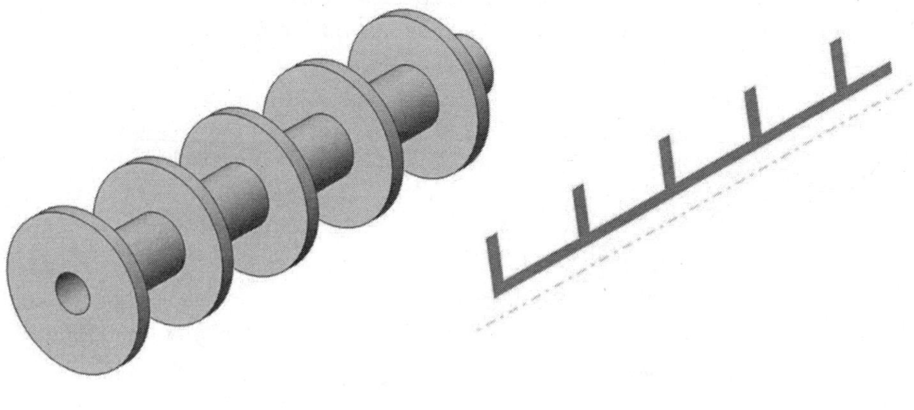

Full model 2D cross section in the axis of symmetry

Figure 1-11: Axisymmetric model AXISYM may be represented by a 2D cross section.

Notice that models DOUBLE SYM (Figure 1-10) and AXISYM (Figure 1-11) are suitable for analysis of temperature, but because of sharp re-entrant edges, they are not suitable for analysis of heat flux in the vicinity of the sharp re-entrant edges because heat flux there is singular. This is in direct analogy to sharp re-entrant edges causing stress singularities in structural models.

One you acquire sufficient familiarity with thermal analysis you are encouraged to analyze models BRACKET TH, HEAT SINK01, DOUBLE SYM and AXISYM using thermal parameters of your choice.

Let's wrap up this review with an important observation which will serve as a guide to all thermal analysis problems. In structural analysis we define a load path by defining loads and supports. In a heat transfer problem, we define a mechanism of heat transfer; we must know how heat enters the model, how it travels through the model and how it exits the model.

Types of thermal analysis

Thermal analysis may be linear or nonlinear, steady state or time-dependent as shown in Figure 1-12.

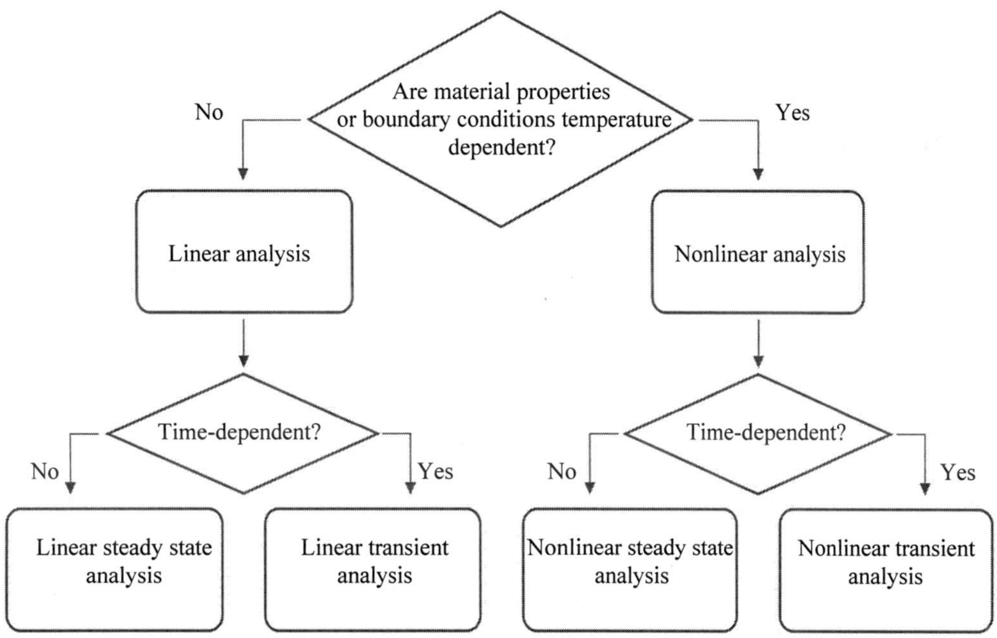

Figure 1-12: Types of thermal analyses.

In linear analysis, the conductivity matrix does not change during the solution process, in nonlinear analysis it must be modified because material properties and/or boundary conditions are temperature dependent. In steady state analysis, material conditions and boundary conditions do not change with time; in time dependent (transient) they do change.

We will be working with all of types of thermal analyses shown in Figure 1-12.

Thermal analysis with SolidWorks Simulation

SolidWorks Simulation uses methods of finite element analysis to solve both structural and thermal problems. CAD models prepared in **SolidWorks** are discretized (meshed) into finite elements which type depends on the type of geometry prepared in **SolidWorks**. Solid bodies are meshed into solid elements; Surface bodies are meshed into shell elements; 2D axisymmetric and extruded models are meshed into corresponding 2D elements. Types of finite elements, meshing techniques and other mesh specific considerations are discussed in details in the pre-requisite text "**Engineering Analysis with SolidWorks Simulation 2012**". Here we limit our review to thermal analysis specific issues.

Elements available in thermal analysis with **SolidWorks Simulation** are shown in Figure 1-13. Notice that beam elements are not available in thermal analysis.

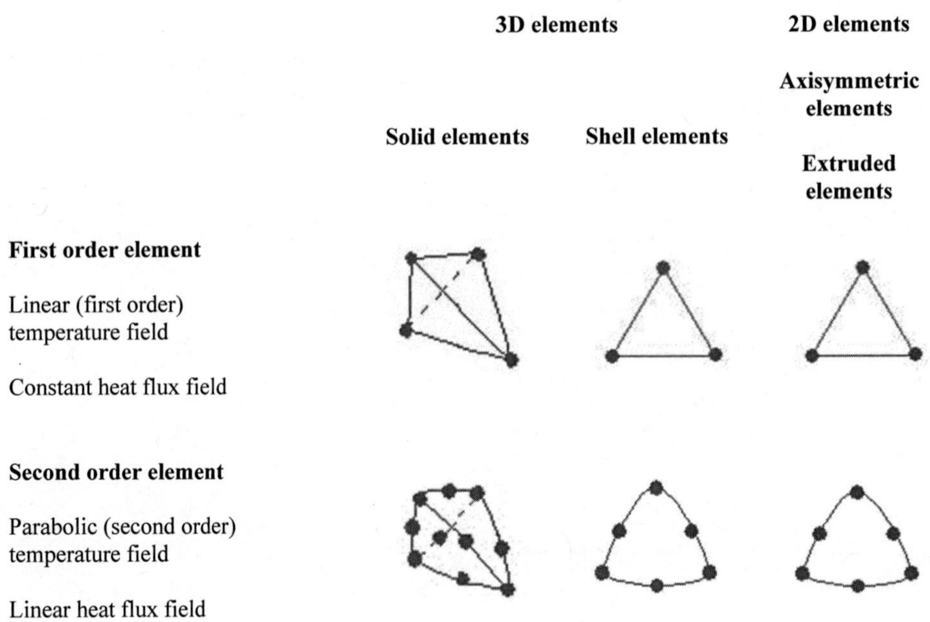

Figure 1-13: Elements available in thermal analysis with SolidWorks Simulation.

The majority of analyses use the second order tetrahedral element.

First order elements do not offer any advantages in either structural or thermal analysis and beam elements are neither applicable nor available in thermal analysis. Therefore we are left with second order solids and second order shells to model 3D problems and second order plate elements to model 2D axisymmetric or extruded problems.

Prior to commencing work with thermal problems, make sure that **Solid Bodies** and **Surface Bodies** are visible in the **SolidWorks** Feature Manager (Figure 1-14).

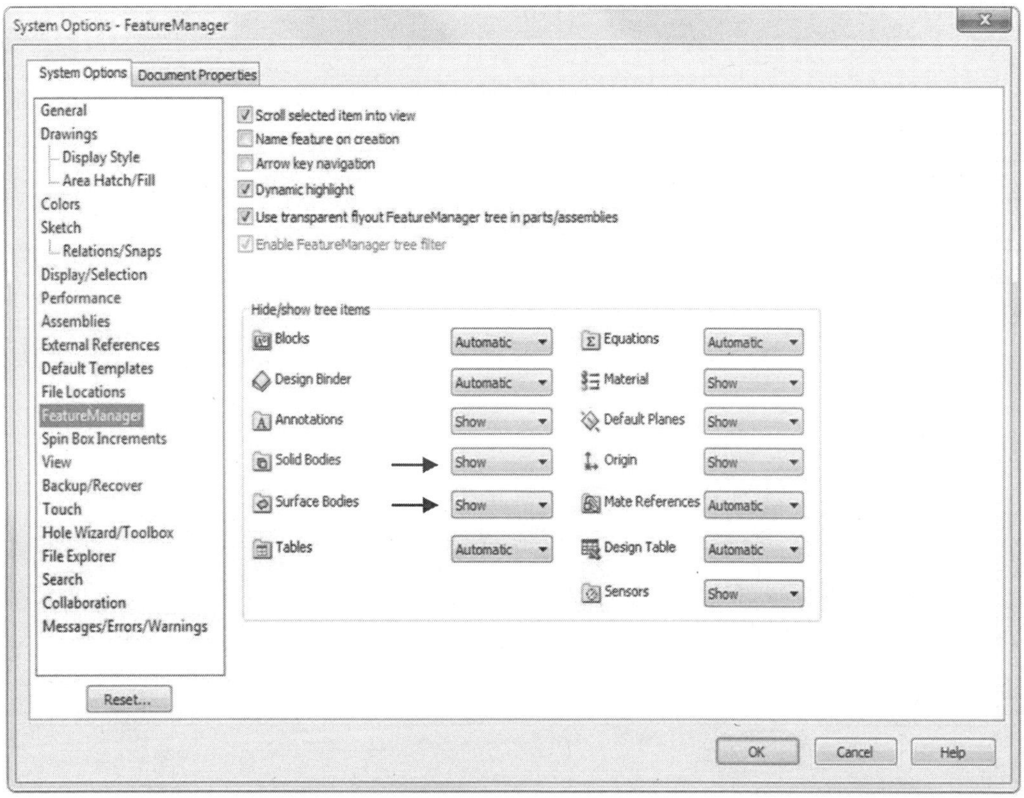

Figure 1-14: Settings of Feature Manager.

To facilitate working with Simulation models make sure that Solid Bodies and Surface Bodies are always visible.

Notes:

2: Hollow plate

Topics covered

- Heat transfer by conduction
- Heat transfer by convection
- Different ways of presenting results of thermal analysis
- Convergence analysis in thermal problems
- Solid elements in heat transfer problems
- Shell elements in heat transfer problems

Project description

We'll conduct thermal analysis of simple models to study the effects of discretization error and the use of different types of elements. In this chapter we use our expertise in structural analysis gained from "**Engineering Analysis with SolidWorks Simulation 2012**". We use HOLLOW PLATE TH, similar to the model from this introductory textbook where it is used in structural analysis examples.

Open model HOLLOW PLATE TH and review the two configurations: *01 solid* where the model is represented as a solid body and *02 shell* where the model is represented as a surface body. Stay in the *01 solid* configuration and create a thermal study called *01 solid.* Apply the prescribed temperature boundary conditions as shown in Figure 2-1; these prescribed temperatures will induce heat flow from hot to cold.

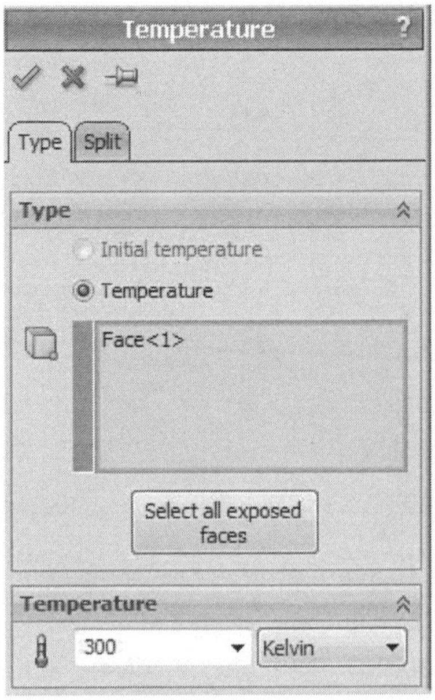

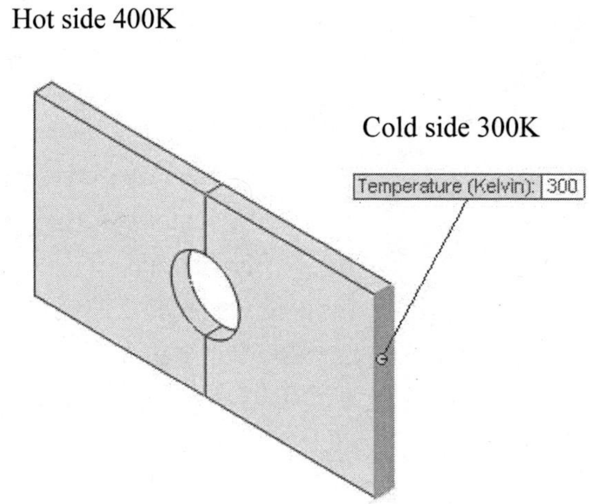

Figure 2-1: Prescribed temperatures boundary conditions applied to the cold side.

No convection is defined anywhere in the model meaning that all faces are insulated except where temperature boundary conditions are defined.

Repeat the definition of the prescribed temperature on the hot side where it is 400K. Mesh the model with a coarse mesh as shown in Figure 2-2.

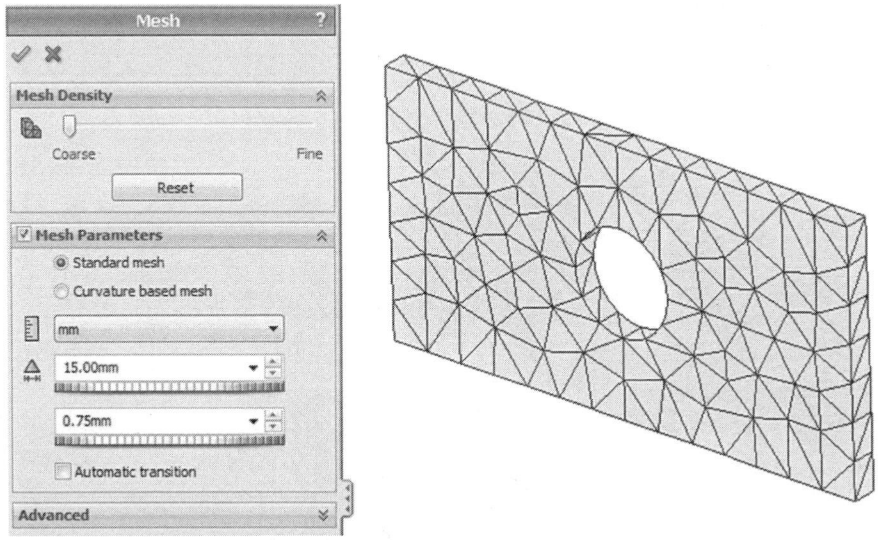

Figure 2-2: Coarse mesh created with 15mm element size

Use Standard mesh; do not use Draft quality elements. This mesh is coarse; it is used only as the first step in the convergence process.

Run the solution and create two plots: **Temperature** and **Resultant Heat Flux**, probe results as shown in Figure 2-3 and Figure 2-4.

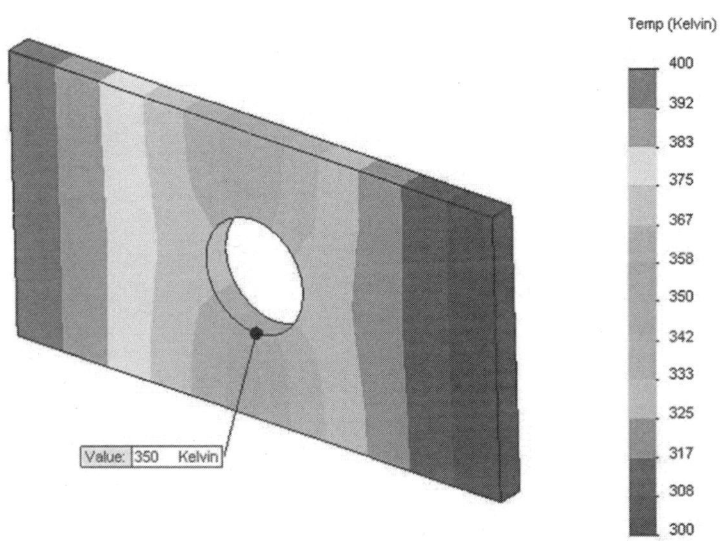

Figure 2-3: Temperature results: 350K in the probed location.

Probe at the vertex created by the split line.

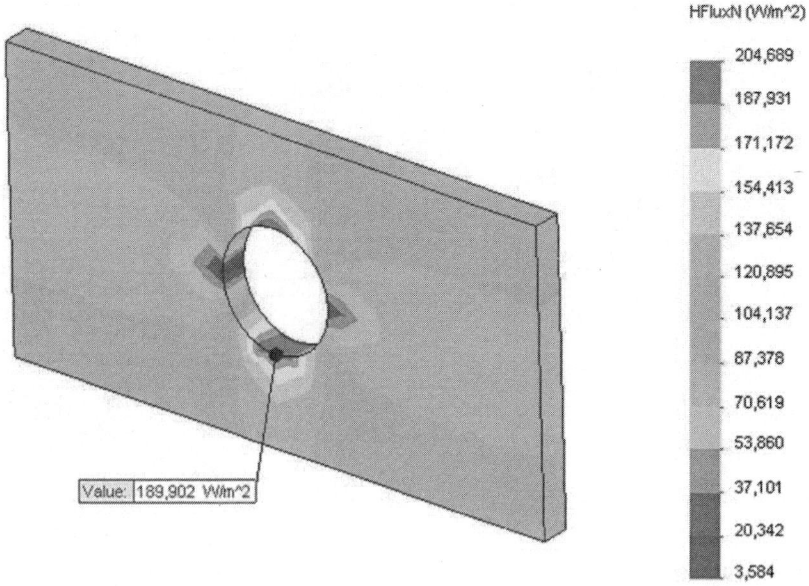

Figure 2-4: Resultant heat flux results: 189902W/m^2 in the probed location.

Probe at the vertex created by the split line.

Repeat the analysis using a mesh of default size 5.72mm (study *02 solid*) and a fine mesh with element size 2mm (study *03 solid*). Optionally try meshing the model with 1mm element size but be prepared for a long run. Notice that while temperature results are almost insensitive to mesh refinement, the resultant heat flux changes with mesh refinement as shown in Figure 2-5.

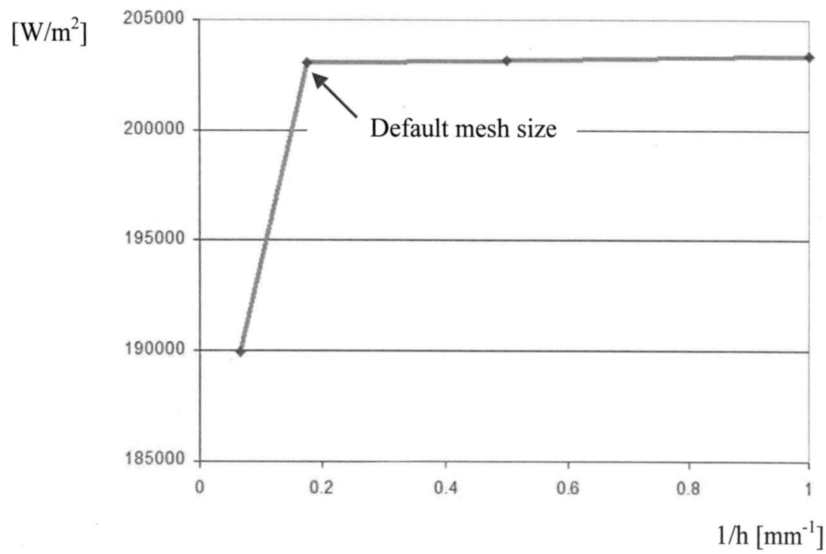

Figure 2-5: Resultant heat flux in the probed location as a function of the inverse of element size.

Four points are connected by line only to visually enhance the graph.

As the graph in Figure 2-5 demonstrates, the heat flux converges to a finite value and the default element size produces acceptable results. What should also be noticed is that every given mesh introduces artificial thermal resistance; the coarser the mesh the larger that added resistance is and that causes lower heat flux. This is the effect of discretization error in direct analogy to structural models where artificial stiffness is added to model by discretization (meshing).

Copy study *02 solid* (the one with default mesh) into study *05 solid convection.* We'll use it to demonstrate convective heat transfer out of the plate. Delete prescribed temperature on the cold size. In its place define **Convection** as shown in Figure 2-6.

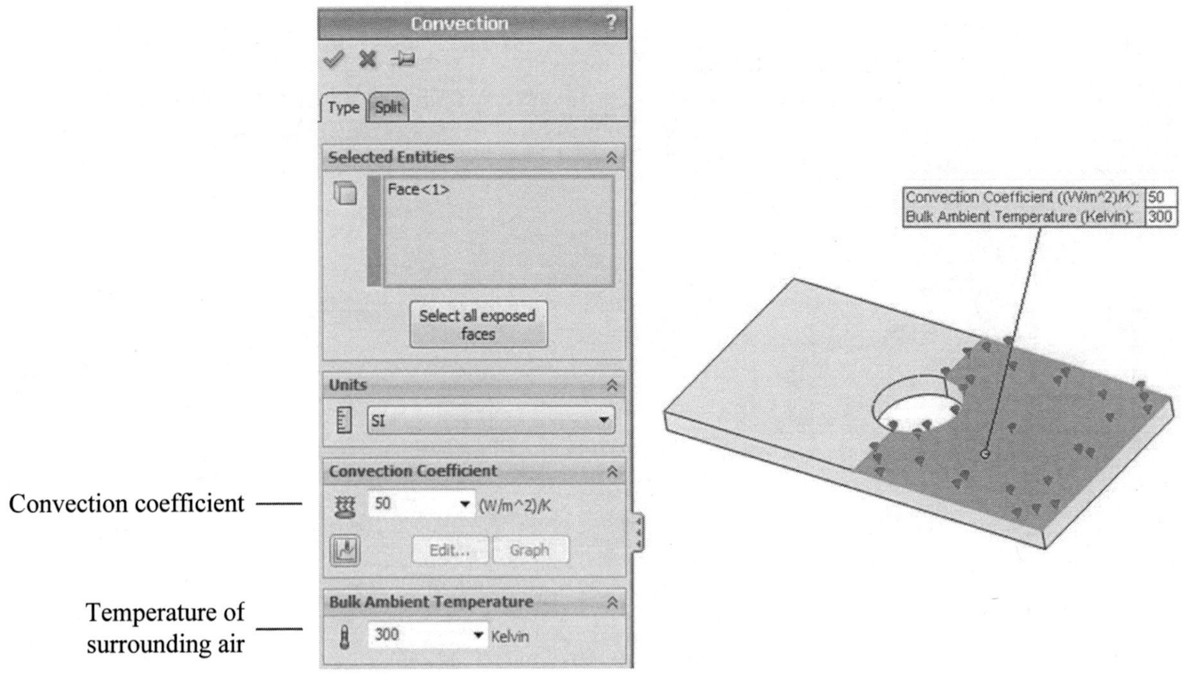

Figure 2-6: Definition of convection on ½ of one side.

As always, definition of convection requires a convection coefficient and bulk temperature which is the temperature of the fluid surrounding the model.

A convection coefficient of 50W/m²/K corresponds to free convection with air.

Run the solution of study *05 solid convection* and obtain results as shown in Figure 2-7.

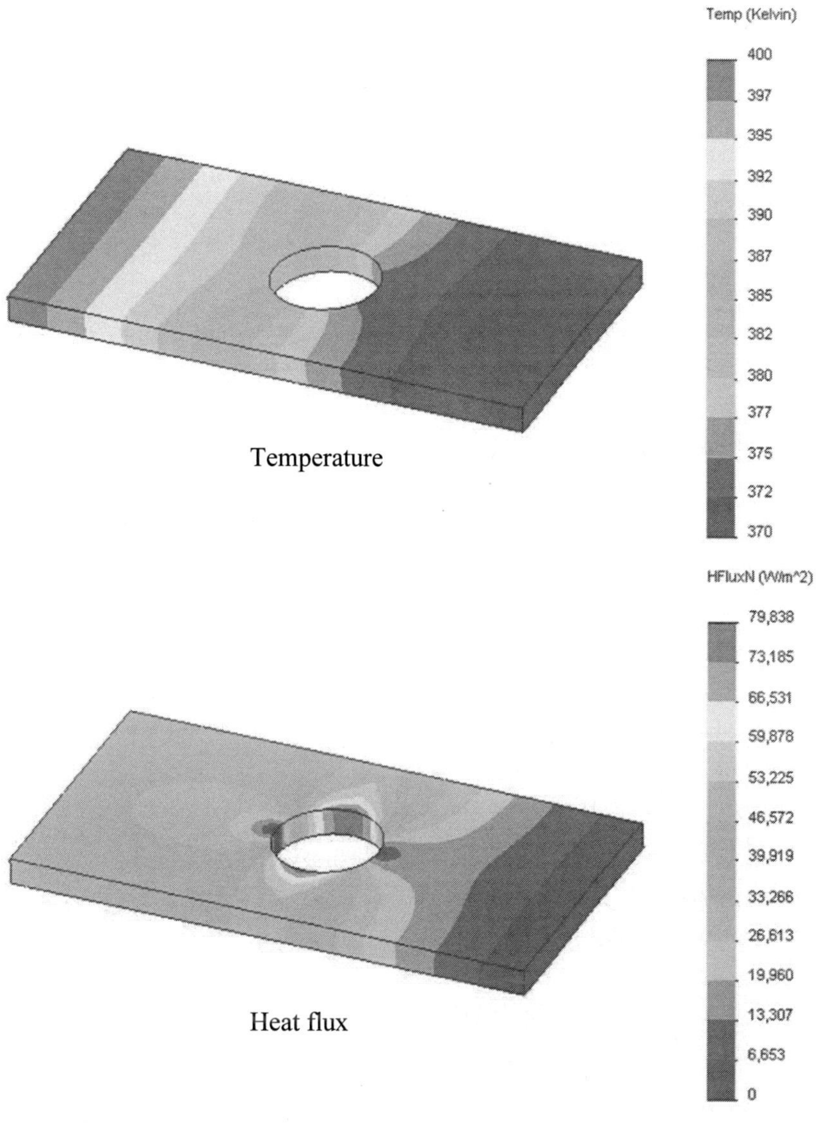

Figure 2-7: Temperature and heat flux results in the presence of convection.

Temperature is a scalar value and can be only plotted using a fringe plots above. Heat flux is a vector value; presenting it as a fringe plot shows only the magnitude but not the direction of heat flow.

Modify the heat flux plot into a vector plot as shown in Figure 2-8.

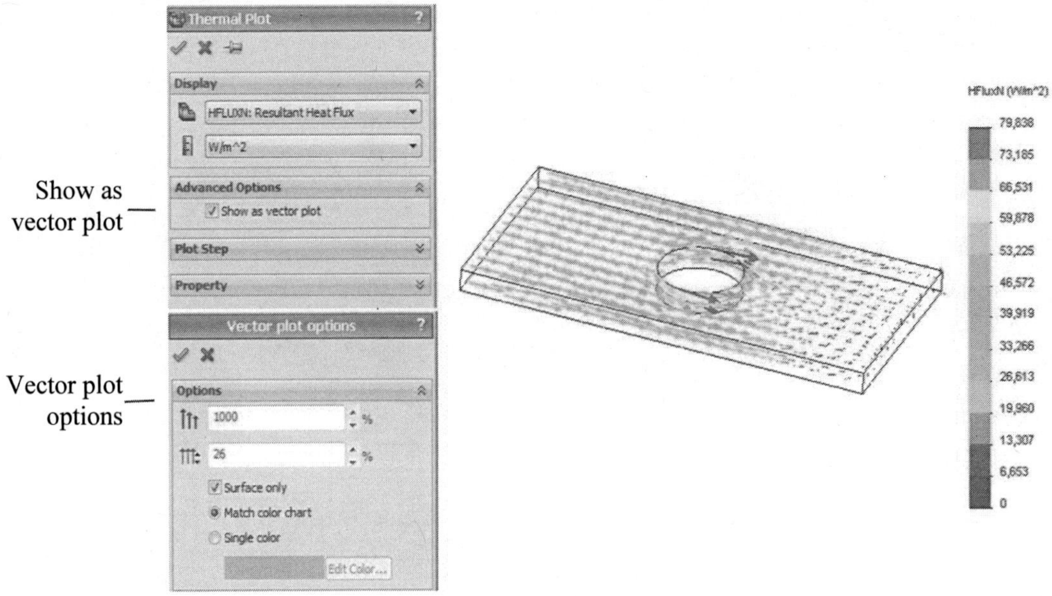

Figure 2-8: Heat flux results presented as a vector plot display the direction of heat flow.

Rotate the plot as required to see vectors "coming out" of the model through the face where convection conditions have been defined.

You may want to review the results of other studies with heat flux results shown as a vector plot.

Having demonstrated analogies between the convergence process in structural and thermal analyses using solid elements, we'll now study the use of shell element in thermal analysis.

Stay with model HOLLOW PLATE TH but switch to *02 surface* configuration. Create a thermal study *06 surface convection*. Define the surface thickness as shown in Figure 2-9.

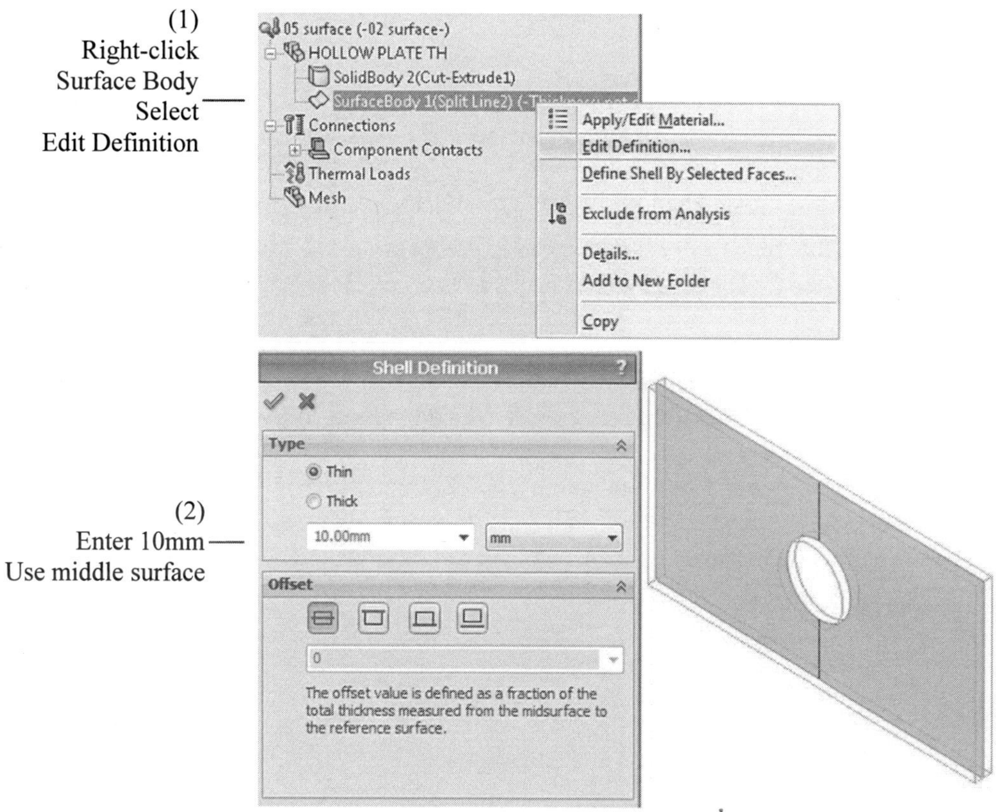

Figure 2-9: Definition of surface thickness.

The definition of thickness is required because thickness is not specified in the surface CAD model. Thermal analysis does not distinguish between Thin and Thick shell element formulation.

Follow steps in Figure 2-10 to eliminate the **Solid Body** from the analysis.

Right-click
Solid Body
Select
Exclude from Analysis

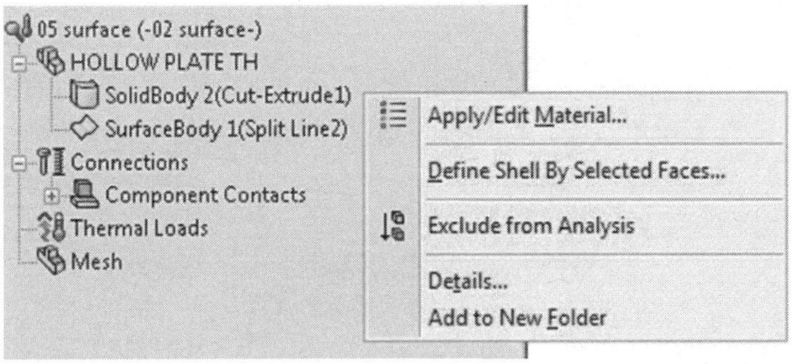

Figure 2-10: Exclusion of the Solid Body from the analysis.

Even though the Solid Body was made invisible in the CAD model, it still forms a part of the CAD geometry and needs to be excluded from the analysis.

Apply thermal boundary conditions as in study *05 solid convection*: a prescribed temperature of 400K on the hot side (the edge) and convection to the side face as shown in Figure 2-6. Use the default element size to mesh the model into shell elements, obtain a solution and present **Temperature** and **Heat Flux** results using fringe plots (Figure 2-11).

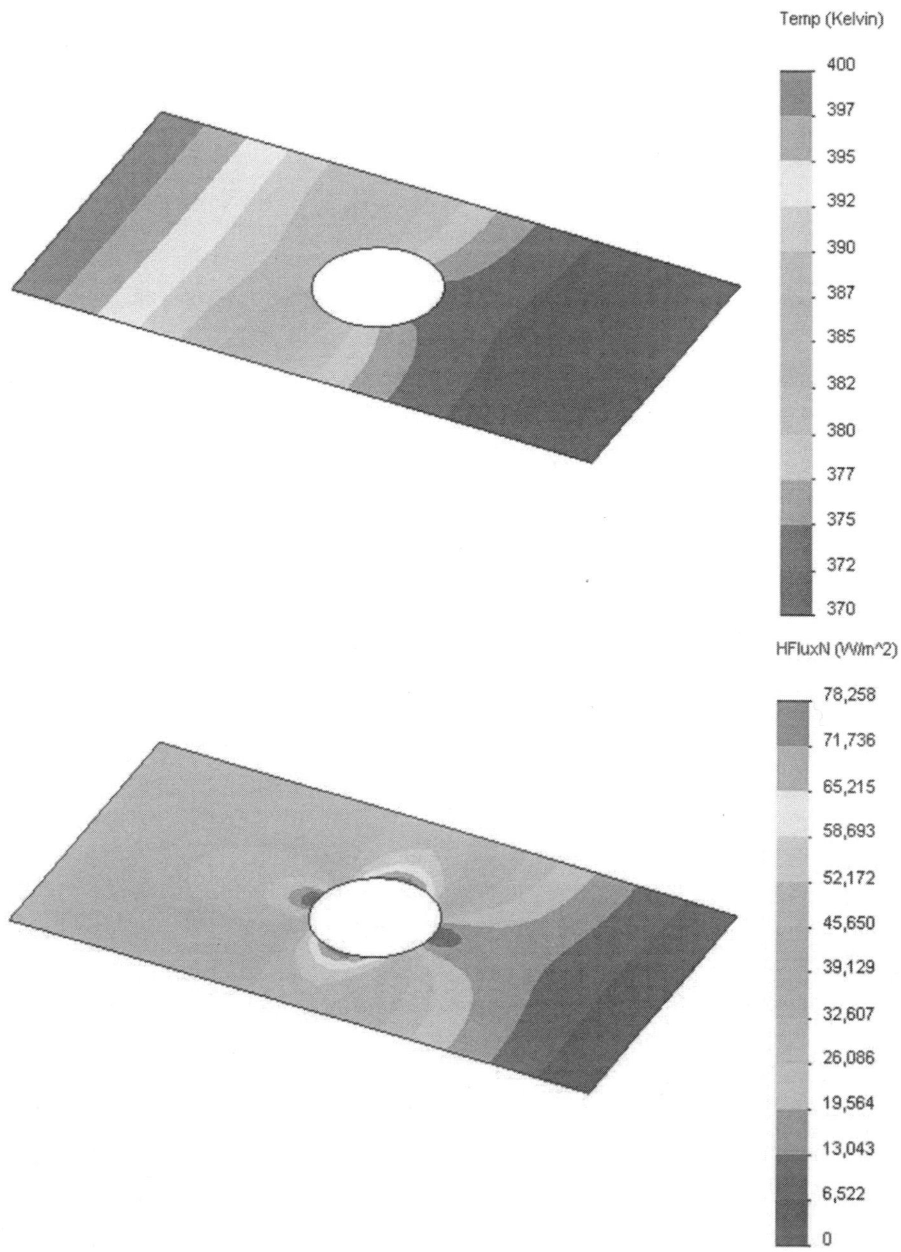

Figure 2-11: Temperature and heat flux results from the shell element model presented as fringe plots.

These results are very similar to the results produced by the solid element model.

While fringe plots show little difference between results obtained from the solid element and shell element models, vector plots do show important differences (Figure 2-12).

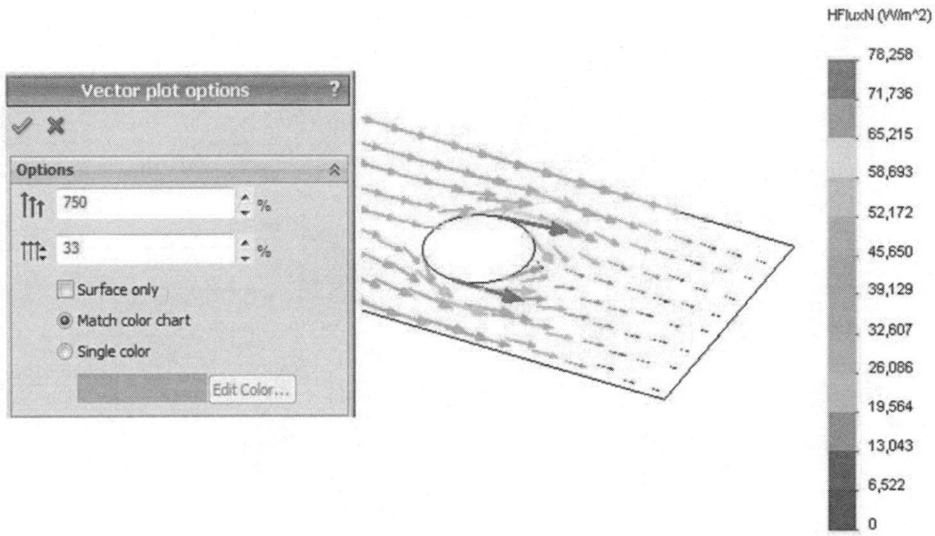

Figure 2-12: Heat flux results in the shell element model presented with vector plots.

Rotate the plot to see that heat flux vectors do not "come out" of the model.

In structural analysis shell elements differentiate between top and bottom and different stress results are read on opposite sides. In thermal analysis shell elements do not differentiate between sides. Therefore, the shell element model cannot show to which side heat escapes from the model. As shown in Figure 2-12, heat flux vectors "fade away" without "coming out" of the model.

Since in thermal analysis shell elements do not differentiate between sides, you cannot apply different thermal boundary conditions to the sides of face meshed with shell elements.

3: L bracket

Topics covered

- Heat transfer by conduction
- Use of 2D models
- Singularities in thermal problems

Project description

We'll conduct a thermal analysis of a simple model to study heat flux singularities. Demonstration of heat flux singularities requires the use of very small elements, consequently models are large and expensive to solve. However, our model lends itself toward a 2D representation. Using 2D thermal elements, we'll demonstrate a heat flux singularity at a fraction of the computational effort that would be required if a 3D analysis were performed. Open model L BRACKET TH shown in Figure 3-1; make sure it is in the *01 sharp edge* configuration.

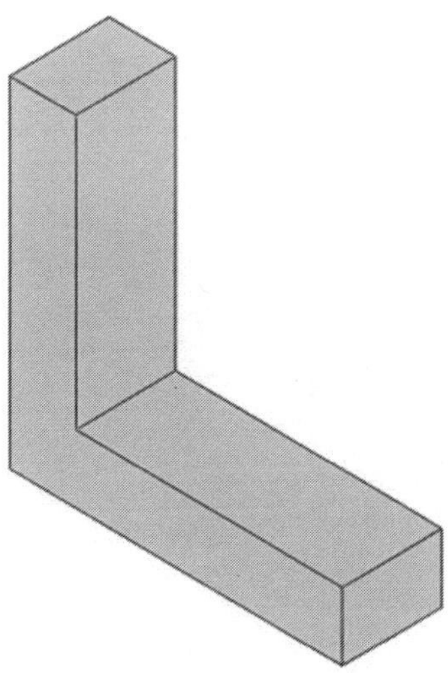

Configuration
01 sharp edge

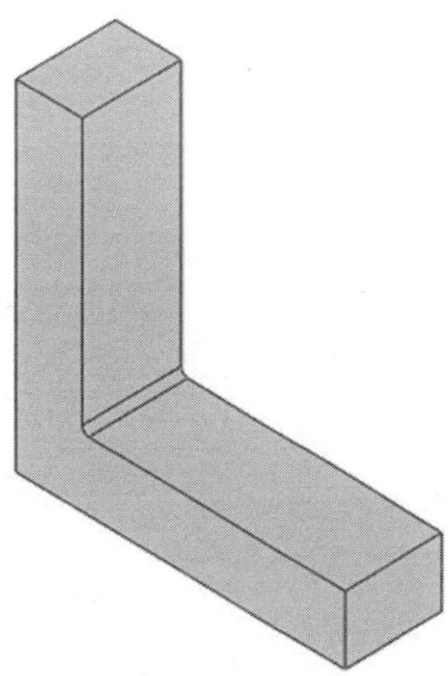

Configuration
02 round edge

Figure 3-1: Model L BRACKET TH comes in two configurations: with a sharp edge and with a round edge.

Demonstrating heat flux singularities requires a model with a sharp edge.

Create a thermal study *01 sharp* using 2D Simplification (Figure 3-2).

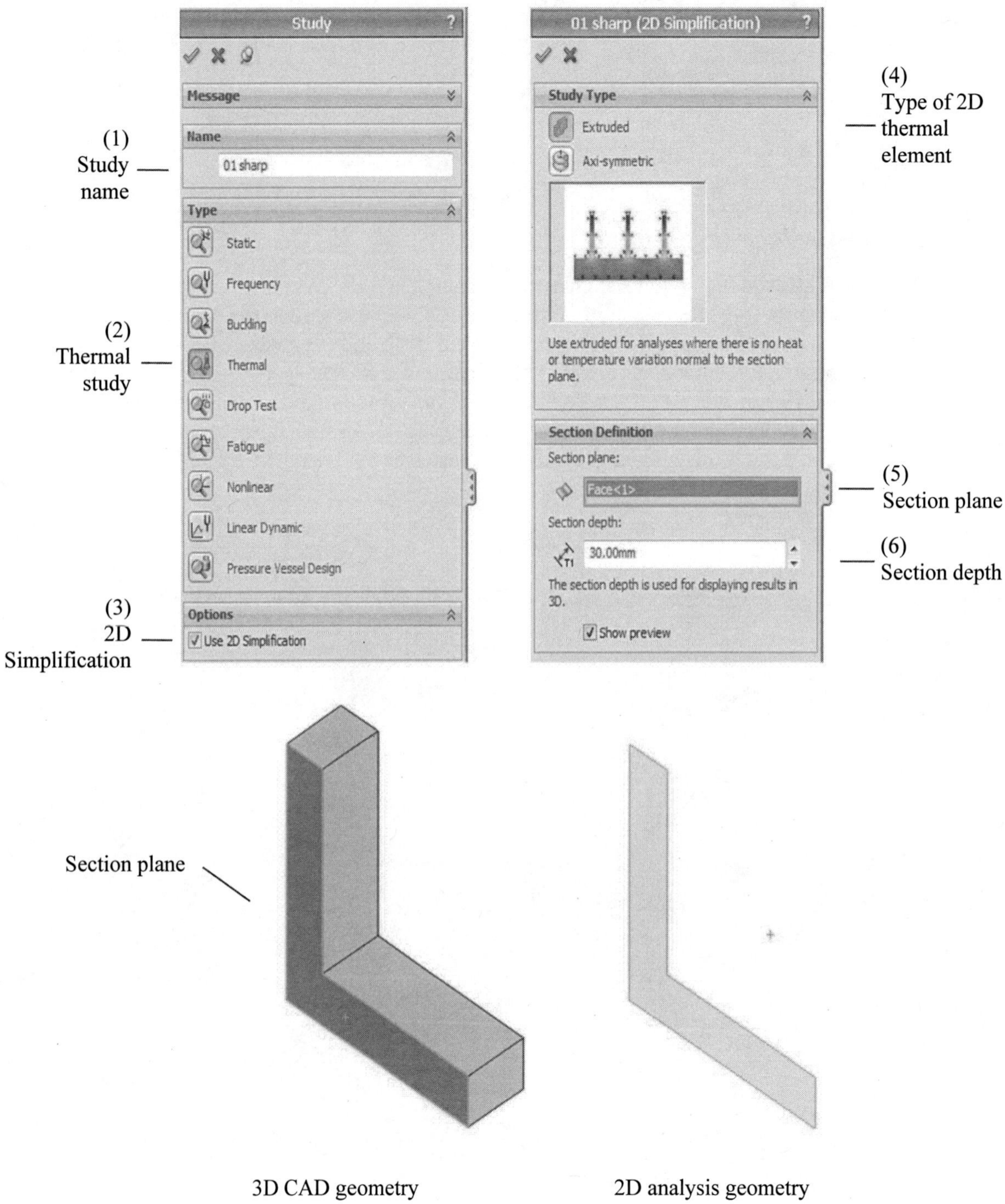

Figure 3-2: Model L BRACKET TH can be represented by a 2D section.

Section depth is the thickness of the CAD model.

To demonstrate the heat flux singularity we must define heat flow in the model. The easiest way to do that is to define prescribed temperatures as boundary conditions as shown in Figure 3-3.

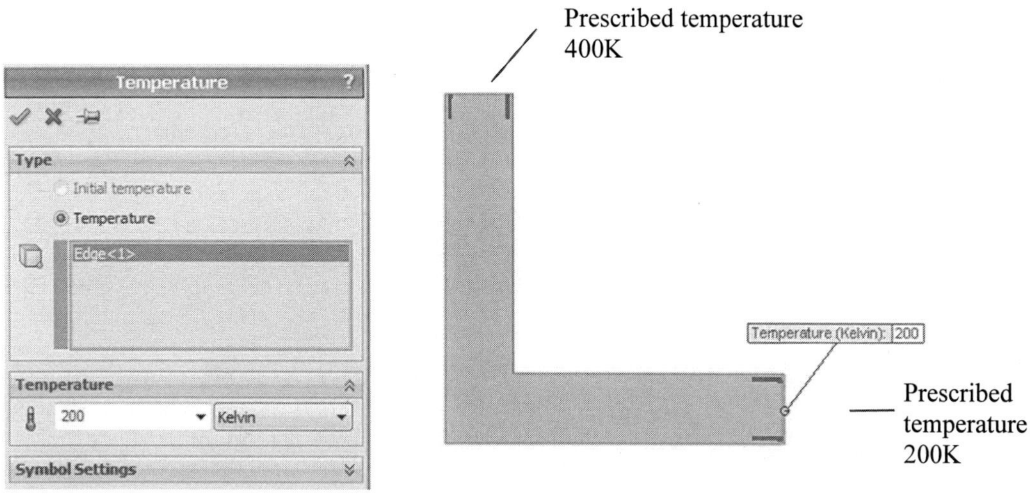

Figure 3-3: Definition of prescribed temperatures in 2D thermal model; top edge: 400K, right edge: 200K.

The temperature window shows the definition of a 200K prescribed temperature.

Mesh the model with an element size of 2mm, run the solution and display a **Heat Flux** result (Figure 3-4).

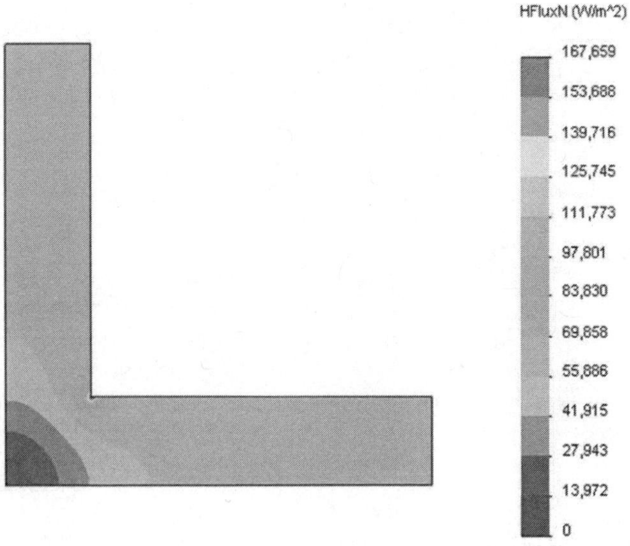

Figure 3-4: Heat flux results obtained with 2mm show the maximum heat flux 168kW/m^2.

Review this plot using vector display.

Notice that the location of the maximum heat flux coincides with the sharp corner.

Copy study *01 sharp* into study *02 sharp*; add a mesh control to the corner (Figure 3-5):

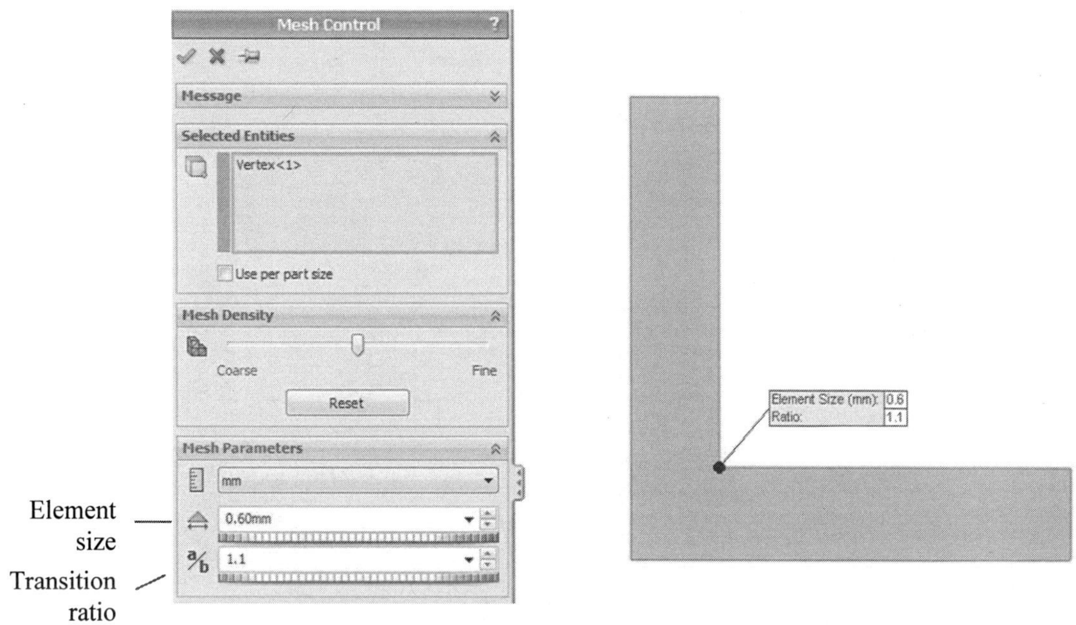

Figure 3-5: Mesh control in the sharp corner in study *02 sharp*.

Use an element size of 0.6mm, and a transition ratio of 1.1 to ensure a smooth transition from dense elements in the corner to coarse elements (2mm) everywhere else in the model.

Run the analysis then repeat it using progressively smaller elements in the corner; study *03 sharp*: 0.4mm, study *04 sharp:* 0.2mm and study *05 sharp*: 0.1mm. Collect heat flux results in the corner (this will also be the maximum heat flux) from all studies and present them in a graph showing the maximum heat flux as a function of 1/h where h is the element size in the corner (Figure 3-6).

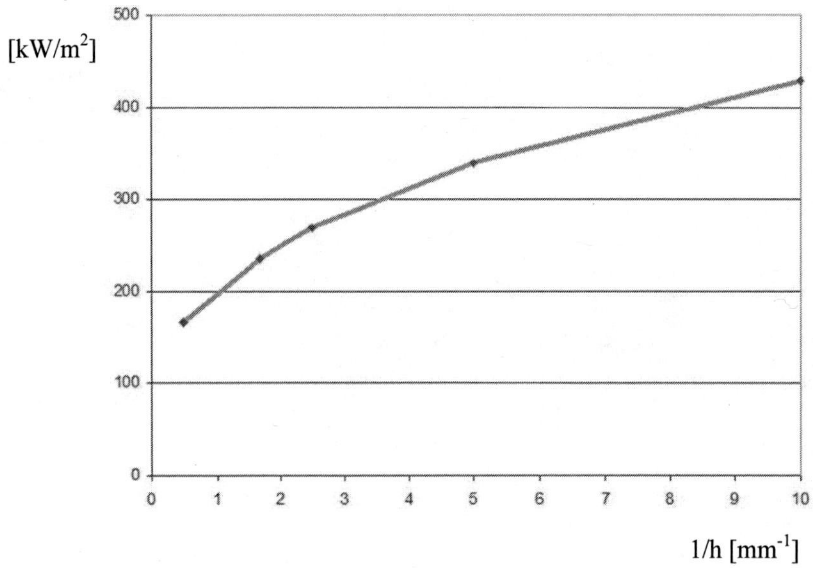

Figure 3-6: Maximum heat flux as a function of the inverse of the element size, h.

Five points are connected by line only to visually enhance the graph.

The summary of results presented in Figure 3-6 demonstrates divergence of heat flux results in the presence of a sharp corner. This is in direct analogy to stress divergence in sharp corners in 2D models or sharp edges in 3D models.

Divergence of heat flux results will be further discussed using the HEATING DUCTS model in chapters 5 and 6.

4: Thermal analysis of a round bar

Topics covered

- Heat transfer by conduction
- Thermal conductivity
- Heat transfer by convection
- Convection boundary conditions
- Thermal resistance
- Prescribed temperature boundary conditions
- Heat power
- Heat flux

Project description

A round steel rod has one end in boiling water at 100°C and the other end in melting ice (0°C). The cylindrical face is insulated; no heat is exchanged through that face (Figure 4-1).

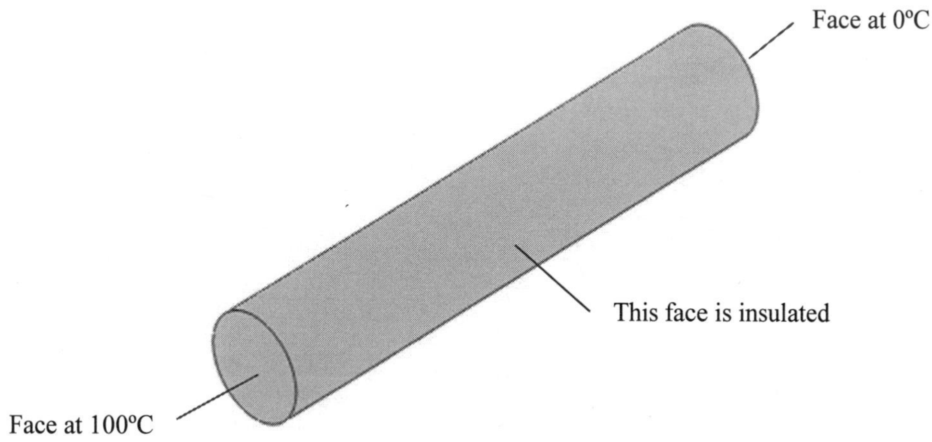

Figure 4-1: The STEEL ROD model with prescribed temperatures as boundary conditions.

If no boundary conditions are defined on a face, it means that no heat is exchanged through that face; the face is insulated.

Our objective is to find the total heat transferred by the rod from the hot to cold side. Notice that conduction is the only heat transfer mechanism present in the model.

Create a thermal study *01 conduction* and define prescribed temperatures as boundary conditions as shown is Figure 4-2.

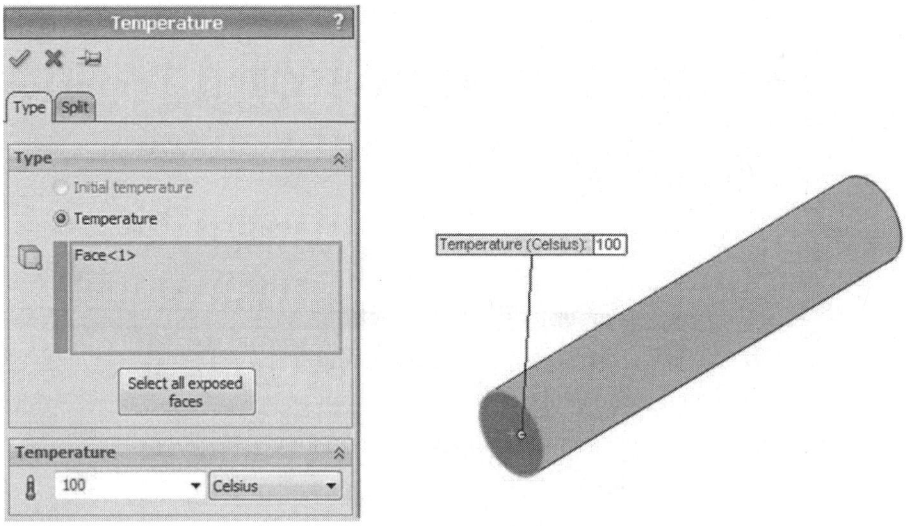

Figure 4-2: Prescribed temperature defined on the hot side of the rod.

Define a prescribed temperature of 0°C on the other side.

Obtain a solution using a default mesh size and review the **Temperature** plot. Follow steps in Figure 4-3 to find the total heat traveling through the rod.

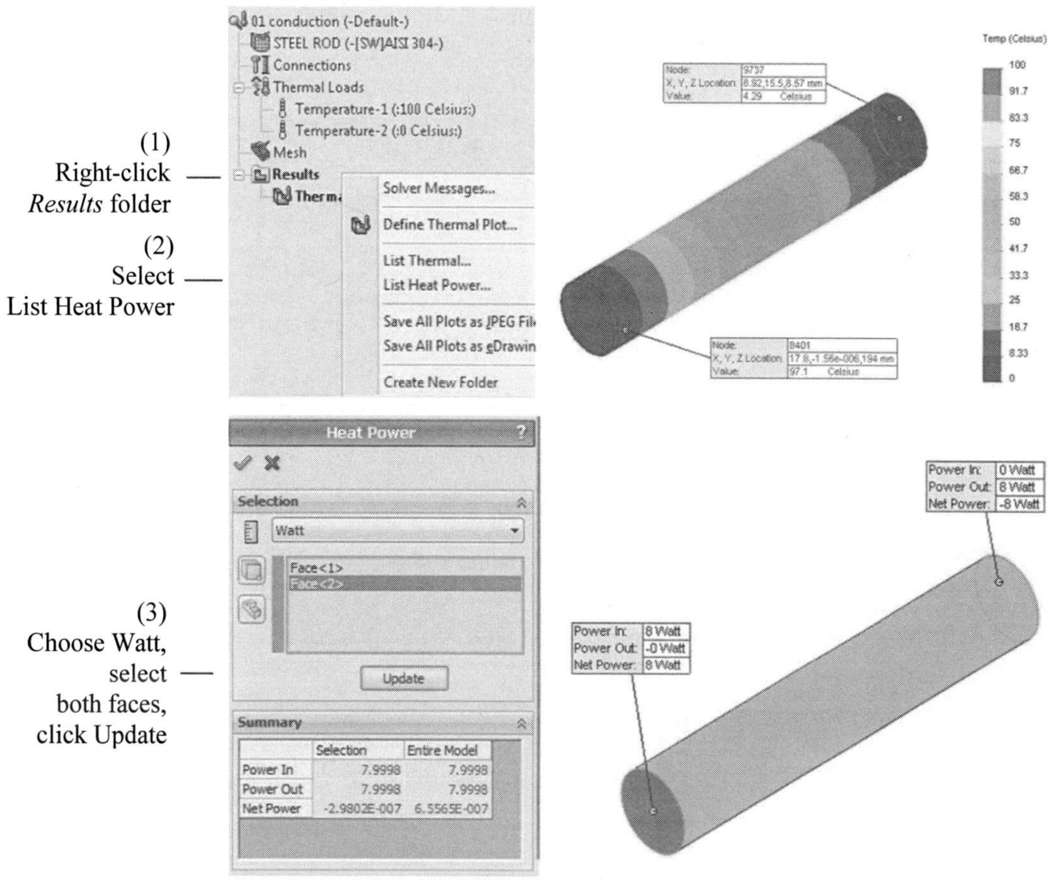

<u>Figure 4-3: Listing Heat Power.</u>

Heat power in is 8W, heat power out is 8W.

Probe the temperature plot near the ends of the model to see the temperature gradient along the rod.

Heat Power window does not have to be called from a result plot. You may right-click results folder and select Heat Power form the pop-up menu.

We use this simple model to compare our heat power result to the analytical solution:

$$Q = \frac{kA(T_{HOT} - T_{COLD})}{L} = \frac{16 \times 0.001 \times (100 - 0)}{0.2} = 8W$$

Where:

k – Thermal conductivity of steel: 16W/m/K

A – Cross section area: 0.001m^3

T_{HOT} – Temperature of boiling water: 100°C

T_{COLD} – Temperature of melting ice: 0°C

L – Length of rod: 0.2m

To complete the review of the results of study *01 conduction*, create a **Heat Flux** plot presented as vectors (Figure 4-4).

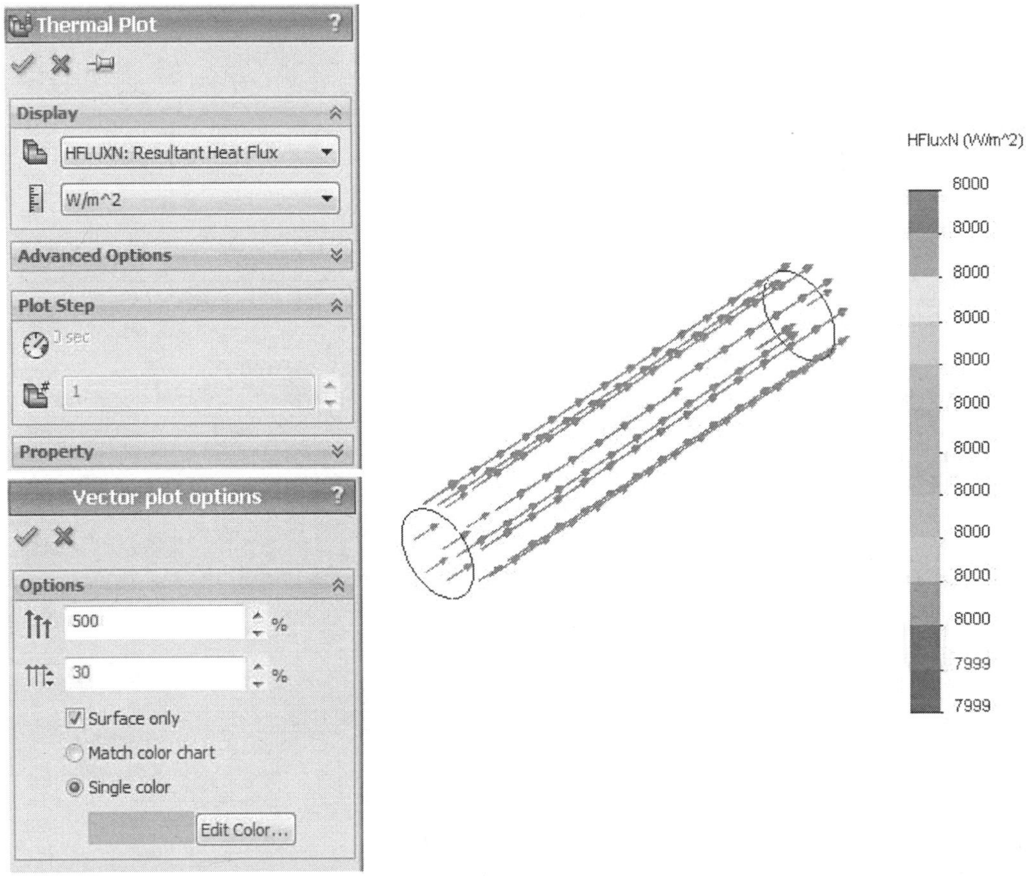

Figure 4-4: The resultant heat flux presented as vector plot with Vector plot options shown above.

Heat flux is uniform throughout the model as shown by the numbers at the color legend. The only reason for minute differences is the discretization error introduced by meshing.

Next we introduce heat transfer through convection. Copy *study 01 conduction* into *02 convection* and delete the prescribed temperature of the cold side. We want to replace this prescribed temperature boundary condition with a convection boundary condition that will give the same temperature distribution along the length of the rod and the same heat flow 8W. What should be the convection coefficient?

First, let's consider what ambient temperature should be defined. We want the cold end of the rod to be at 0°C (273K). If we defined the ambient temperature equal to the previously used prescribed temperature 0°C (273K), then the convection coefficient would have to be infinitely large so the ambient temperature must be lower than 0°C. The lower the ambient temperature, the lower will be the required convection coefficient while 8W of heat power travels through the road. Let's assume the ambient temperature is -10 °C.

Heat transferred by convection is:

$$Q = hA(T_S - T_F)$$

Where:

Q – Heat power (8W) - given

h – Unknown convection coefficient [$W/m^2/K$]

A – Area participating in convective hear transfer ($0.001m^2$) - given

T_S – Temperature of surface (273 K) - given

T_F – Temperature of surrounding fluid (263K) - assumed

From the above equation, the required convection coefficient is:

$$h = \frac{Q}{A(T_S - T_F)} = \frac{8}{0.001 \times 10} = 800 \frac{W}{m^2 K}$$

Using this result define convection coefficient as shown in Figure 4-5.

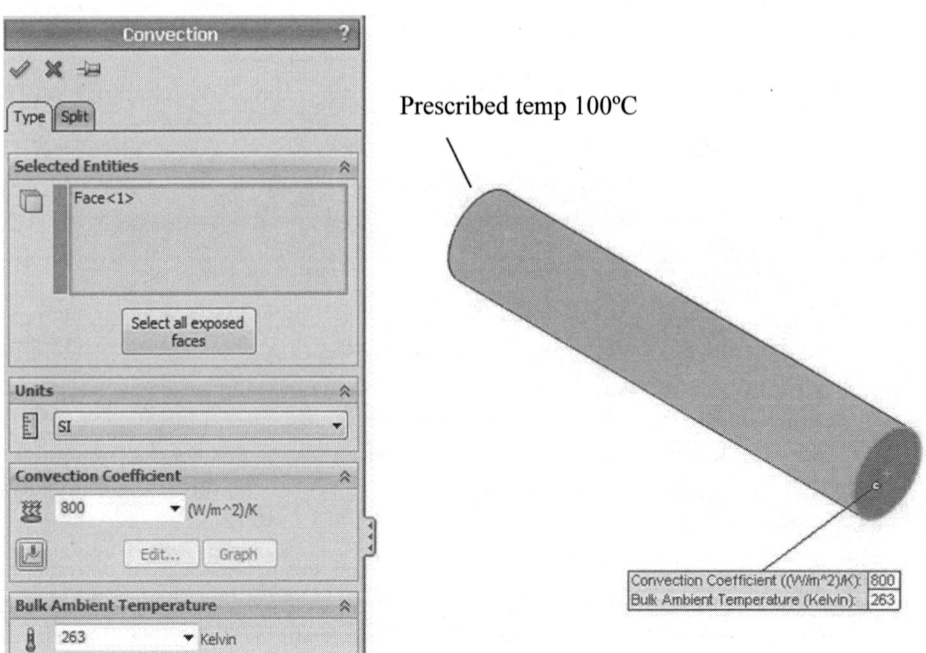

Figure 4-5: Convection coefficient on the cold side.

The convection coefficient replaces the previously used prescribed temperature boundary condition.

Obtain the solution and find the heat power as shown in Figure 4-6.

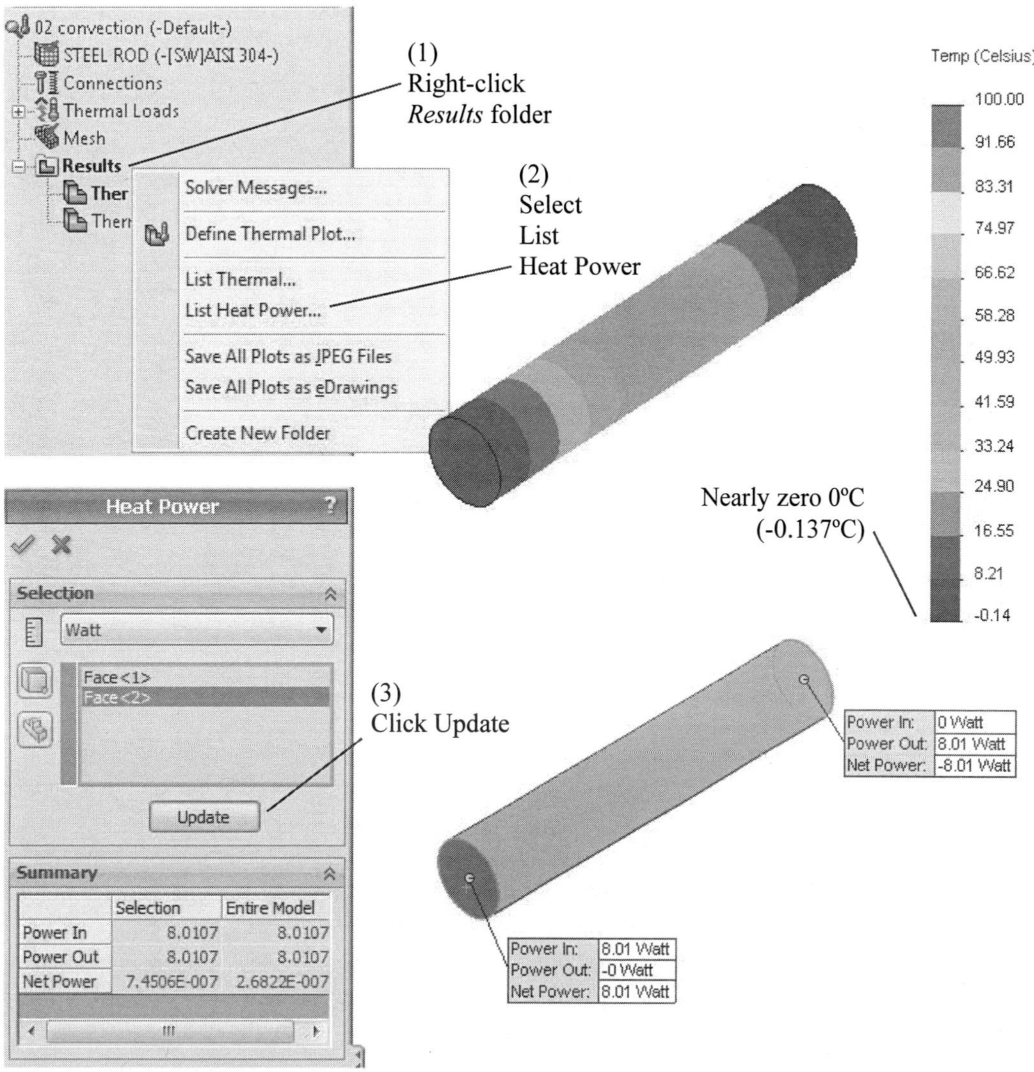

Figure 4-6: Heat power in model with prescribed temperature on the hot side and convection on the cold side.

Compare this with the results shown in Figure 4-3.

As Figure 4-6 shows, the convection coefficient of $800 W/m^2/K$ combined with the temperature gradient between the face and surrounding fluid is equivalent to the prescribed temperature of 273K. From a practical point of view we should notice that the convection coefficient of $800 W/m^2/K$ is quite high, however, it would be possible to get that convection between metal and moving water with melting ice.

Open assembly TWO RODS; the assembly consists of two identical copper rods 100mm long glued with a layer of epoxy resin. The thickness of the glue is 0.5mm; not a very good design but makes for an interesting exercise (Figure 4-7).

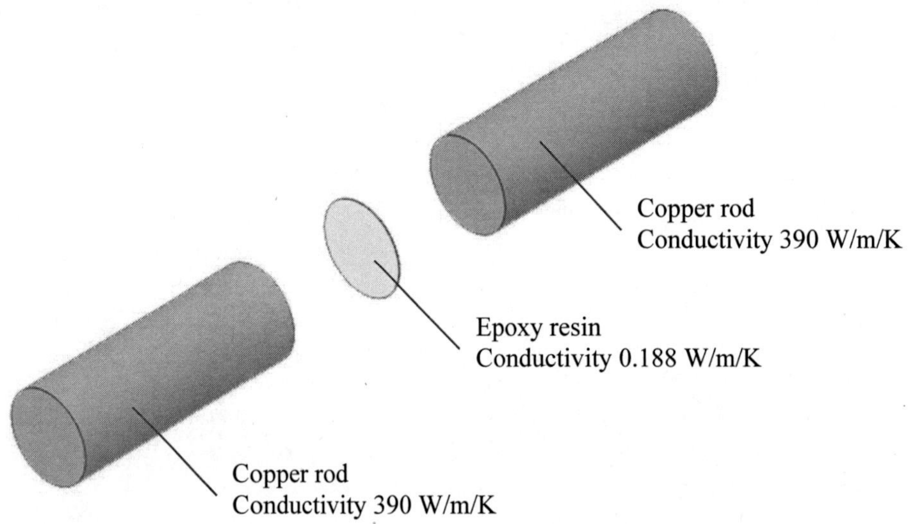

Figure 4-7: The TWO RODS model features two copper rods glued by epoxy glue.

The rod material (copper) and glue material (epoxy resin) have vastly different thermal conductivities. Assembly shown in an exploded view.

Our objective here is to study the effect of thermal resistance caused by the layer of epoxy. Even though the layer of epoxy is very thin, it has a major effect on heat transfer through the assembly because of its low thermal conductivity. The thinness of the epoxy layer will also cause significant meshing difficulties.

Make sure the assembly is in the *01glue* configuration and create a thermal study called *01 glue.* To ensure a correct aspect ratio of elements meshing the glue layer, apply a **Mesh Control** to the glue component as shown in Figure 4-8.

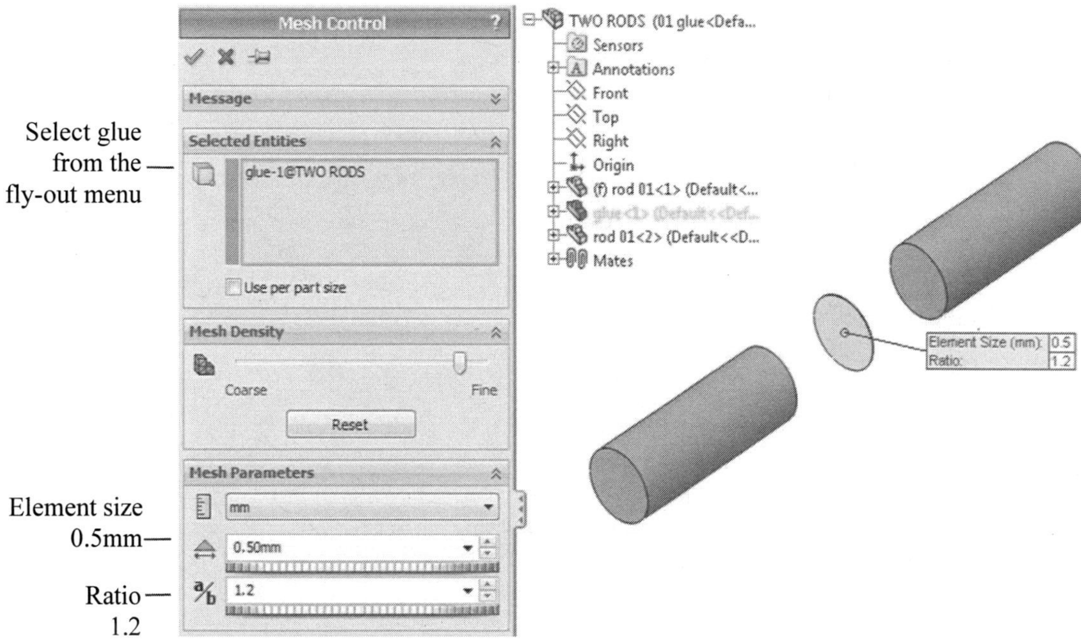

Figure 4-8: Mesh Control applied to glue assembly component.

A low a/b ratio assures a smooth transition between large elements that mesh the rods, and small elements that mesh the glue. Assembly shown in exploded view.

The mesh control shown in Figure 4-8 produces one layer of elements in the glue. Second order elements are capable of modeling second order temperature fields and first order (constant) temperature fields. Given that the expected temperature gradient is constant across the epoxy layer, one layer of element will suffice.

Mesh the assembly with the default element size. Apply prescribed temperatures identical to the STEEL ROD exercise: 100°C on one end, 0°C on the other end (Figure 4-9).

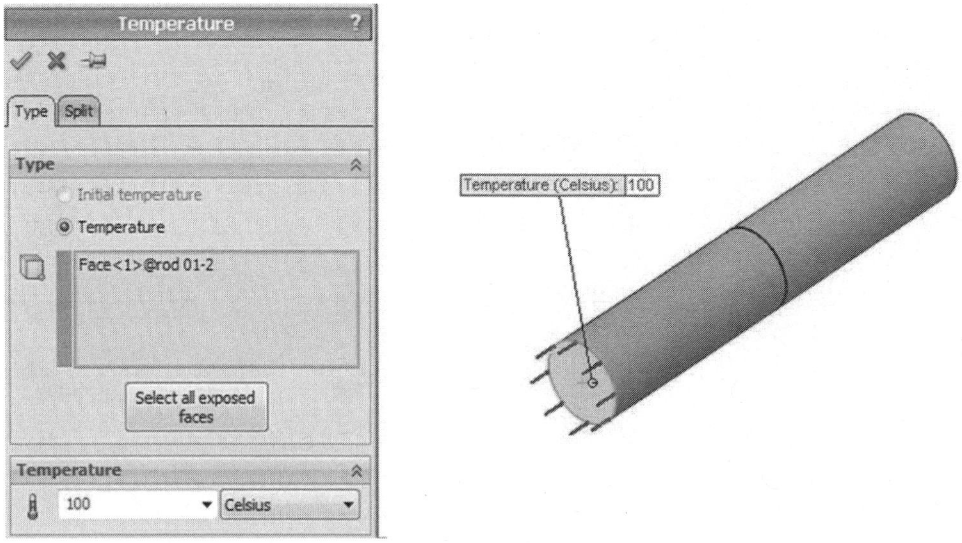

Figure 4-9: Prescribed temperature definition at the hot end.

A prescribed temperature of 0°C on the other end is not shown.

Run the solution and review the **Temperature** plot. Notice the temperature drop of 8°C over the distance of 100mm in the bar. Compare this to a drop of 84°C over the distance of 0.5mm in glue (Figure 4-10).

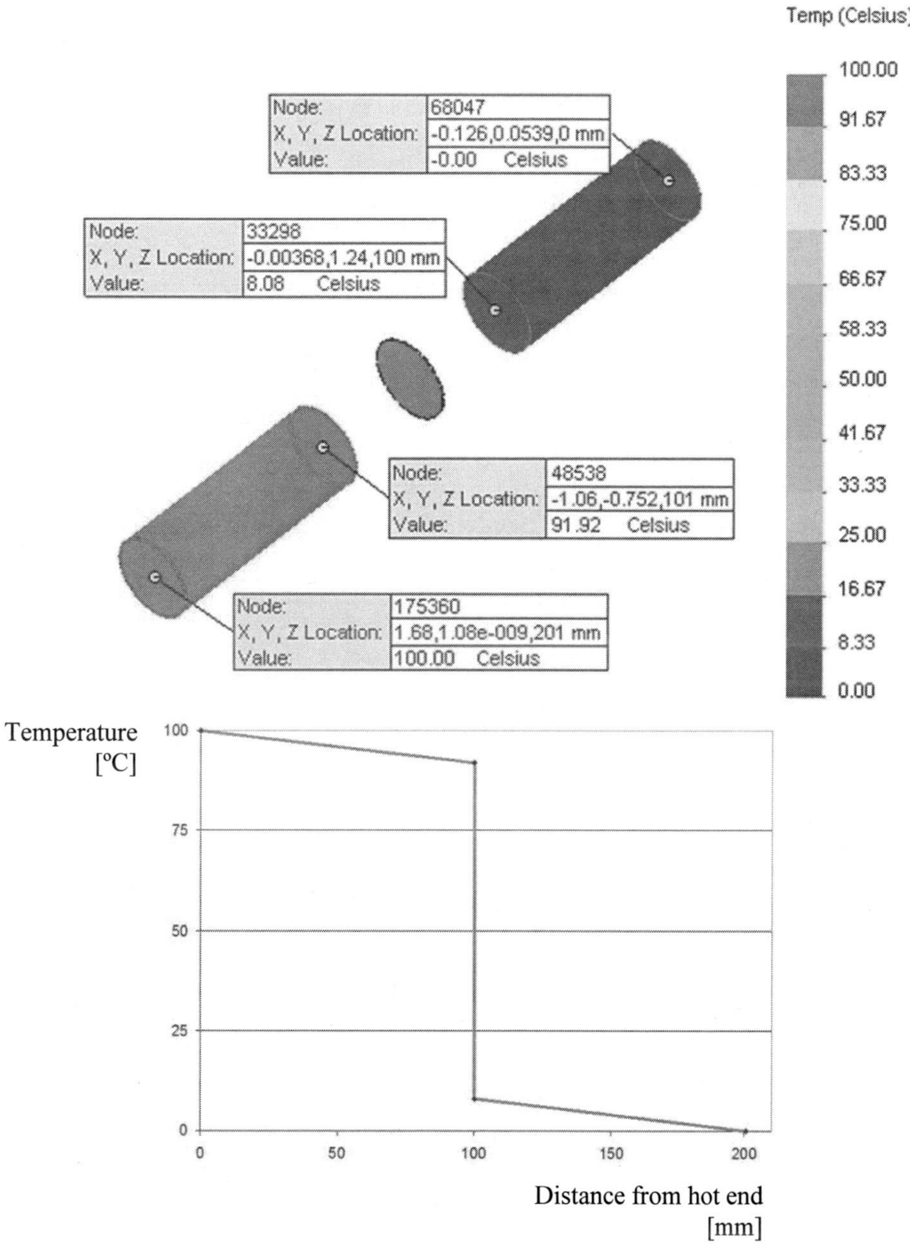

Figure 4-10: Temperature drop along the length of the assembly.

A rapid temperature drop is caused by a low thermal conductivity of the epoxy glue.

Total heat flow in the assembly can be displayed as shown in Figure 4-11.

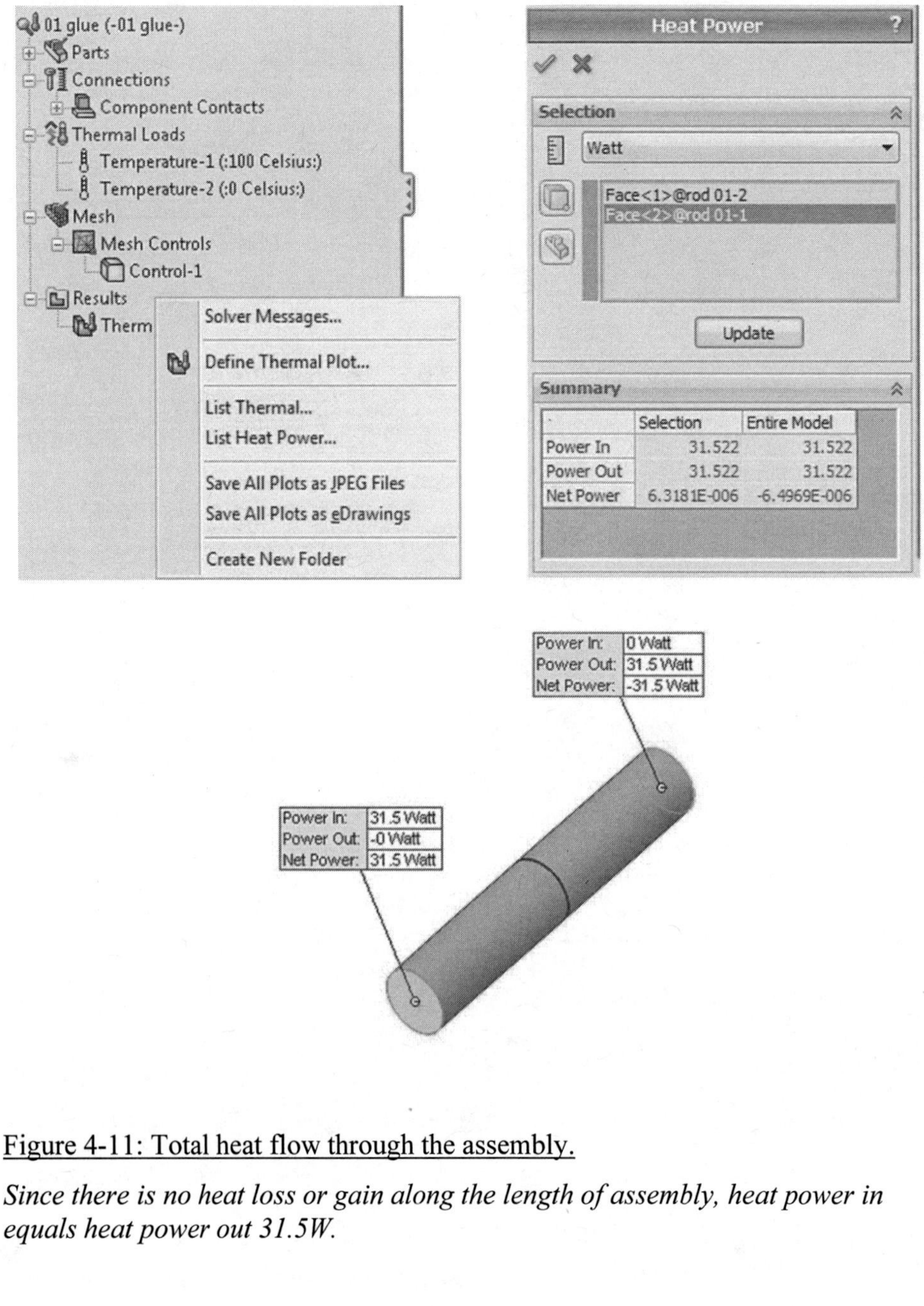

Figure 4-11: Total heat flow through the assembly.

Since there is no heat loss or gain along the length of assembly, heat power in equals heat power out 31.5W.

The thermal resistance of epoxy causes temperature a drop of 83°C over the distance of 0.5mm. Heat flowing through the epoxy is 31.5W. The cross sectional area of the epoxy is 1000mm^2. Knowing the above we may easily calculate the thermal resistance of epoxy layer:

$$R = \frac{\Delta TA}{P} = \frac{83 \times 0.001}{31.5} = 0.026\frac{Km^2}{W}$$

Where:

R – Distributed (per area) thermal resistance Km^2/W

ΔT – Temperature drop across the layer 83K

A – Cross sectional area: 0.001m^3

P – Heat flow (heat power) through the layer

The glue part of the assembly is very small in comparison to the rods, yet it causes a major obstacle in heat flow because of its poor heat conductivity. It also poses major modeling difficulties; we had to apply a mesh control that increased the number of elements in the model very significantly.

The objective of this exercise is to introduce the concept of the layer of thermal resistance. We saw that explicit modeling of the layer of thermal resistance is difficult and gets even more so when the layer gets very thin. Fortunately, there is a better way of modeling the layer of thermal resistance.

Stay with the TWO RODS assembly but switch to the *02 no glue* configuration. The assembly now consists of two parts only. Create a thermal study *02 thermal resistance*. The layer of thermal resistance will be modeled as a **Contact Condition**. Follow Figure 4-12 to define a **Thermal Resistance Contact Condition**.

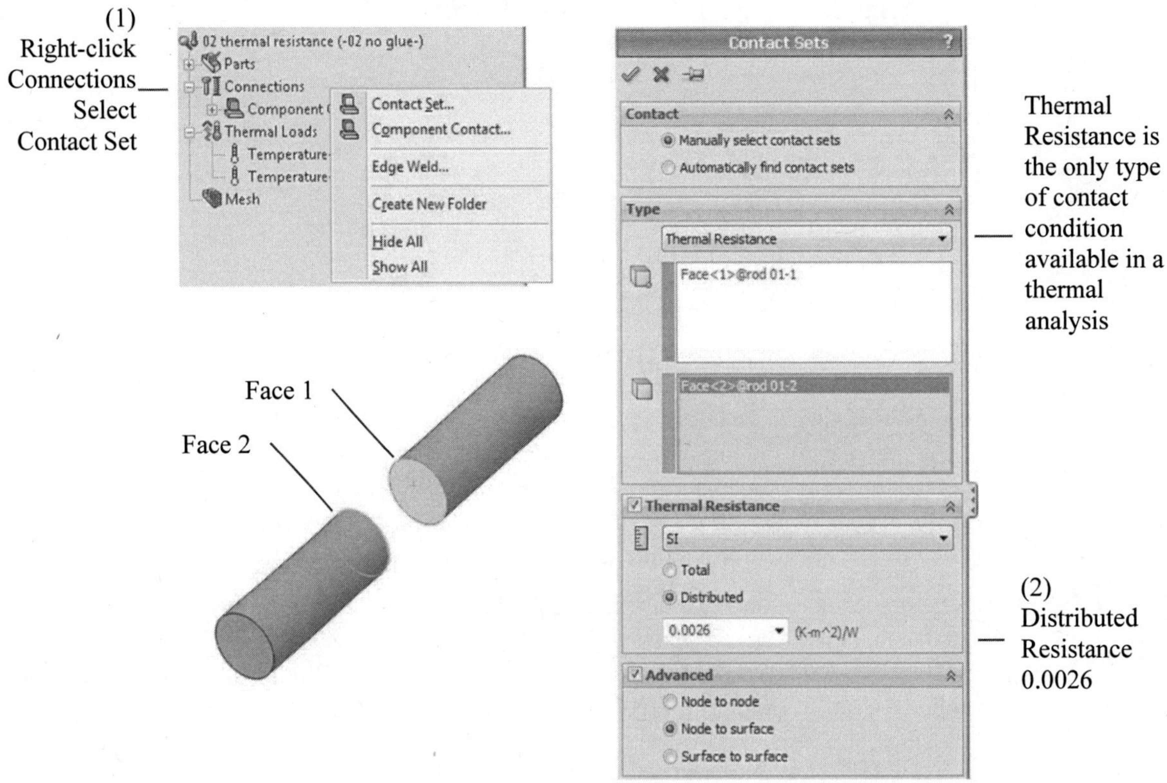

Figure 4-12: Definition of a Thermal Resistance Contact Condition.

Use exploded view.

The value of thermal resistance, 0.0026 Km^2/W comes from a calculation based on the results of the previous study where the layer of thermal resistance was modeled explicitly.

Mesh the assembly with the default element size; no mesh control is needed. Obtain a solution and review the **Temperature** plot.

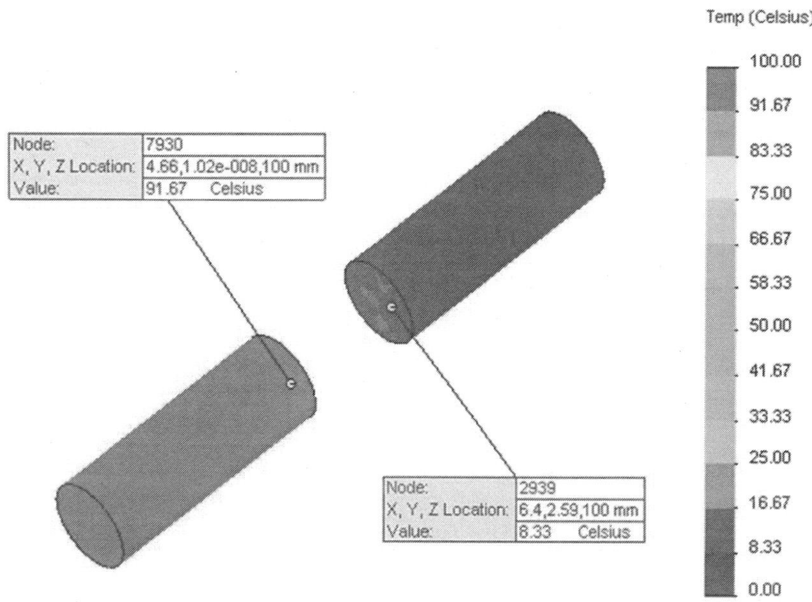

Figure 4-13: Temperature results in the model with a layer of thermal resistance.

The temperature drop across the layer of thermal resistance is 83°C.

The results of study *01 glue* (Figure 4-10) and study *02 thermal resistance* (Figure 4-13) are practically the same. The layer of epoxy glue produces the same temperature drop when modeled either explicitly or as a layer of thermal resistance.

The use of **Thermal resistance Contact Conditions** allows for a very significant simplification of the model, and a faster solution time compared to explicit modeling, as long as the value of thermal resistance in known. If it is not known, it can be found using simple models such as TWO RODS in the *01 glue* configuration. The analysis of real design problems can then be done using **Thermal Resistance**.

Notes:

5: Floor heating duct – part 1

Topics covered

- Heat transfer by conduction
- Prescribed temperature boundary conditions
- Heat power
- Heat flux
- Heat flux singularities
- Analogies between structural and thermal analysis

Project description

A ceramic floor panel used to heat the room is modeled in assembly HEATING DUCTS (Figure 5-1). Hot air flows in the ducts transferring heat to the panel. Heat is dissipated by the panels top faces. We assume that the side and bottom faces are insulated, therefore no thermal boundary conditions are defined there: no prescribed temperatures, no convection coefficients and no radiation coefficients.

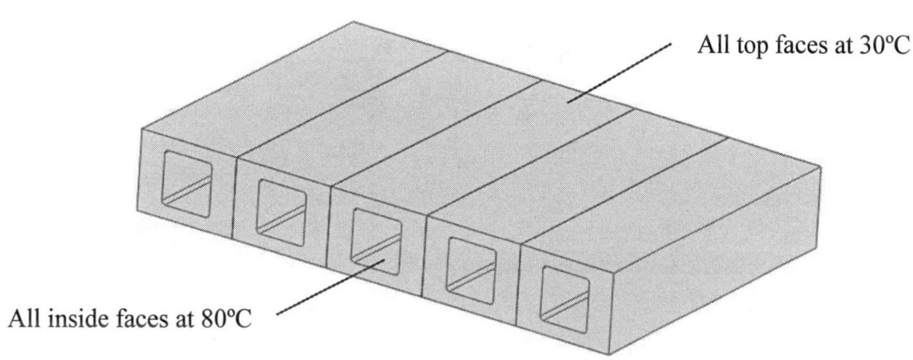

Figure 5-1: HEATING DUCTS assembly model of a ceramic floor panel.

The assembly consists of five identical parts. The model is shown in 01 CAD configuration.

Notice that the temperatures shown in Figure 5-1 are prescribed temperatures which are thermal boundary conditions; we will investigate heat flow induced by these boundary conditions. Side faces and bottom faces don't have any prescribed temperature defined but that does not mean that they won't have any temperature. Temperature there will establish itself as a result of heat flow induced by prescribed temperatures shown in Figure 5-1.

We will perform a thermal analysis of this floor panel to find out how much heat is transferred to the room. Because of repeatable geometry and no thermal boundary conditions on either side, the model can be simplified to just one segment. Also, because there is no temperature gradient along the length of ducts (uniform prescribed temperature is defined) the analysis can be further simplified by using a 2D model. A 2D model will also make it easy to demonstrate the heat flux singularity in the presence of sharp edges.

Switch to the *02 Analysis Part1* configuration to review the model (Figure 5-2).

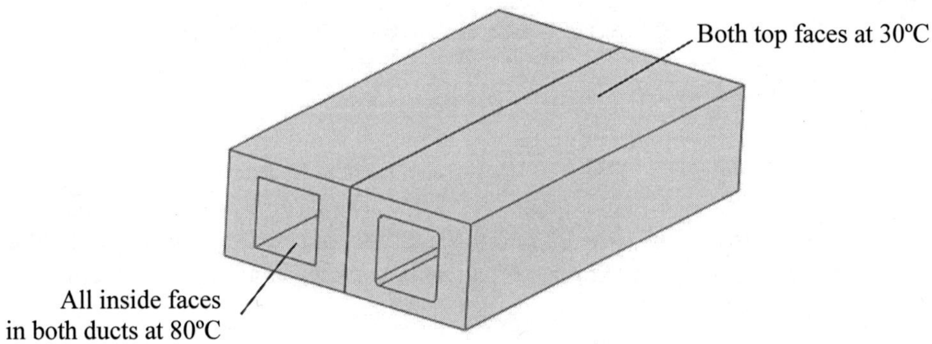

Figure 5-2: HEATING DUCTS assembly in *02 FEA* configuration.

Notice round edges in the duct on the right.

Why do we use two segments for analysis even though only one segment could be used? We do that to study the effect of sharp re-entrant edges on heat flux; notice that the left segment has sharp edges; the right one has rounded edges.

The analyzed segment consisting of two ducts is part of a larger assembly, no heat flows through the side faces, therefore no boundary conditions are defined there. The side faces are treated as if they were insulated.

Procedure

Make sure the model is in configuration *02 Analysis Part 1* and define a thermal study *01 2D* using **2D Simplification**. Follow the steps shown in Figure 5-3.

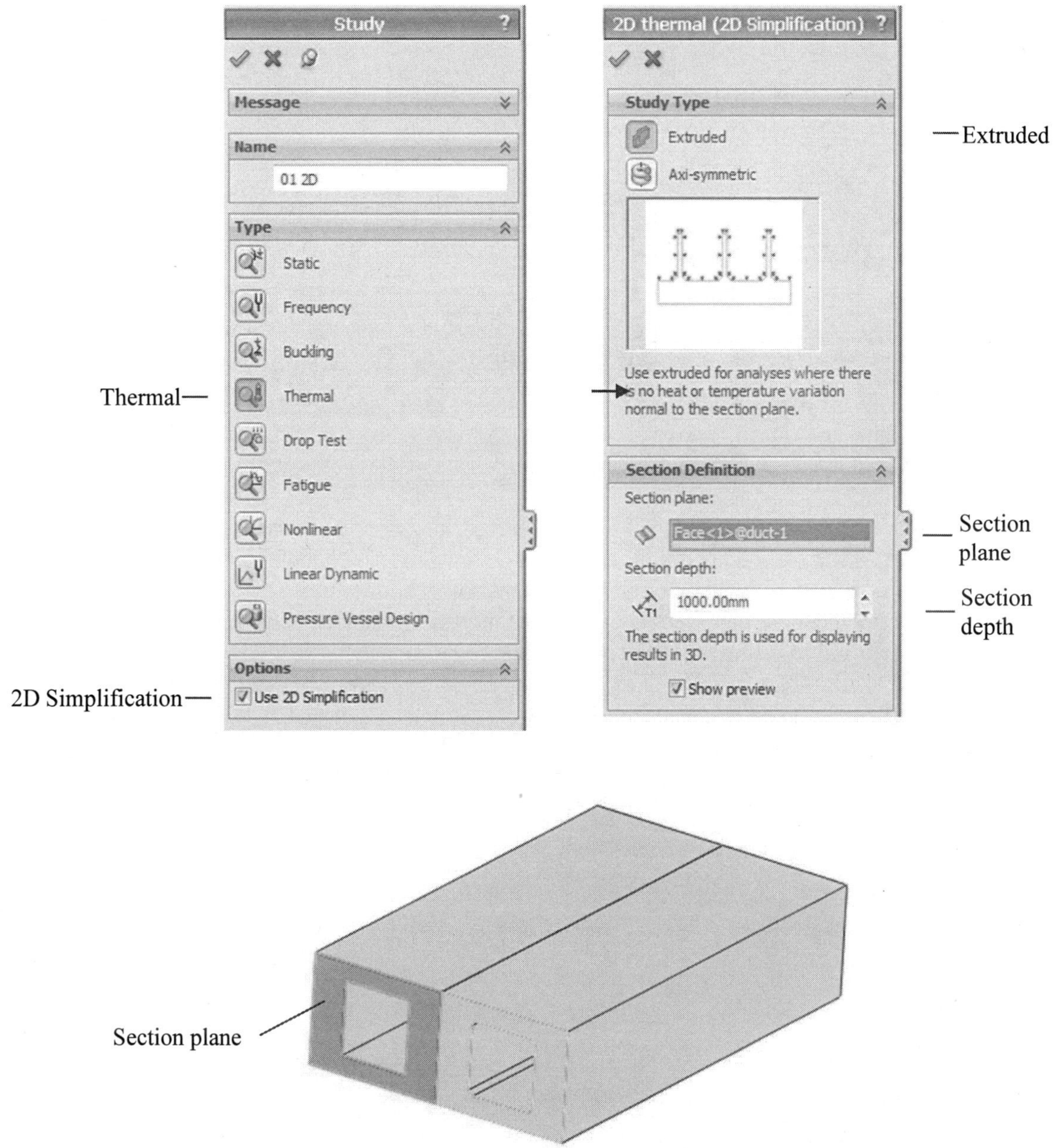

Figure 5-3: Thermal study definition using 2D Simplification.

Section depth is equal to the length of floor panel 1000mm; this can be measured in the CAD assembly model.

Geometry ready to be meshed with 2D elements is shown in Figure 5-4.

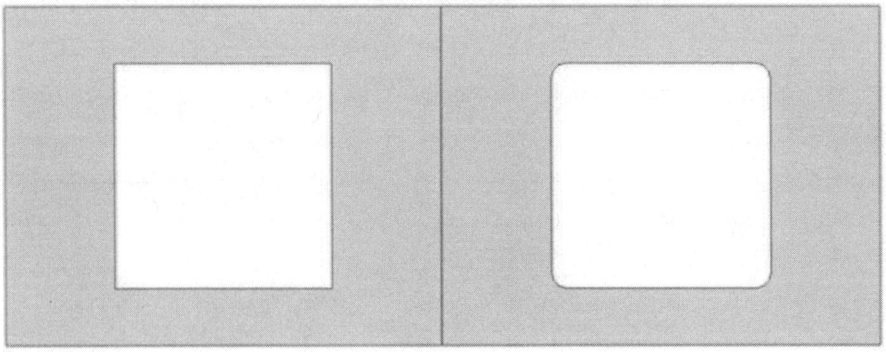

Figure 5-4: 2D geometry ready to be meshed with 2D elements.

The left segment has sharp re-entrant corners, the right segment has rounded corners.

Follow the steps in Figure 5-5 to define prescribed temperatures on the inside edges of the 2D model and Figure 5-6 to define prescribed temperatures on the outside edges of the 2D model. Notice that contact conditions remain as default **Bonded** meaning that there is no layer of thermal resistance between two segments. No action is required on contact conditions.

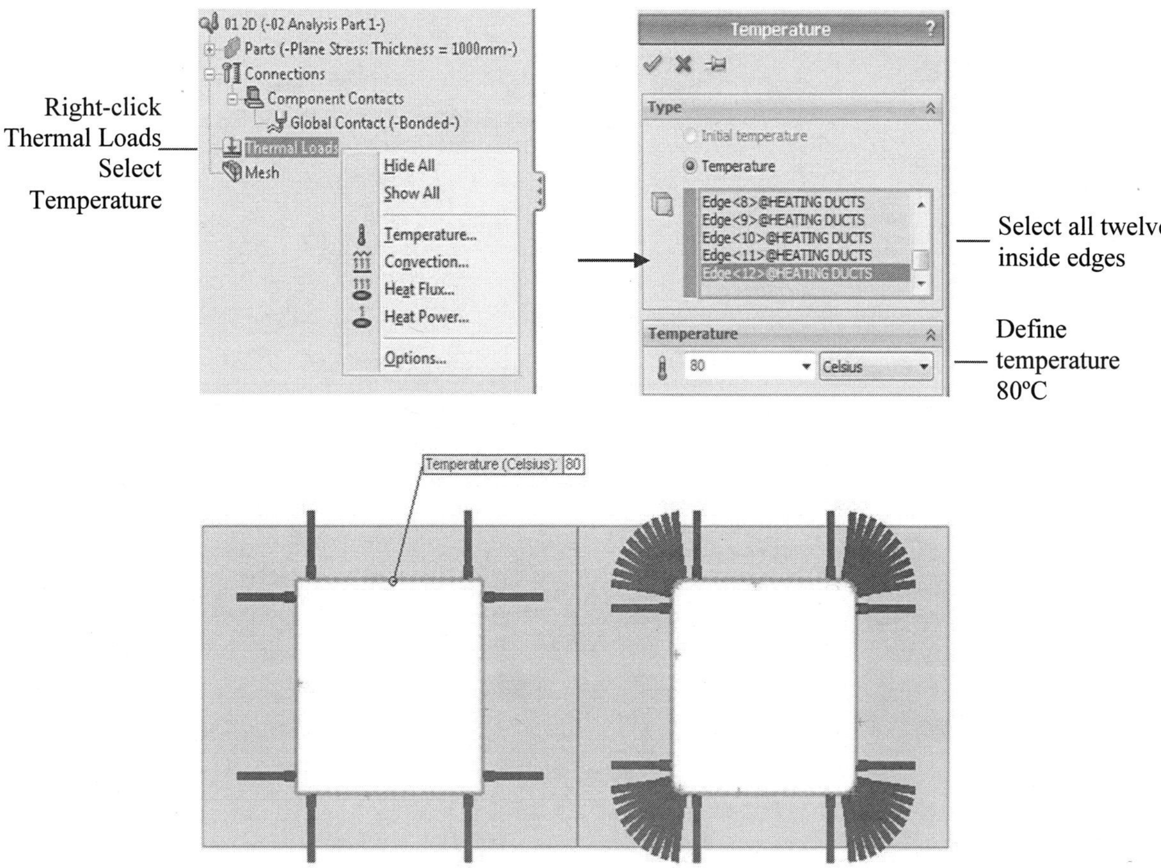

Figure 5-5: Definition of prescribed temperature on the inside edges.

A prescribed temperature of 80°C is applied to twelve inside edges: four edges in the left segment and eight edges in the right segment.

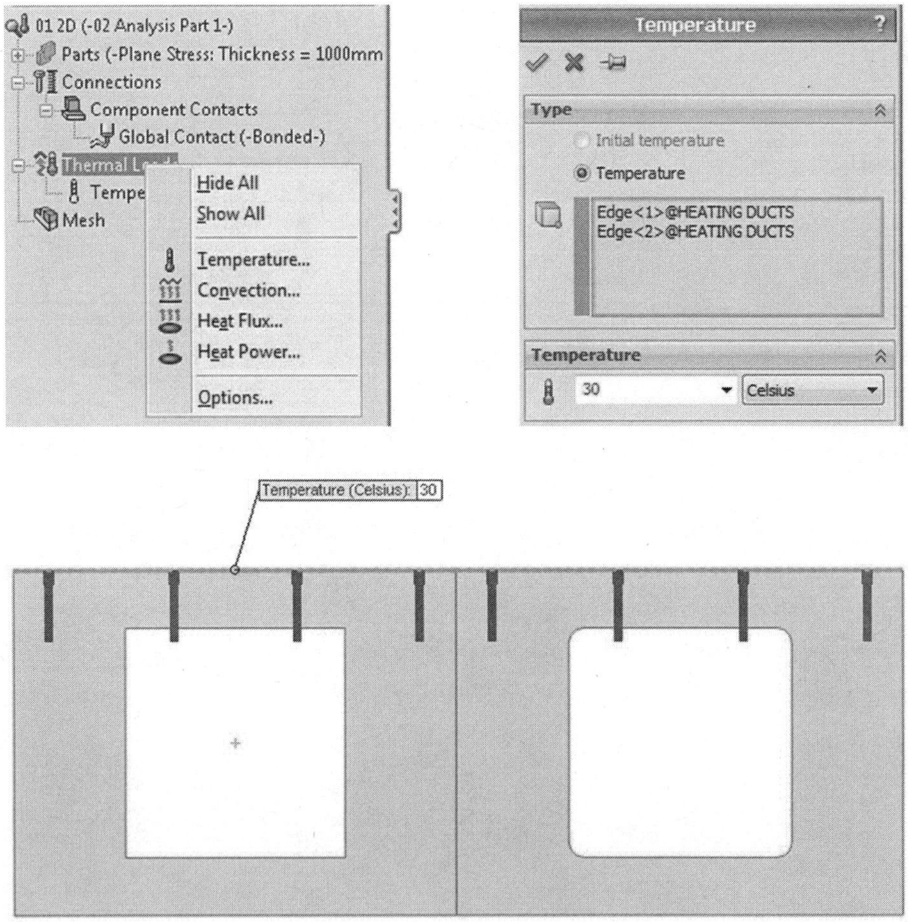

Figure 5-6: Definition of prescribed temperature on the outside edges.

A prescribed temperature of 30°C is applied to the two outside edges.

Symbols of previously defined prescribed temperatures are not shown here for clarity of this illustration.

Having defined prescribed temperatures on the inside and outside edges we have established a mechanism of heat transfer. Now, mesh the model with a default element size to create a mesh as shown in Figure 5-7.

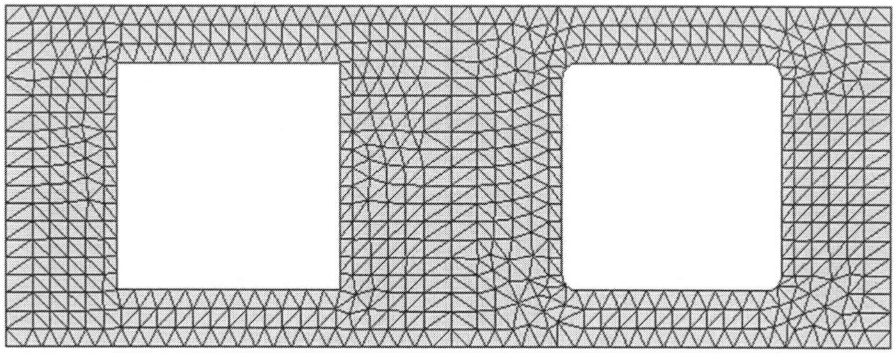

Figure 5-7: Model meshed with default element size.

Notice the high turn angle in elements meshing round corners.

Obtain a solution noticing almost instantaneous results; 2D thermal models solve very fast because of a low number of elements due to the 2D formulation and to the fact that there is only one degree of freedom (temperature) per node. Review temperature result as shown in Figure 5-8.

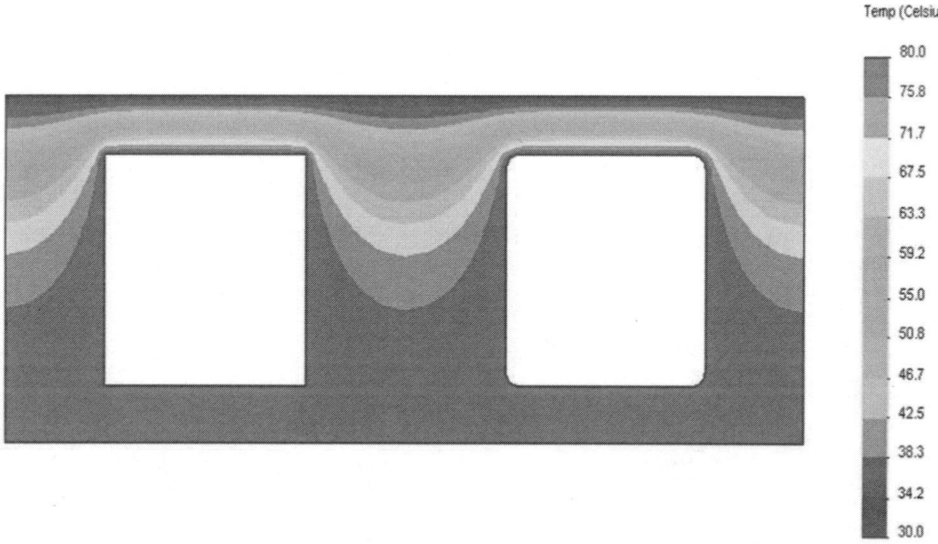

Figure 5-8: Temperature results from study *2D thermal 01*.

Temperature is a scalar value; temperature results can be only presented as a fringe plot.

As Figure 5-8 illustrates, there is little difference between sharp and round corners. The temperature on the inside edges is equal to 80°C; the temperature on the outside edges is equal to 30°C. Everywhere else, a steady state temperature establishes itself as a result of heat flow from hot (80°C) to cold (30°C) edges. Now, create Heat Flux plot as shown in Figure 5-9.

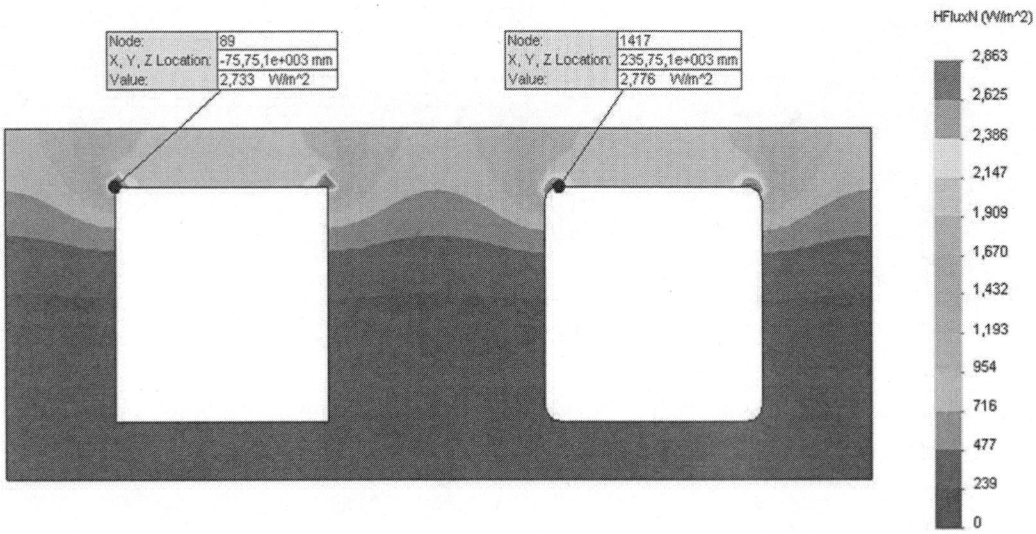

Figure 5-9: Heat Flux results from study *2D thermal 01*. The probed result in the sharp corner is 2733W/m^2; the probed result in the round corner is 2776W/m^2.

The fringe plot is used to present Heat Flux results. Results in round corners are probed where the horizontal straight line meets the arc.

Figure 5-9 shows next to no difference in **Heat Flux** between the sharp and round corners, but this will change once we use a more refined mesh.

Heat Flux is a vector value; fringe plots show the magnitude but not the direction. To see the direction of heat flow, create a vector plot of **Heat Flux** as shown in Figure 5-10.

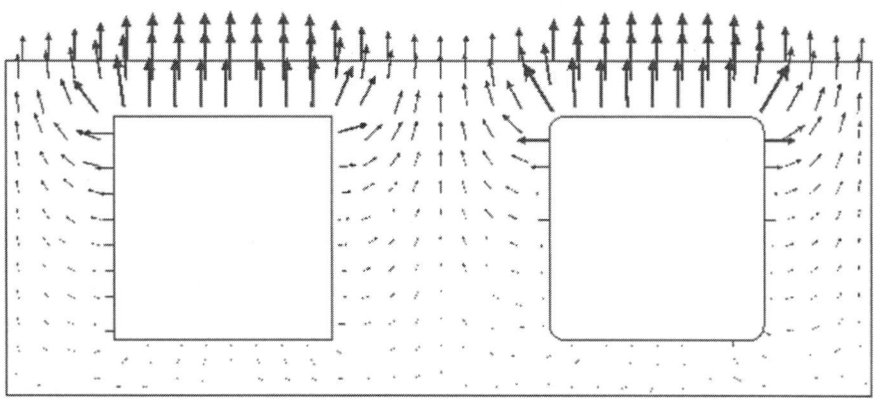

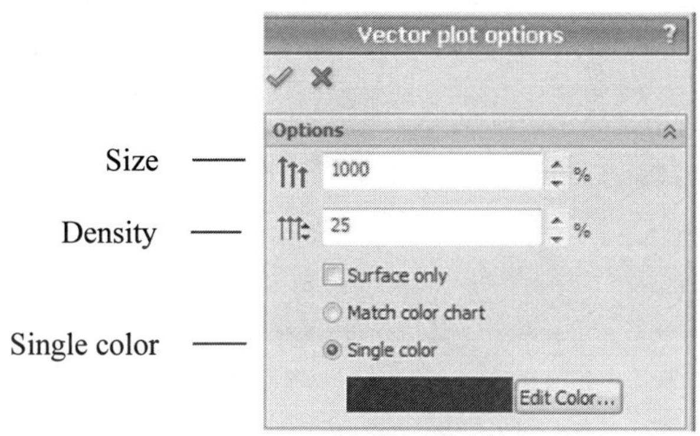

Figure 5-10: Heat Flux results from study *2D thermal 01.*

The vector plot may be modified using Vector plot options shown on the left. Color information is suppressed. Experiment with different Vector plot options.

Figure 5-10 makes it clear that heat enters and escapes the model only through the edges where prescribed temperatures have been defined. No heat enters or escapes the model through the bottom or sides. No heat is exchanged between the two segments.

Copy study *01 2D* into *02 2D* and add mesh controls as shown in Figure 5-11.

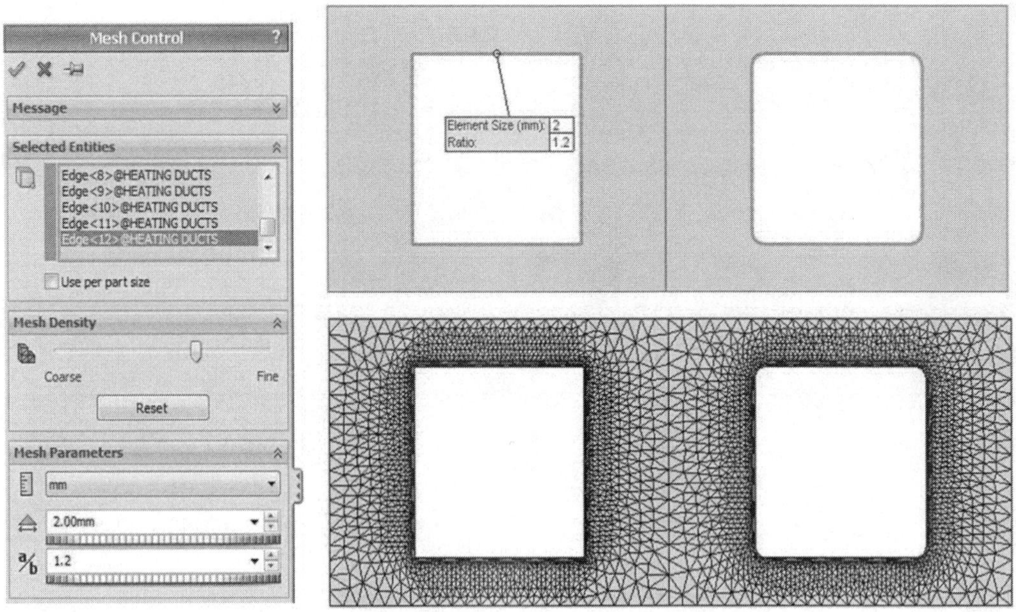

Figure 5-11: Mesh controls and mesh in study *2D thermal 02.*

An element size of 2mm is defined on all inside edges. A transition of 1.2 creates a large transition zone.

Also shown is the mesh created using these controls.

Using a small element size as shown in Figure 5-11 will demonstrate a very important difference between heat flow in the presence of a sharp and round corner. Obtain the solution of *02 2D* and review the **Temperature** and **Heat Flux** results shown in Figure 5-12 and Figure 5-13.

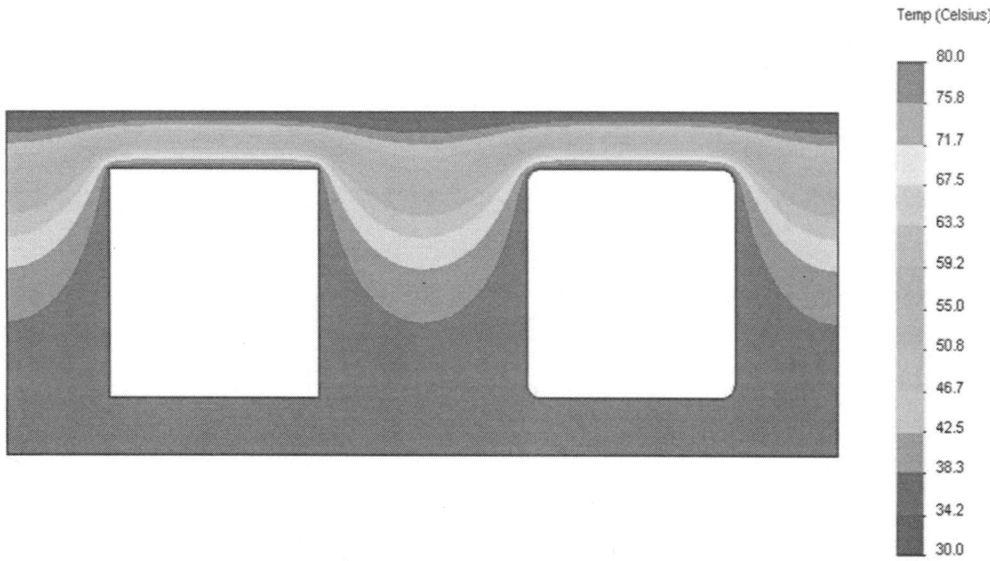

Figure 5-12: Temperature results from study *2D thermal 02.*

These results are indistinguishable from the results of study 2D thermal 01.

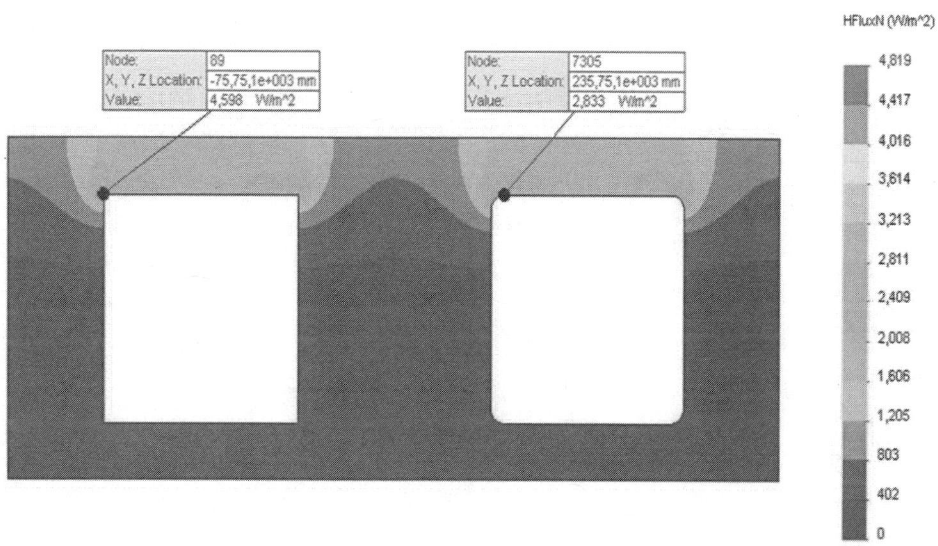

Figure 5-13: Heat Flux results from study *2D thermal 02.* A probed result in the sharp corner shows 4588W/m^2; a probed result in the round corner shows 2833W/m^2.

There is a distinct Heat Flux concentration in sharp corners.

The small elements used in study *02 2D* reveal a heat flux concentration in the sharp corners. The concentration was previously masked by large elements. To investigate this concentration, we will run three more studies with progressively more aggressive mesh biases as shown in Figure 5-14.

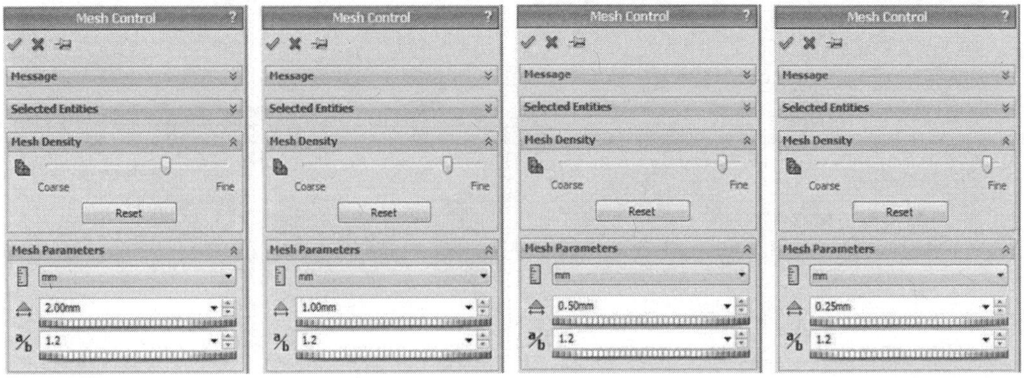

02 2D *03 3D* *04 3D* *05 3D*

Figure 5-14: Mesh control in studies *02 2D* through *05 2D.*

There is no Mesh Control in study 01 2D. The global element size (12mm) is the same in all studies.

The summary of all results is shown in Figure 5-15.

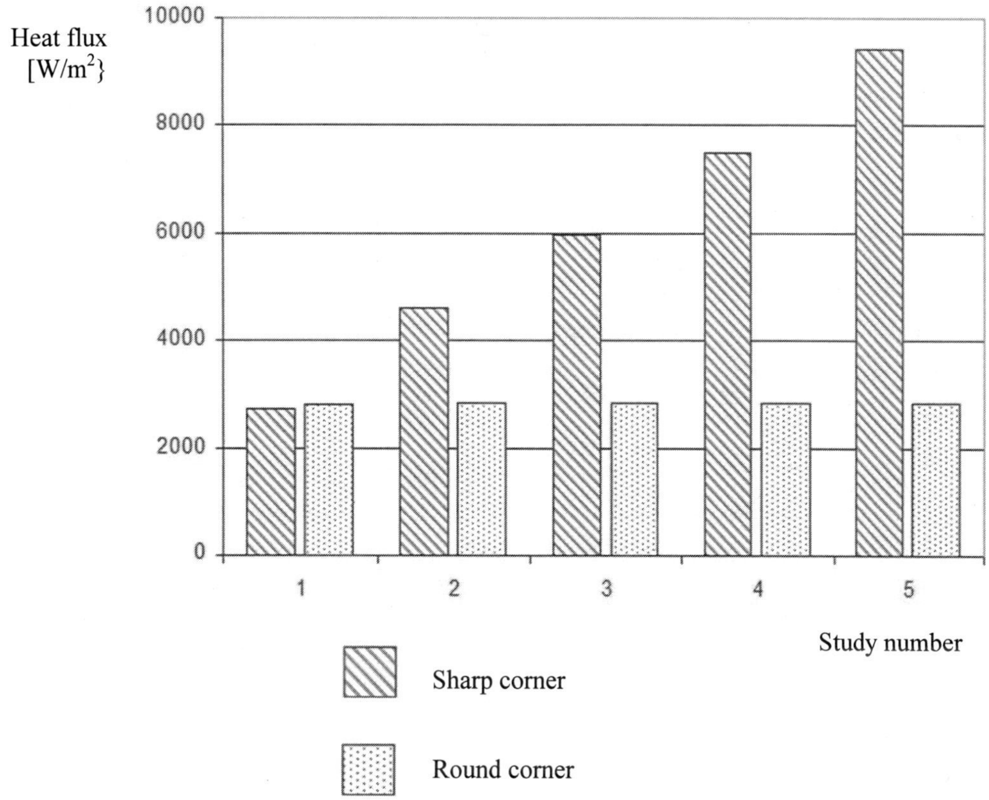

<u>Figure 5-15: Summary of Heat Flux results in five studies.</u>

The Heat Flux magnitude diverges with mesh refinement in the sharp corner while mesh refinement has no effect on Heat Flux in the round corner.

Divergent heat flux results in a sharp corner are caused by a singularity. The mathematical model has no heat flux solution in a sharp corner; a mathematician would say that the solution is singular there; an engineer would say that heat flux is infinite in a sharp re-entrant corner. Meshing introduces a discretization error which masks the singularity and may give an appearance of correct results especially when large elements are used as in study *01 2D*. Mesh refinement reveals the singularity demonstrating divergent results (Figure 5-15). Numerical values of heat flux in sharp and round corners seen in study *01 2D* are close by coincidence. We can't say which study provides "the best" heat flux results in sharp corners because all these results are meaningless. Heat flux results in locations coinciding with sharp corners (or edges in case of 3D models) are entirely dependent on the choice of discretization and by manipulating the mesh size we can produce as high result as we want!

Notice that sharp corners have no effect on temperature results. Sharp re-entrant corners (in 2D models) or sharp re-entrant edges (in 3D models) may be acceptable if the data of interest is temperature. They can be also acceptable if heat flux results are sought away from the singularity. However, if the maximum heat flux is the data of interest, rounds must be modeled no matter how small they are. Notice that a sharp (zero-radius) corner or edge is a mathematical abstract, in reality a round is always present even though it may be very small.

To demonstrate the divergence of heat flux results (singularity) we had to use very small elements. It was possible to execute a number of studies in a short time because we used a 2D model. Divergent heat flux can be also demonstrated with a 3D model but at a higher computational effort.

We'll now look at the heat power of the floor panel. Heat power is not sensitive to mesh refinement or heat flux singularities so we may use any of the five studies created so far. Heat power is analogous to the reaction force in a structural analysis.

To list heat power for two segments we use results from study *01 2D* and follow the steps shown in Figure 5-16.

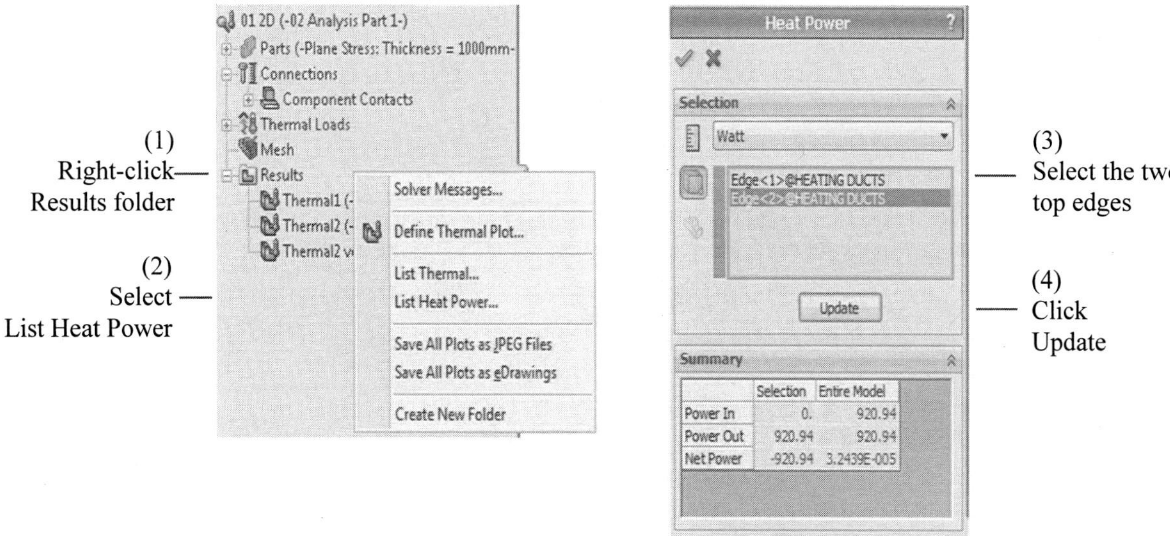

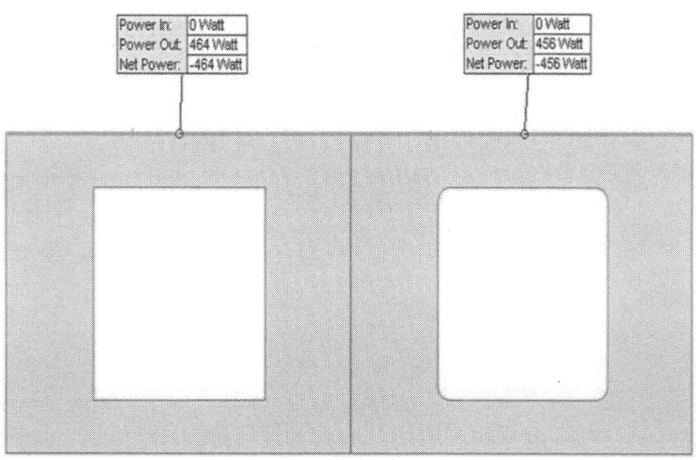

Figure 5-16: The heat power of the segment with sharp corners is 464W, and 456W for the segment with round corners. The total heat power of the two segments is 920W.

The difference in heat power is due to the different amount of conducting material, not the heat flux singularity.

To wrap up the analysis of the floor panel with prescribed temperatures for boundary conditions we'll create one more study: *06 3D* where a 3D model will be analyzed to find the total heat power.

Use a standard mesh with element size 20mm to create mesh as shown in Figure 5-17.

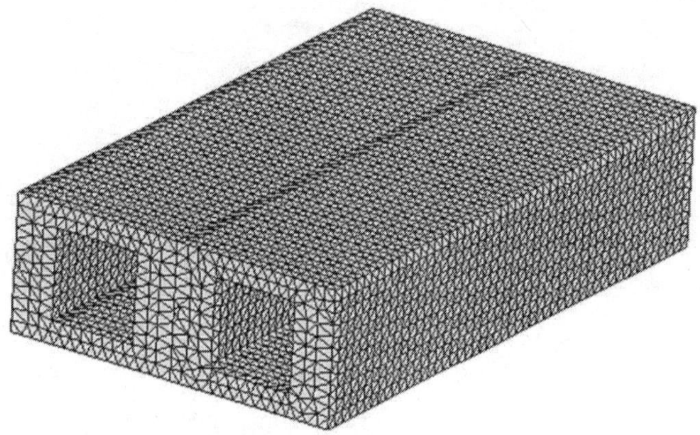

Figure 5-17: Solid element mesh of the 3D model with two segments.

The elements in the rounds have poor turn angles. It's acceptable for the analysis of heat power on the outside of the model but would require intervention if heat flux results on the inside faces were of interest.

Heat Power results are shown in Figure 5-18.

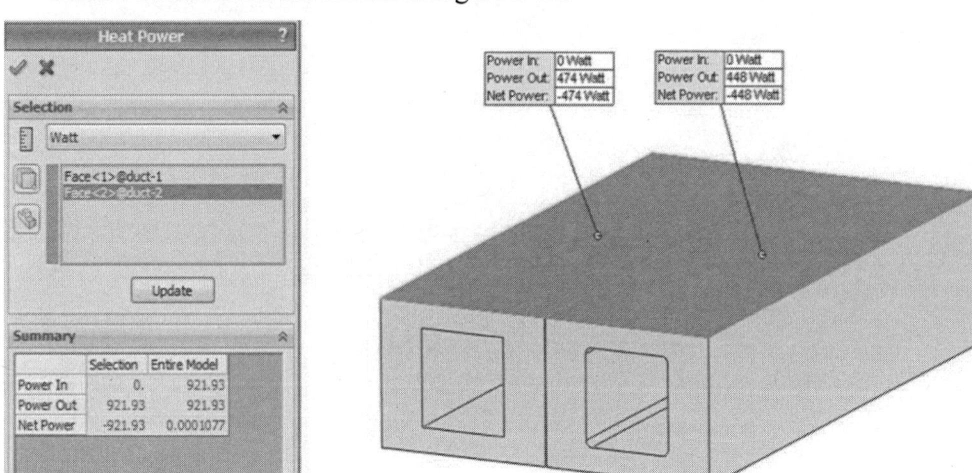

Figure 5-18: The heat power of the segment with sharp corners is 474W, and 448W for the segment with round corners. The total heat power of the two segments is 922W.

A small difference of results between the 2D model (Figure 5-16) and the 3D model (Figure 5-18) is caused by discretization error which differs between 2D and 3D models.

6: Floor heating duct – part 2

Topics covered

- Heat transfer by convection
- Free and forced convection
- Convection coefficient
- Ambient (bulk) temperature

Project description

We have completed part 1 of the floor heat panel analysis modeling heat flow induced by prescribed temperatures: 80°C on the hot side and 30°C on the cold side. Now, we'll take this analysis one step further.

Assume that we have taken the following temperature measurements: air inside: 85 °C, inside faces: 80°C, air outside: 17°C, outside face: 30°C. Notice that the face temperatures are the prescribed temperatures from part 1 of this analysis.

Given the above temperature information we want to find out what convection conditions must be present on the hot and on the cold side to keep these steady state temperatures. For that we use the same assembly model HEATING DUCTS and switch to configuration *03 Analysis Part2*; this configuration has only one segment (Figure 6-1).

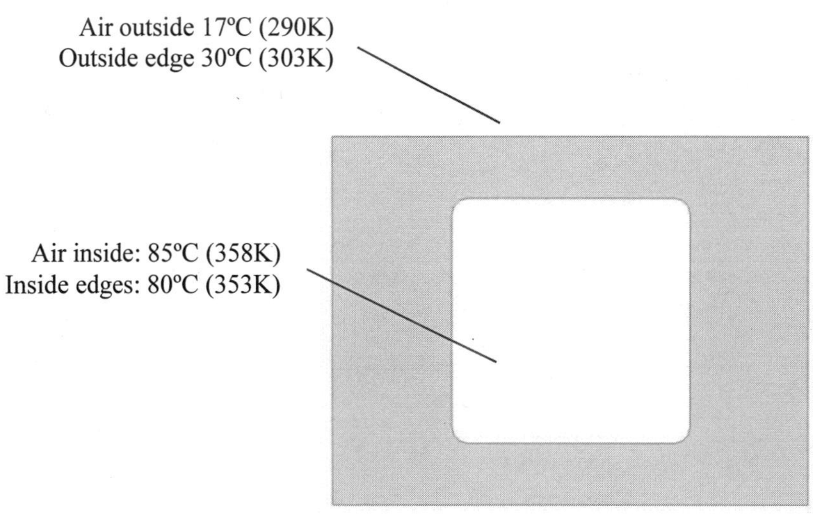

Figure 6-1: HEATING DUCTS assembly model in *03 Analysis Part3* configuration.

A 2D Simplification of a segment with round corners used.

The bottom outside face is assumed to be insulated and side faces don't exchange heat because this segment is a part of larger assembly, therefore no thermal boundary conditions are defined on these faces. We'll proceed in two steps using the 2D model; refer to Figure 6-1 for the location of inside and outside edges.

Step 1 (study *07 2D*):

Thermal boundary conditions on the inside edges are prescribed temperatures of 80°C, this is unchanged from part 1. The convection coefficient on the outside edge will be changed in steps from 10W/m^2/K to 1000W/m^2/K to determine at what value an average outside edge temperature of 30°C is produced.

Step 2 (study *08 2D*):

The convection condition on the outside edge will be the one found in step 1. The convection coefficient on the inside edges will change in steps from 10W/m^2/K to 1000W/m^2/K to determine at what value an average inside edge temperature of 80°C is produced.

Once the convection coefficients on both sides have been found, there won't be a need to define prescribed temperatures, and heat flow will be modeled more realistically.

To prepare study *07 2D,* use **2D simplification**. Define **Convection** as shown in Figure 6-2. Define a prescribed **Temperature** of 80°C on the inside edges as in part 1 of this exercise.

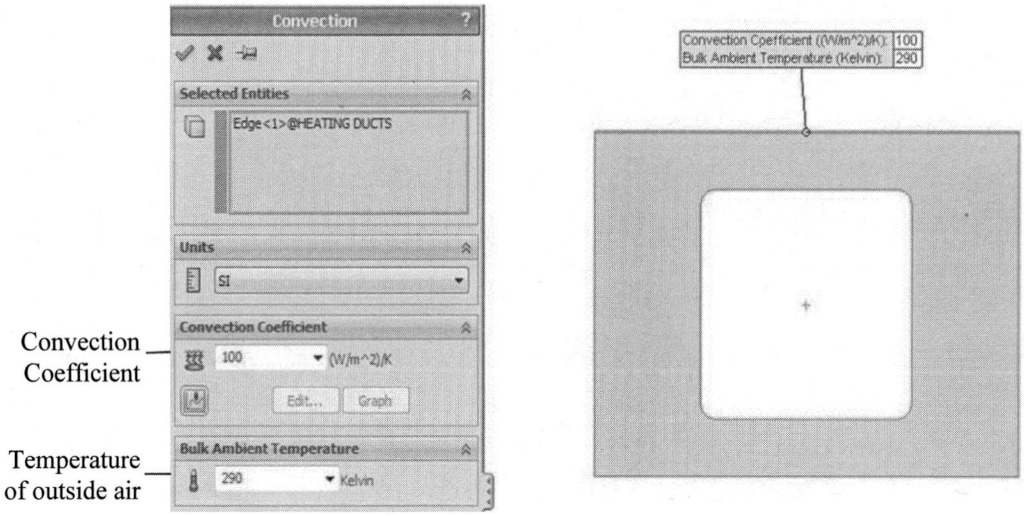

Figure 6-2: Convection coefficient on the outside edge.

A sample value of 100W/m^2/K is shown.

Run study *07 2D* for the following values of convection coefficients on the outside edge: 10, 50, 100, 200, 300, 500, and 1000. For each value, find the average temperature on the outside edge as shown in Figure 6-3.

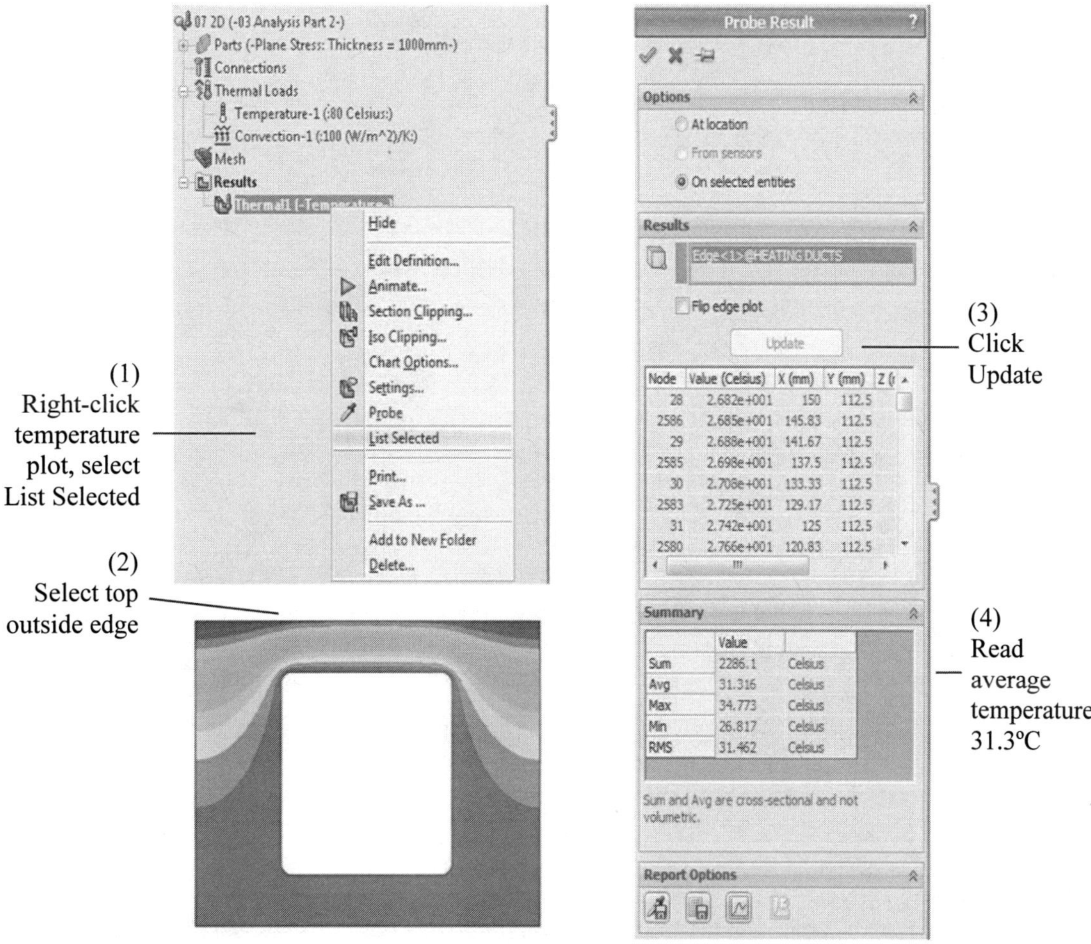

Figure 6-3: Average temperature on the outside edge.

With a convection coefficient of 100W/m²/K, the average temperature of the outside edge is 31.3°C.

The summary of all runs for convection coefficients on the outside edge of 10, 50, 100, 200, 300, 500, and 1000, is shown in Figure 6-4.

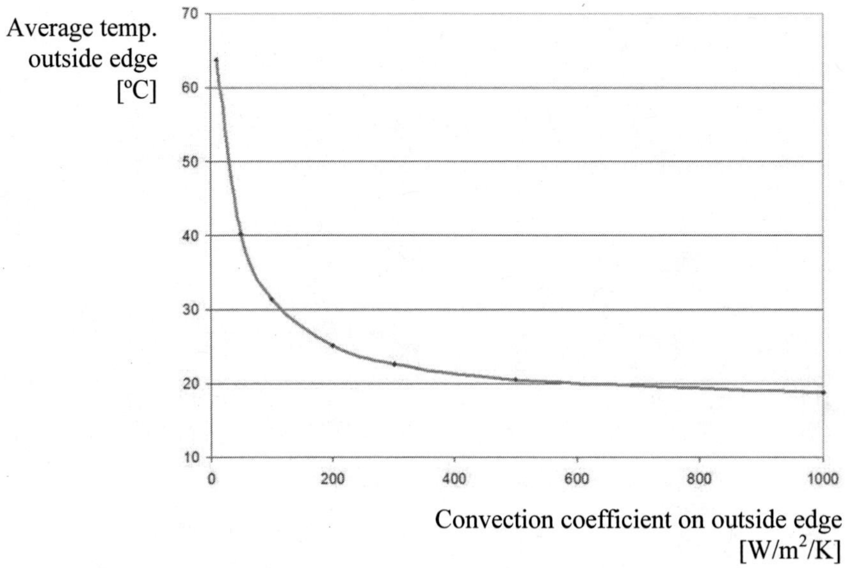

Figure 6-4: Average temperature on the top outside edge as a function of convection coefficient.

A convection coefficient of 100W/m²/K in combination with an ambient temperature of 290K results in an average temperature of the outside edge of approximately 30°C. Compare this with Figure 6-3.

Having found the convection coefficient on the outside edge we proceed to finding convection coefficient on the inside edges. Copy study *07 2D* into *08 2D* and delete the prescribed temperature on the inside edges. Make sure that the **Convection** on the outside edge is characterized by a convection coefficient of 100W/m²/K and an ambient temperature of 290K and keep it unchanged throughout the analysis.

Run study *08 2D* for the following values of convection coefficients on the inside edges: 10, 50, 100, 200, 300, 500, and 1000; refer to Figure 6-5.

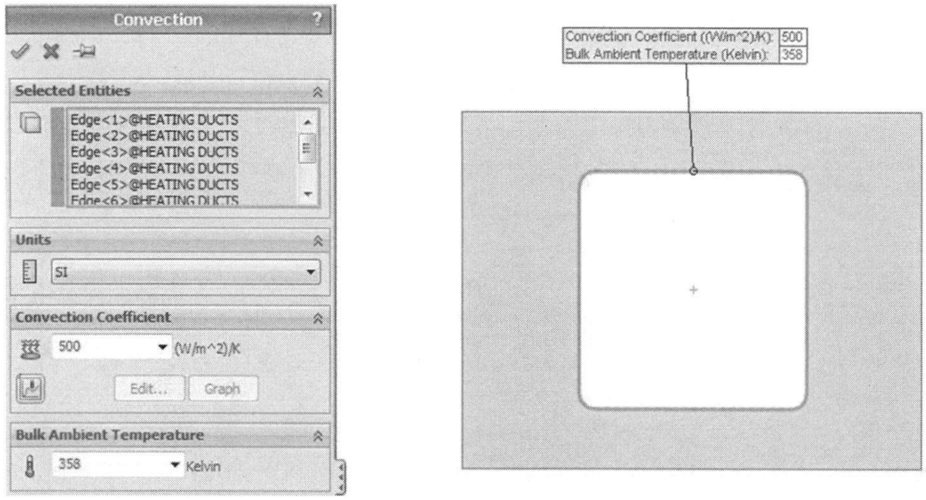

Figure 6-5: Convection coefficient on the inside edges.

Sample value of 500W/m²/K is shown.

For each value of convection coefficient find the average temperature on the inside edge as shown in Figure 6-6.

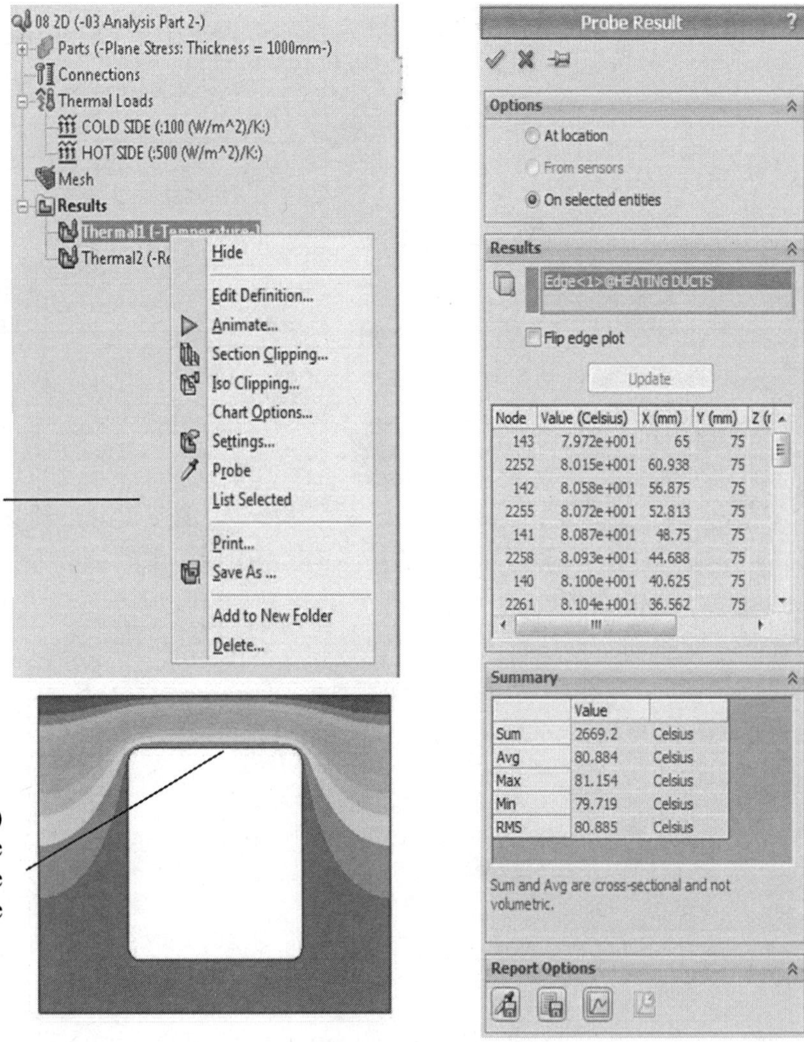

Figure 6-6: Average temperature on the inside edge.

A convection coefficient of 500W/m²/K gives the average temperature of 80.9ºC on the inside edge.

A summary of all runs for convection coefficients on the inside edges of 10, 50, 100, 200, 300, 500, and 1000, is shown in Figure 6-7.

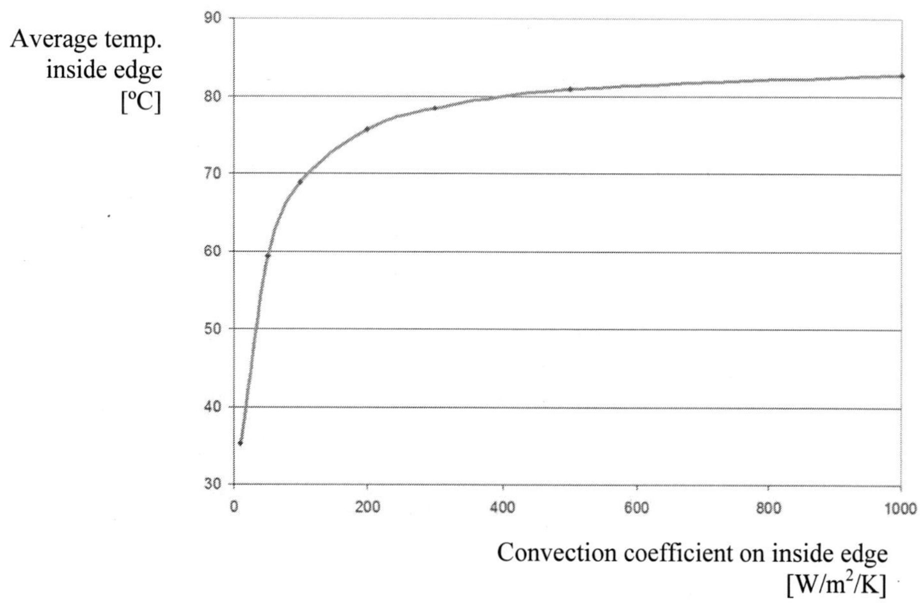

Figure 6-7: Average temperature on the top inside edge as a function of convection coefficient.

A convection coefficient of 400W/m²/K gives an average temperature close to 80°C on the inside edge. Compare this with Figure 6-6 showing results for 500W/m²/K.

Run study *08 2D* one more time with a convection coefficient of 400W/m²/K on the top outside edge and see that the average temperature is 31.4 °C.

In summary, we have found the convection boundary conditions that approximate the prescribed temperature boundary conditions used in part 1 of the HEATING PANEL analysis:

Convection boundary condition on hot side (inside):

Convection coefficient: 400W/m²/K; ambient temp. 85°C (358K);

This boundary condition produces an average temperature 80°C on the top inside edge.

Convection boundary condition on cold side (outside):

Convection coefficient: 100W/m²/K; ambient temp. 17°C (290K);

This boundary condition produces an average temperature 31.4 °C on the top outside edge.

The important difference is that in part 1, the prescribed temperature along the edges is uniform. Using convection boundary conditions, temperature along the edges is no longer uniform, which is more realistic.

Heat Power in the presence of a convection boundary conditions is shown in (Figure 6-8).

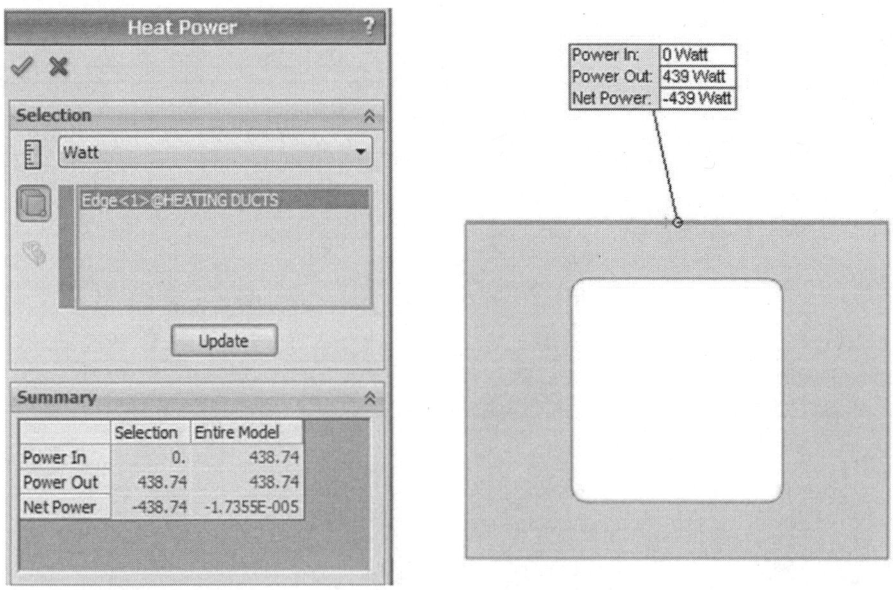

Figure 6-8: Heat power of one segment.

Each segment produces 439W heat power.

Compare this result to the result from part 1 presented in chapter 5.

7: Hot plate

Topics covered

- Transient thermal analysis
- Conductive heat transfer
- Convective heat transfer
- Heat power
- Thermostat
- Thermal inertia

Project description

A ceramic housing has an embedded heating element producing 1000W of thermal power. The power can be cycled on and off by a thermostat so the plate keeps the surface temperature at about 100°C. We will study temperature fluctuations with time for given thermostat settings.

Procedure

Open assembly model HOT PLATE, make sure the assembly is in the *01 heating plate* configuration (Figure 7-1).

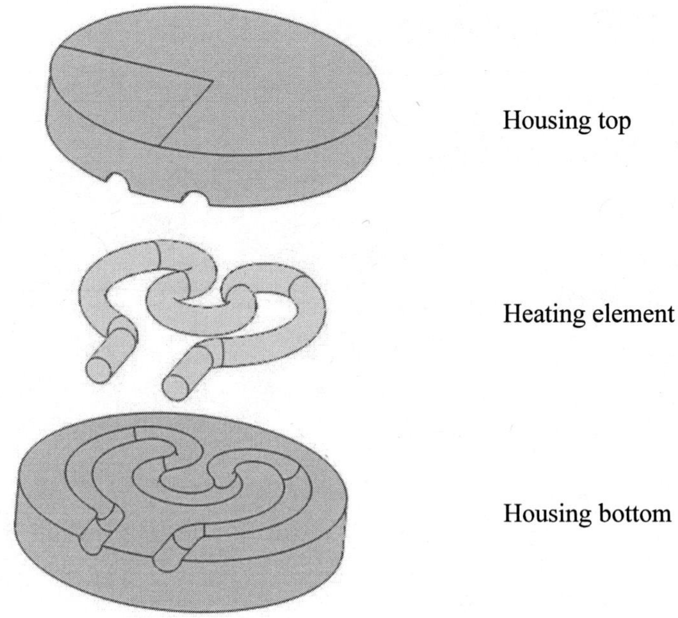

Figure 7-1: HOT PLATE assembly in *01 heating plate* configuration.

The heating plate consists of two identical halves that house a heating element. The exploded view shows all three assembly components. The split line in the housing will be used to define a thermostat position.

Analysis of temperature fluctuations, while power is cycled on and off, requires transient thermal analysis. Create a Thermal study *01 transient* and set the study properties as shown in Figure 7-2.

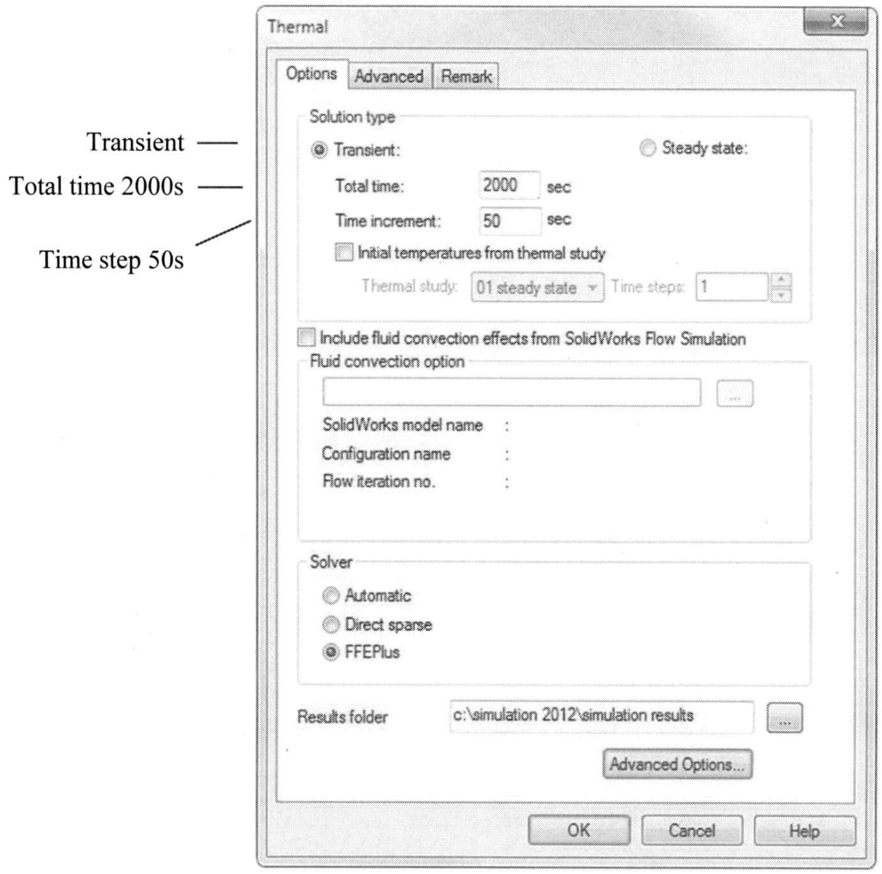

Figure 7-2: Properties of the transient thermal study.

The duration of analysis and time step usually requires some experimenting during trial runs.

Using the transient study settings shown in Figure 7-2, the analysis duration will be 2000s; it will be completed in 50 steps, 40s each.

Define **Heat Power** and a **Thermostat** as shown in Figure 7-3.

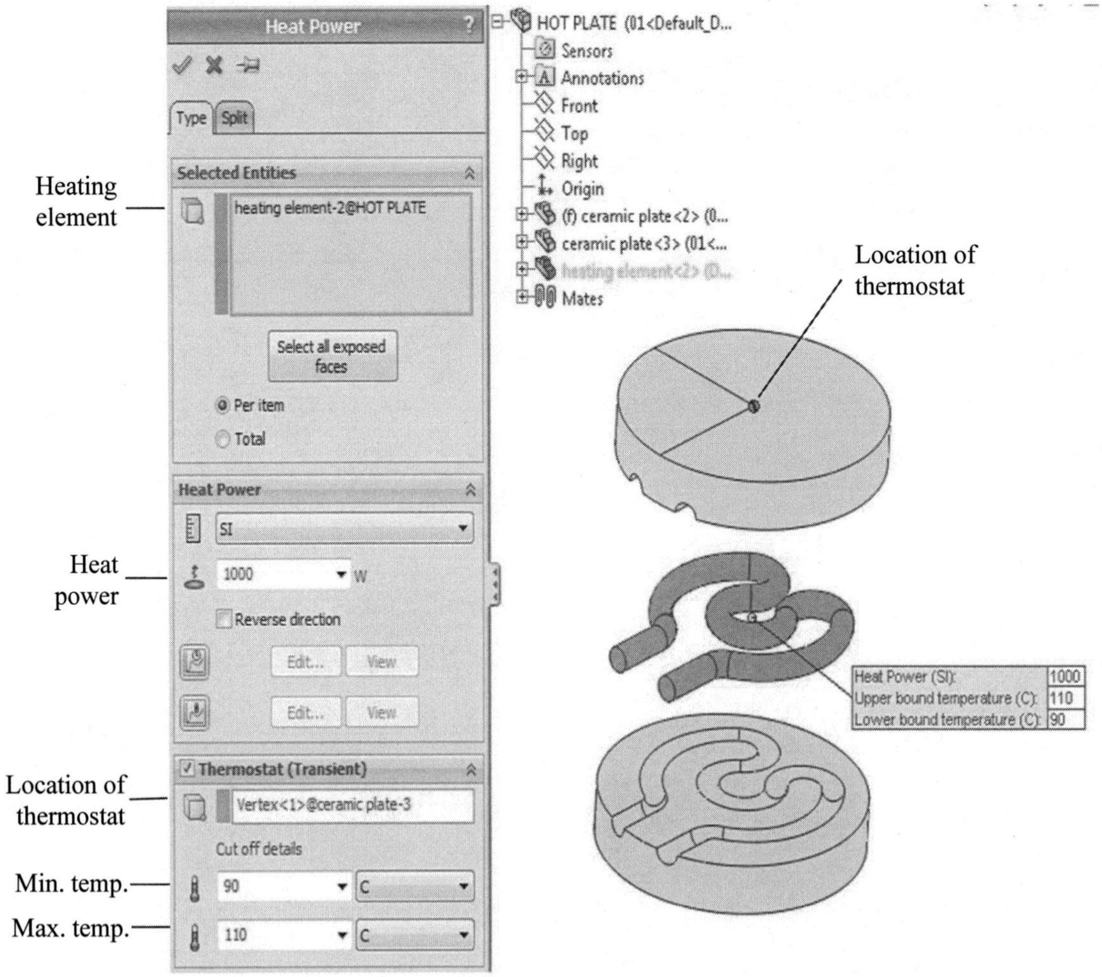

Figure 7-3: Definition of Heat Power controlled by a Thermostat.

Select the heating element from the fly-out menu. Place the thermostat in the corner of the split line. The temperature reading of the location of the thermostat is the temperature reading that will control the power element on and off.

With the **Thermostat** setting set up as in Figure 7-3, power is turned on at time t = 0 and it stays on until the temperature reaches 110°C. At 110°C power is turned off until the temperature drops down to 90°C. Then the power is turned on again. It is important to notice that this is the temperature on the outside of the heating plate, not the temperature of the heating element.

Define **Convection** as shown in Figure 7-4. Select all external faces of the ceramic housing. Do not select any face of the heating element.

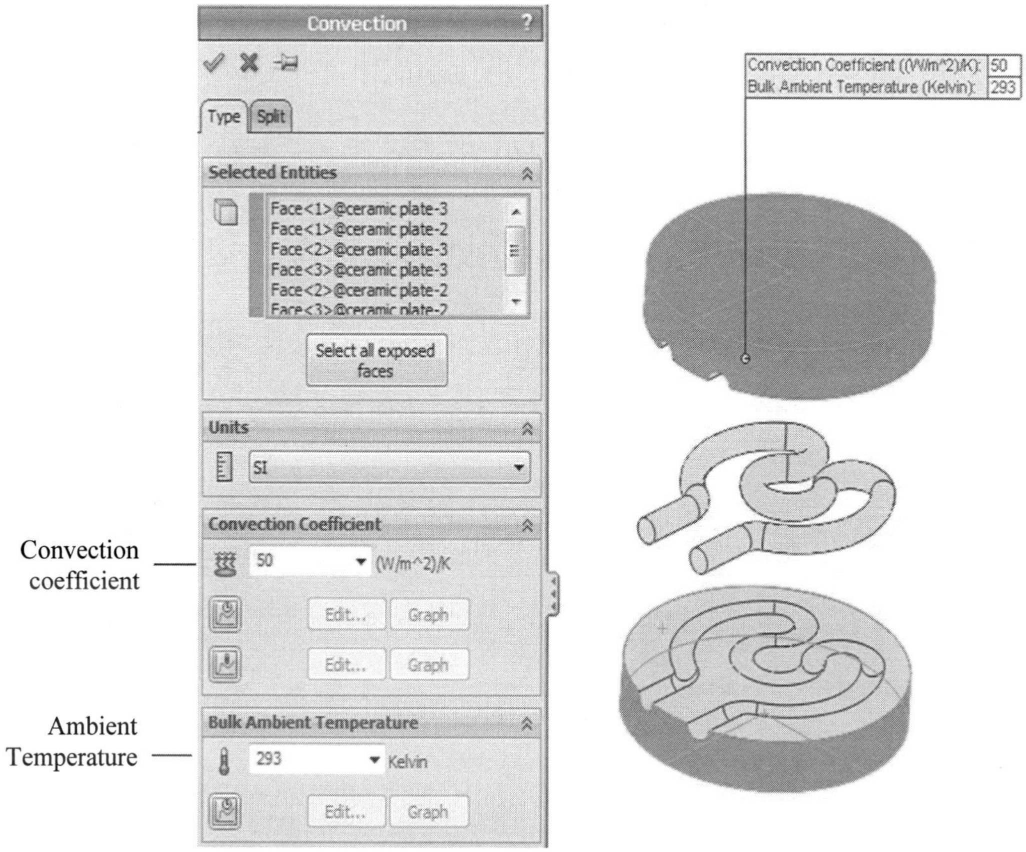

Figure 7-4: Definition of Convection.

The faces of the heating elements that stick out of the housing are insulated; do not define Convection conditions for these faces.

Define an **Initial temperature** to all assembly components as shown in Figure 7-5.

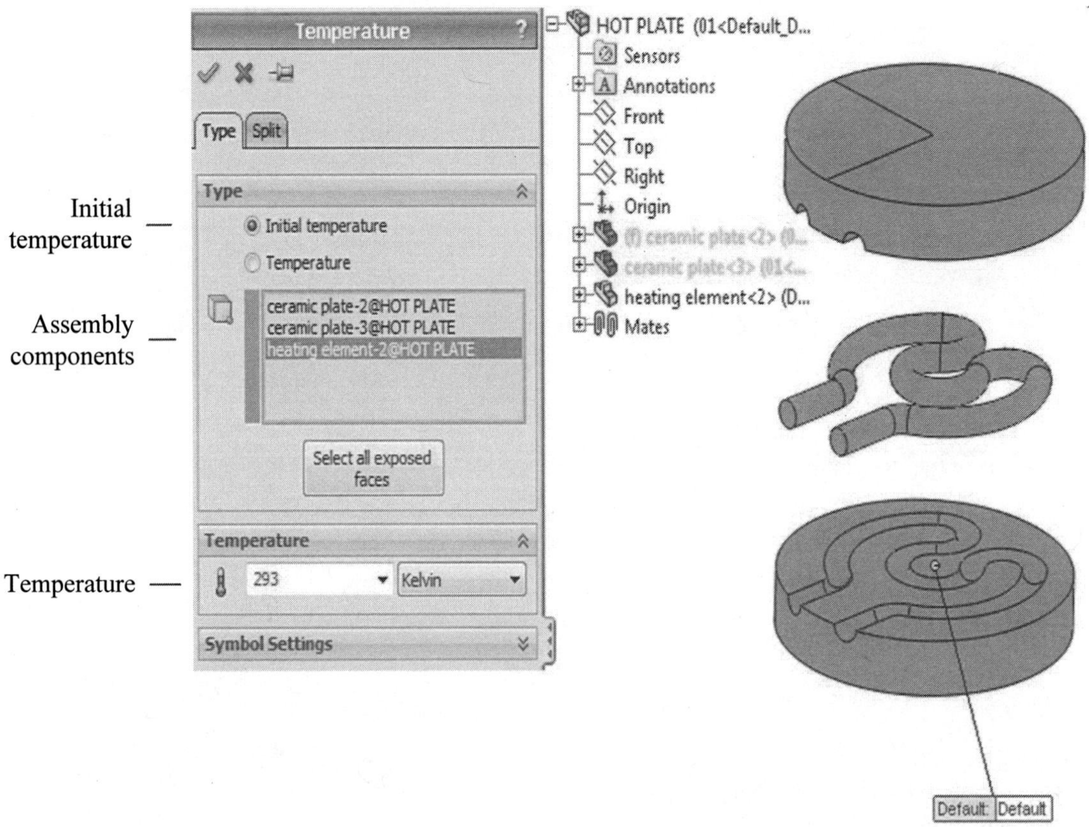

Figure 7-5: Definition of Initial temperature.

Select all three assembly components from the fly-out menu. Alternatively you may select the assembly.

Notice that **Initial temperature** must be defined in **Transient** thermal analysis but not in **Steady State** thermal analysis.

Mesh the model with a **Curvature based mesh** using settings shown in Figure 7-6.

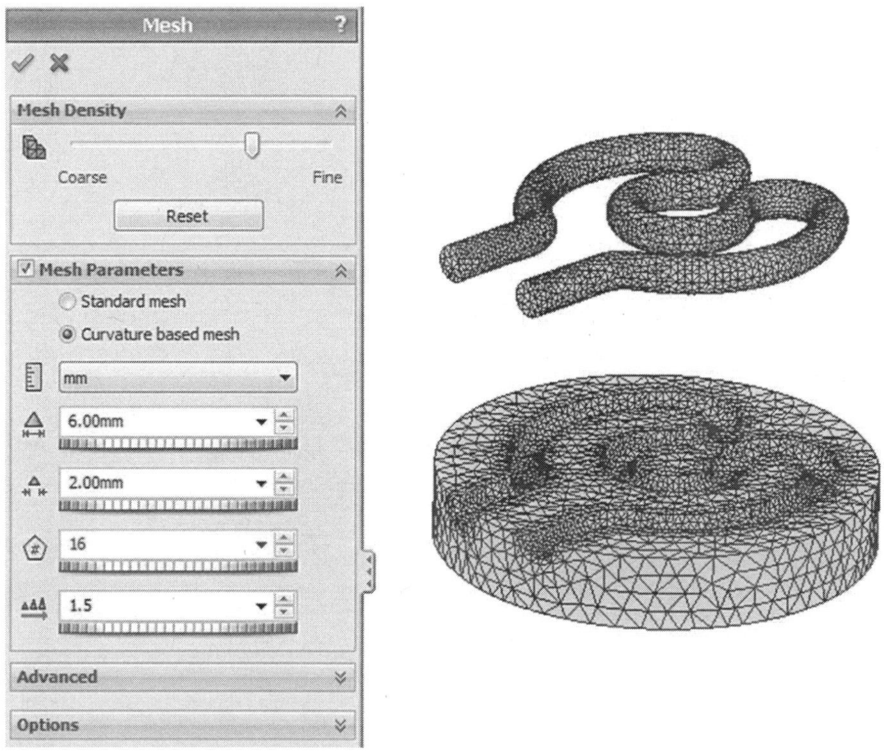

Figure 7-6: Curvature based mesh shown in exploded view, the upper half of the ceramic housing is hidden from view.

The maximum element size is 6mm. A minimum of 16 elements in a circle gives an element turn angle of 22.5°.

A **Curvature based mesh** is more convenient to use because of the many curved faces present in the model. Review the mesh using exploded view to see how the heating element has been meshed. The mesh deficiencies would be easy to miss without the use of exploded view.

We assume an ideal bond between the heating element and ceramic plate; therefore no thermal resistance is defined there.

The solution of study *01transient* completes in 50 time steps. If you want to reduce the solution time, use a less demanding mesh setting and/or switch to **Standard mesh**. You may also reduce the time of analysis. Once a solution completes, show the **Temperature** plot and follow the steps in Figure 7-7 to create a **Temperature Time History** graph.

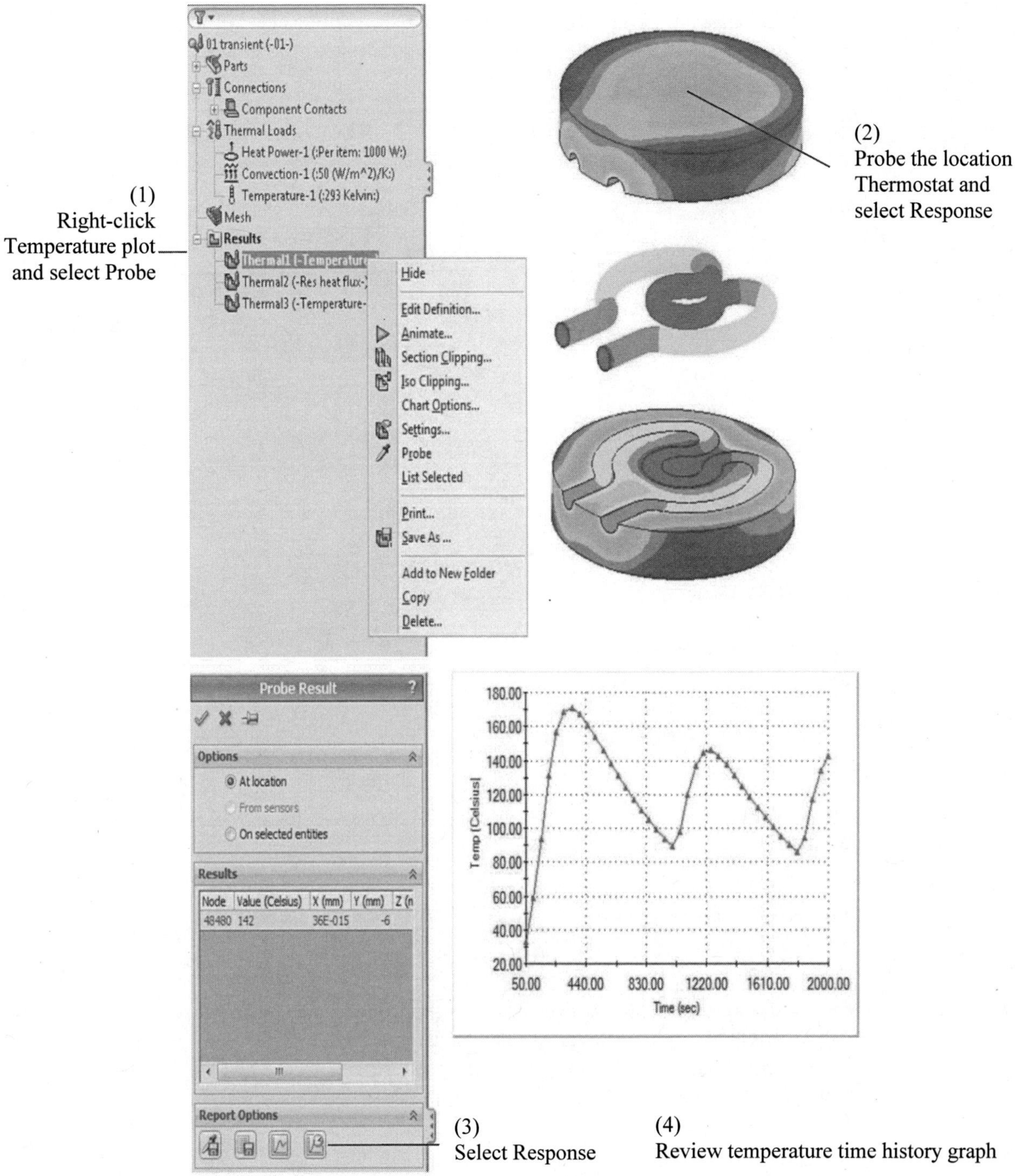

Figure 7-7: Temperature at the Thermostat location during 2000s after power has been first turned on.

After the initial warm-up period, the temperature fluctuates between 85C° and 145°C.

Notice that the range of temperature fluctuation of 85C° to 145°C is wider than what we have defined for our Thermostat. This is due to the effect of thermal inertia; after power has been turned off, the temperature in the thermostat location keeps on climbing for a while. After power has been turned on, the temperature keeps on dropping for a while.

A review of the results for the last performed time step 50 using exploded view is shown in Figure 7-8.

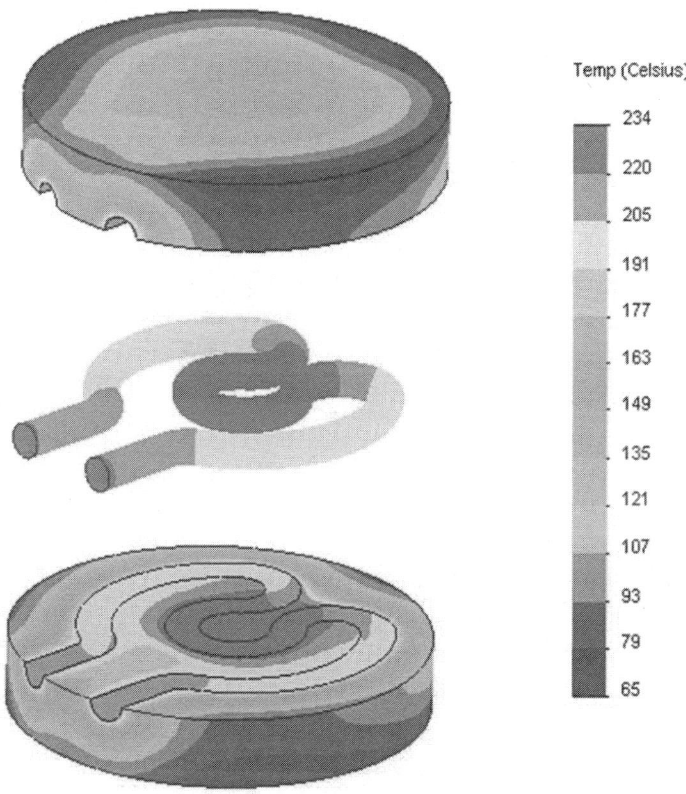

Figure 7-8: Temperature at the end of analysis, time step 50.

Notice the non-uniform temperature of the heating element.

Repeat the analysis with different **Heat Power** and **Thermostat** settings to see the effects of different settings on the temperature time history.

Due to double symmetry of the HOT PLATE assembly in configuration *01 heating plate* we could have conducted the same analysis on one half or one quarter of the assembly model. We will take this approach in the continuation of this exercise, where we analyze the heating plate complete with a coffee pot.

Change configuration to *02 coffee pot* and notice that the assembly now includes the hot plate and a glass bowl filled with water. This assembly has single symmetry. An assembly cut reduces the model to one half (Figure 7-9).

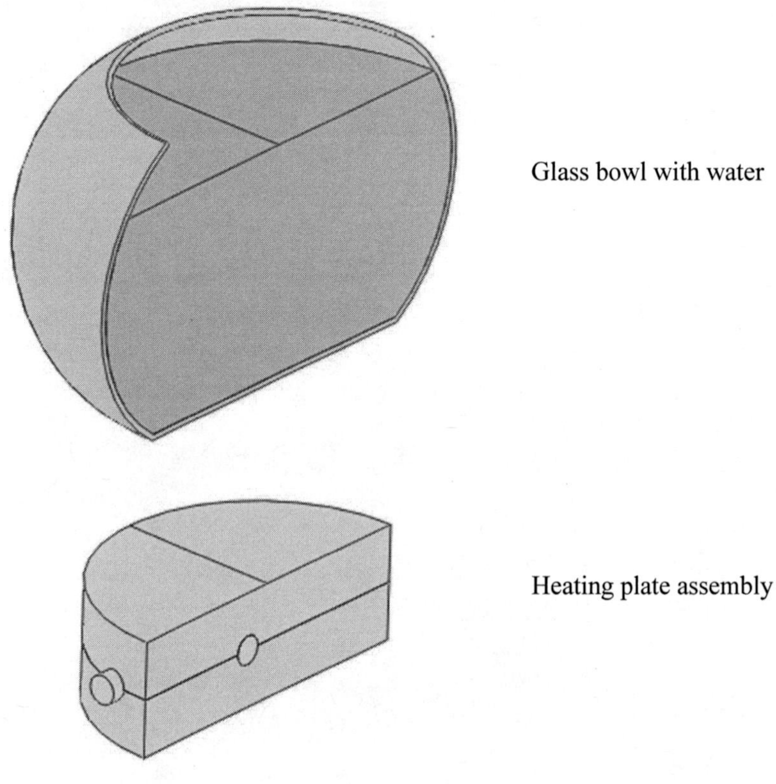

Figure 7-9: HOT PLATE assembly in *01 coffee* configuration.

The model is shown in a partially exploded view.

Our objective is to find the steady state temperature of water when the glass bowl sits on top of the heating plate powered by a constant 200W. Create study *02 steady state*.

The most important part of this exercise is the definition of heat conductivity of water. Water has already defined properties in the CAD model (Figure 7-10), but these properties must be modified in **Simulation**. Why?

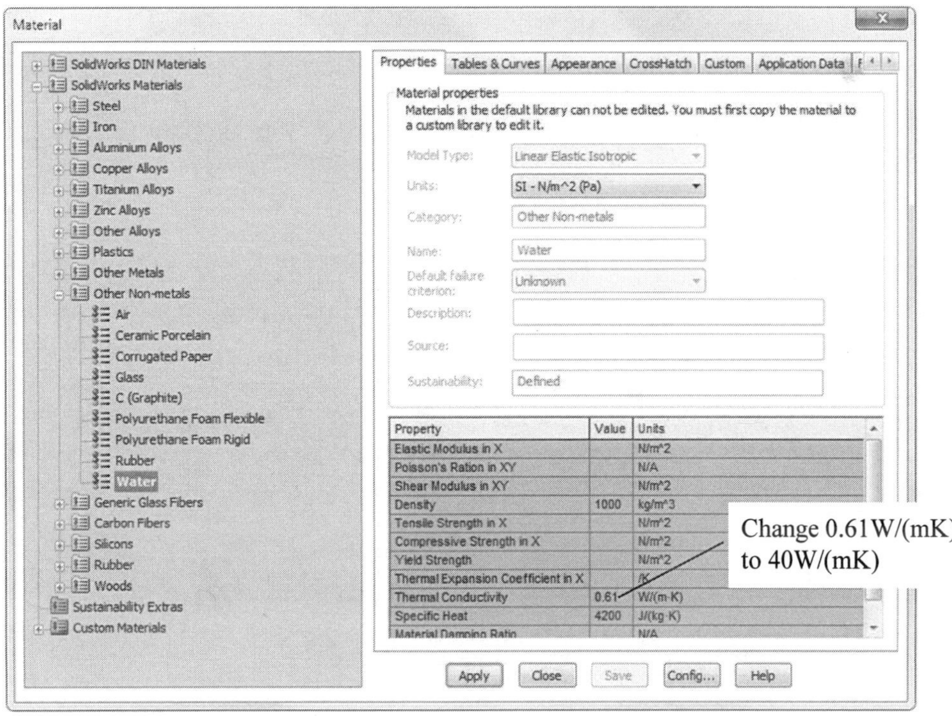

Figure 7-10: Thermal properties of water assigned to CAD model.

The thermal conductivity must be set to 40W/m/K prior to running analysis. To make this change follow steps in Figure 7-11.

The thermal conductivity as shown in Figure 7-10 does not take into consideration that water actually mixes while it is being heated and convection, rather than conduction, is mainly responsible for heat transfer in water. Yet, the only mechanism of heat transfer that can be modeled in a solid body (and this is how water is modeled here) is conduction. To account for convection inside the volume of water which we can't model, we have to define an artificially high thermal conduction of 40W/m/K. This value has been found by testing. Modification of thermal conductivity requires definition of custom material. Follow the steps shown in Figure 7-11. Make sure you do the modification in the **Simulation** study, not in the CAD assembly model.

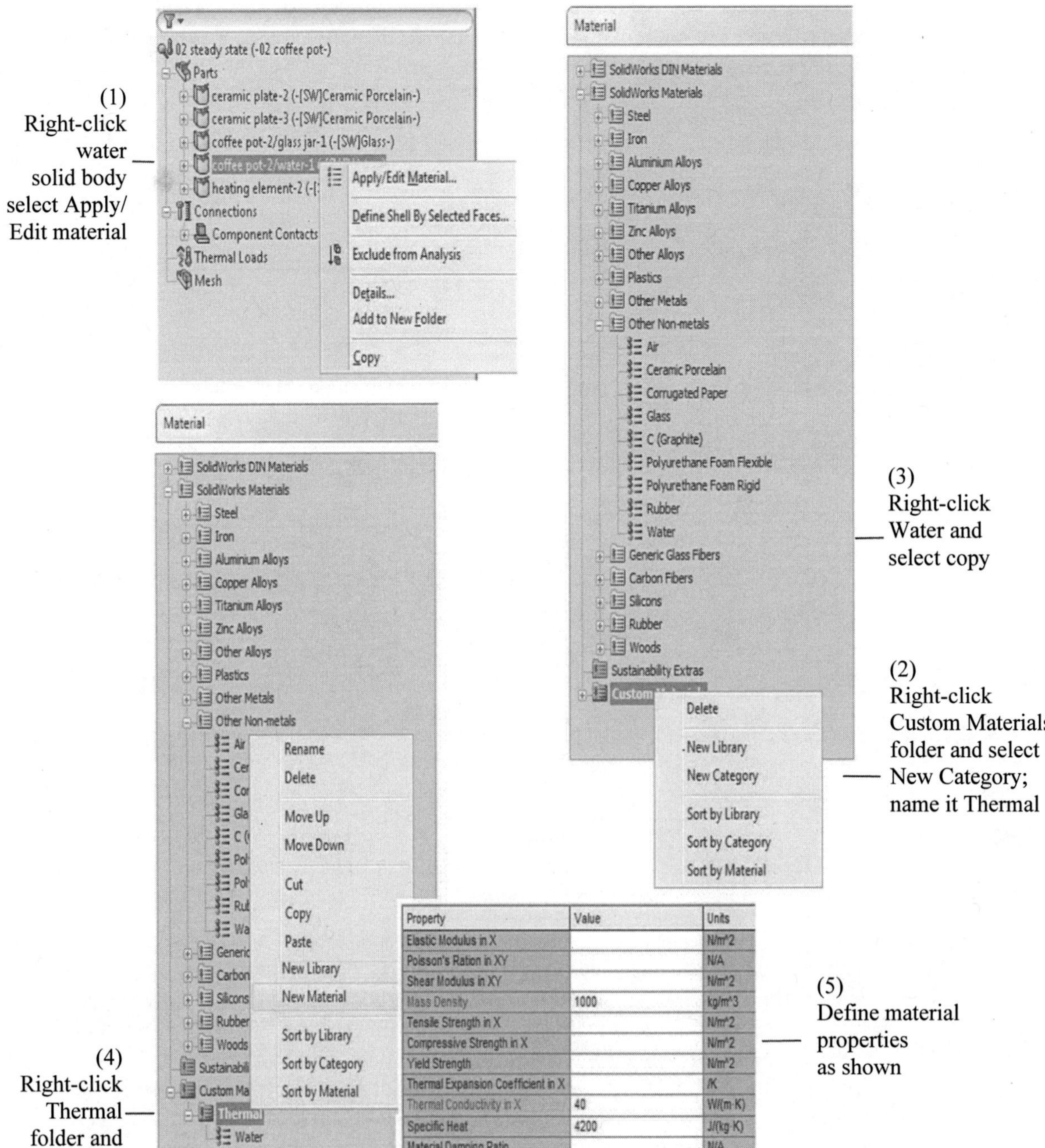

Figure 7-11: Definition of custom material properties of water in the Simulation study.

Define mass a density of 1000kg/m^3, a thermal conductivity of 40W/m/K, and a specific heat of 4200J/kg/.

Notice that mass density and specific heat are not required in steady state thermal analysis. We define them to make the model ready for transient thermal analysis should you wish to run it later.

Contact between the heating plate and glass is not perfect and a **Thermal Resistance** contact condition must be defined as shown in Figure 7-12.

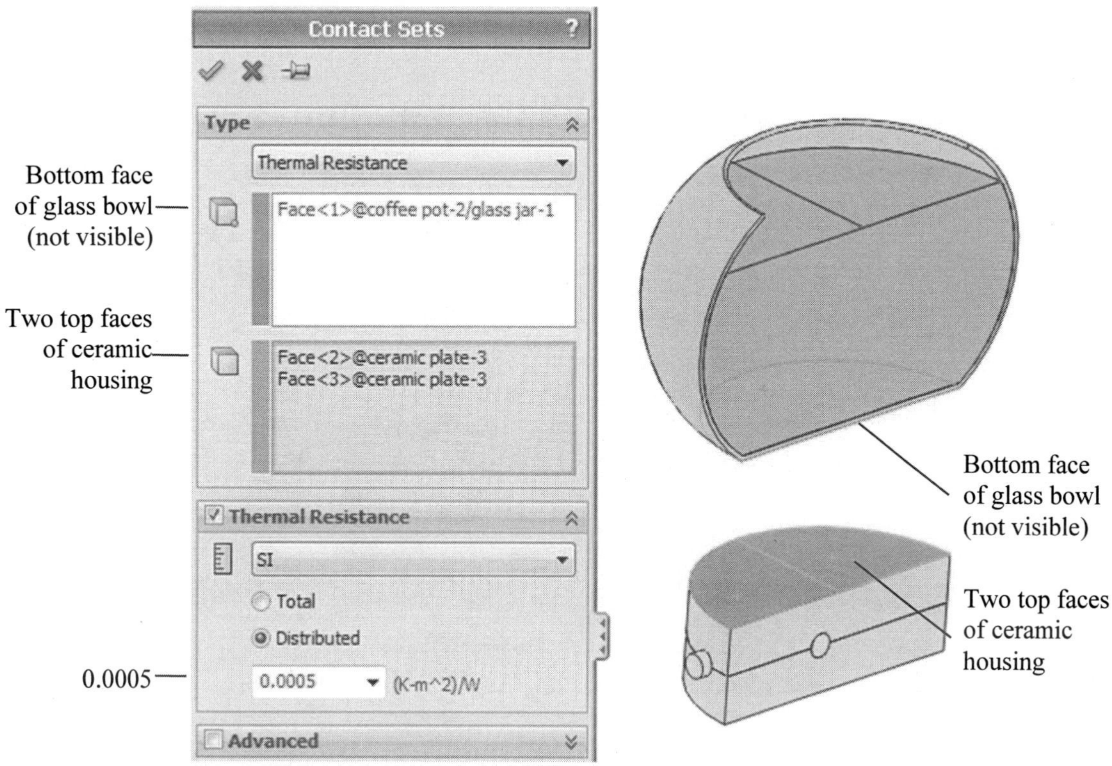

Figure 7-12: Definition of Thermal Resistance between the heating plate and the glass bowl.

The value of Thermal Resistance can be determined in testing by measuring the temperature difference between the faces that remain in contact.

The heating element produces 200W of power. One half of the heating element is modeled, therefore define 100W. To apply **Heat Power**, refer to Figure 7-3. Since this is a **Steady State** analysis, there is no need to define a **Thermostat**.

Apply **Convection** as shown in Figure 7-13.

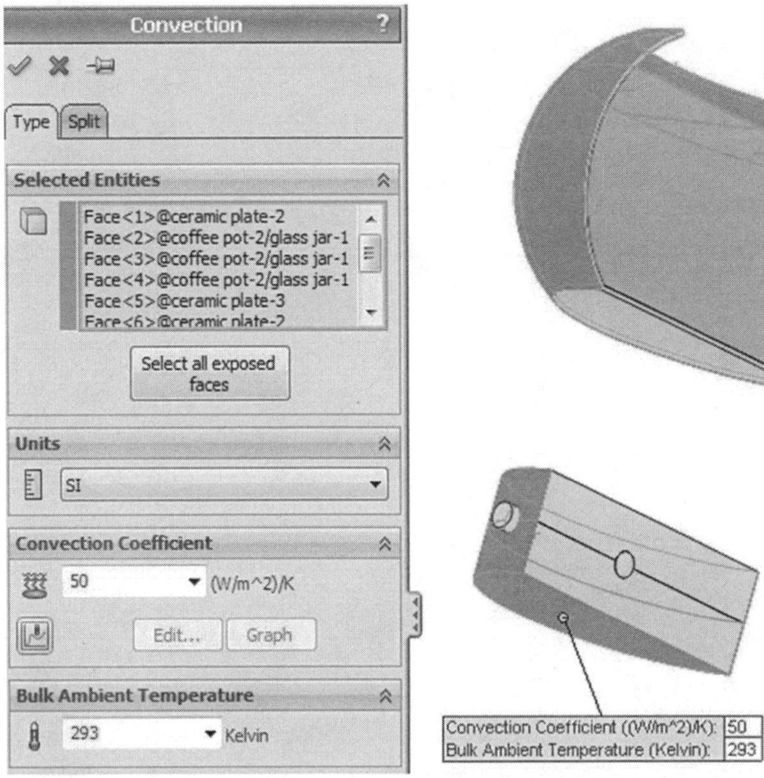

Figure 7-13: Definition of Convection.

Define a convection boundary condition for all faces exposed to air including water and excluding faces of the heating elements that stick out of the housing. Do not apply convection boundary conditions to any face in the plane of symmetry.

Due to symmetry, there is no heat flow in the direction normal to the plane of symmetry. The symmetry boundary condition is enforced by not defining convection on the faces in the plane of symmetry.

We have to point out that while defining **Convection** in **SolidWorks Simulation** is easily done, finding the actual value is often the most difficult part of thermal analysis. Applying the same $50W/(m^2K)$ to all faces including water is a modeling simplification which has to be supported by testing.

Having defined **Heat Power** and **Convection**, we have already defined the mechanisms of heat transfer. No Initial **Temperature** is required in **Steady State** thermal analysis.

Mesh the model using mesh settings shown in Figure 7-6 and run the solution.

Review the **Temperature** plot as shown in Figure 7-14.

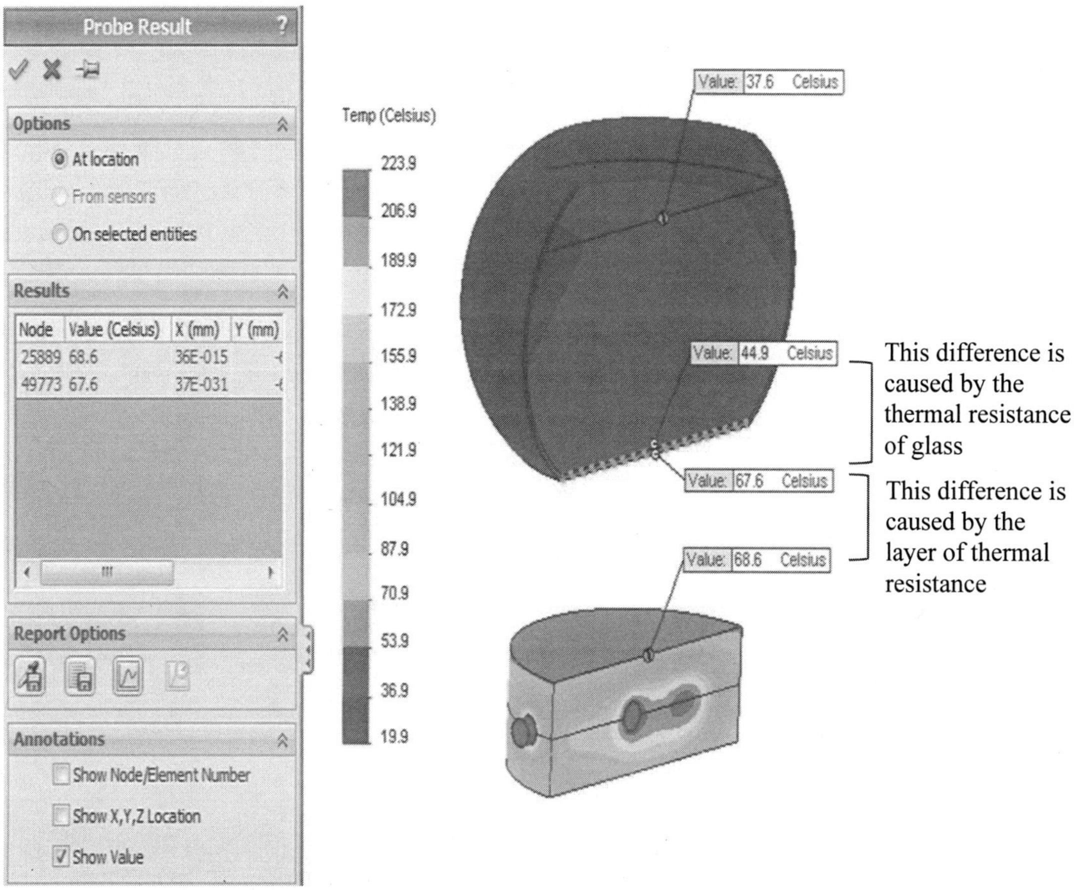

Figure 7-14: Temperature results; probing shows the effect of the layer of thermal resistance and thermal resistance of glass.

Notice that probing location on the side of the hot plate is well defined by split line but on the side of coffee pot you have to "eyeball" probing location. Therefore, you probed result may be slightly different from these shown above.

When probing any results, you may deselect Show Node/Element Number and Show X,Y,Z Location for an uncluttered display.

The thermal resistance illustrated in Figure 7-14 is an inverse of thermal conductivity and has units [K/m^2/W].

In the CAD assembly, hide all parts belonging to the heating plate leaving only the COFFEE POT subassembly visible. Create a resultant **Heat Flux** plot; use **Vector plot options** as shown in Figure 7-15.

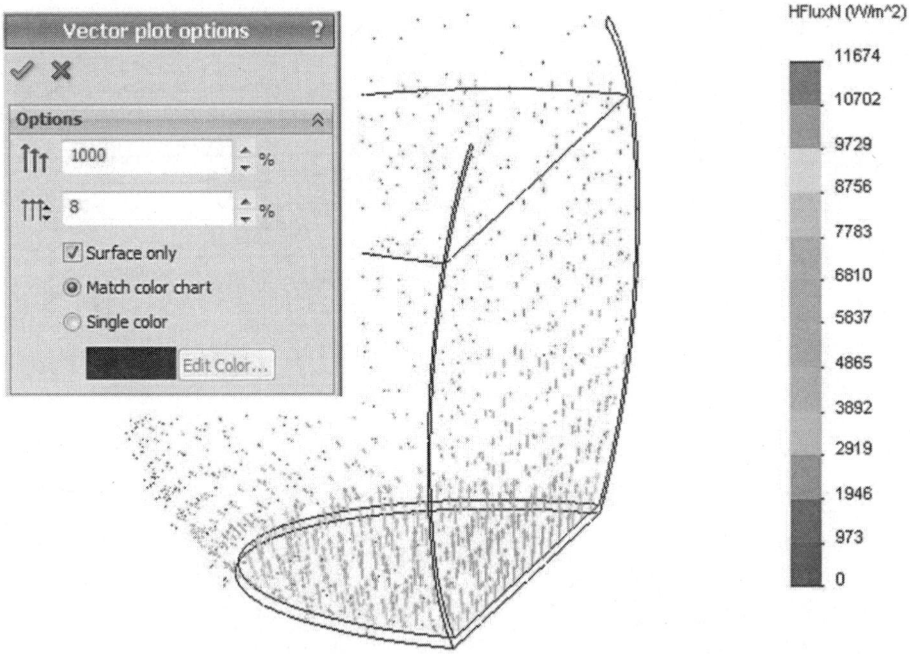

Figure 7-15: Heat Flux results using vector display.

This plots shows poorly in print, experiment with Vector plot options for the best display.

Examine the **Heat Flux** plot and notice that all vectors are tangent to the faces in the plane of symmetry. This demonstrates that there is no heat transfer across these faces. This in turn proves that symmetry boundary conditions in the model work as intended.

8: Thermal and thermal stress analysis of a coffee mug

Topics covered

- Transient thermal analysis
- Thermal stress analysis
- Thermal symmetry boundary conditions
- Structural symmetry boundary conditions
- Use of soft springs

Project description

A ceramic coffee mug at room temperature is filled with boiling water for long enough to reach a steady state temperature, then the water is poured out and the mug is left to cool down. We wish to find thermal stresses in the mug as a function of time during the cooling down process.

Procedure

Open MUG and review the model (Figure 8-1).

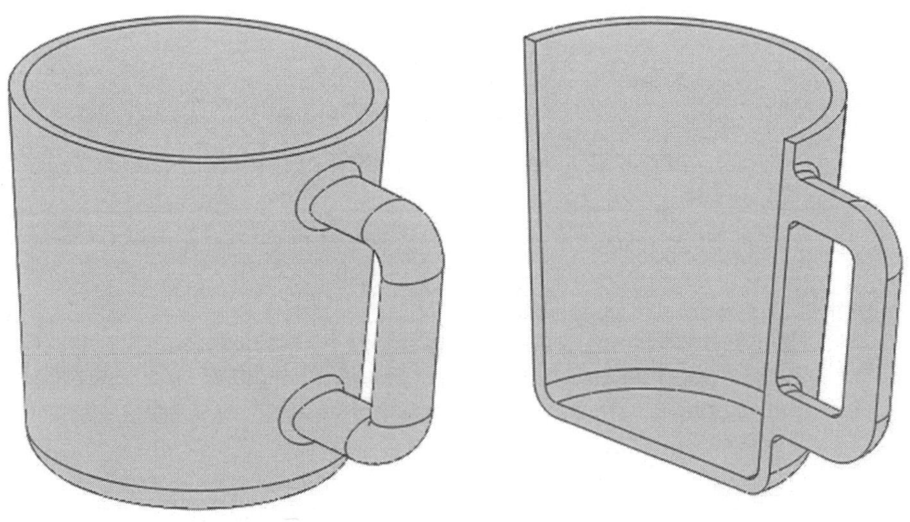

Configuration *01 full* Configuration *02 half*

Figure 8-1: Coffee mug in two configurations.

Split lines on fillets in configuration 02 half are there to define positions of sensors which will be used in this exercise.

Taking advantage of symmetry we'll use the *02 half* configuration.

First we conduct a **Steady state** thermal analysis to find the initial conditions for the cool down process. Switch to *02 half* configuration and create a **Thermal** study called *01 steady state*. Due to a high convection coefficient between water and porcelain, the inside of the mug will reach almost 100°C , the temperature of boiling water. This can be modeled as a prescribed temperature (Figure 8-2).

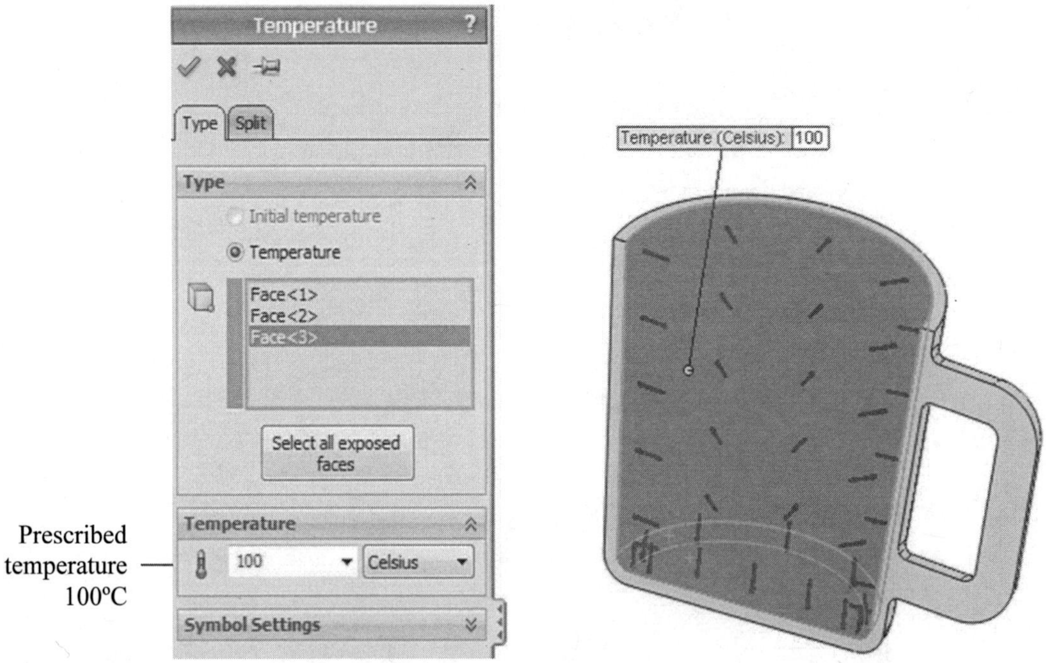

Figure 8-2: Prescribed temperature boundary conditions on inside faces of the mug.

A prescribed temperature is defined for the three inside faces.

Heat enters the mug through faces where prescribed temperature is defined, travels by conduction through the porcelain, and exits to the surrounding air by convection. Define a convection coefficient on the outside faces as shown in Figure 8-3.

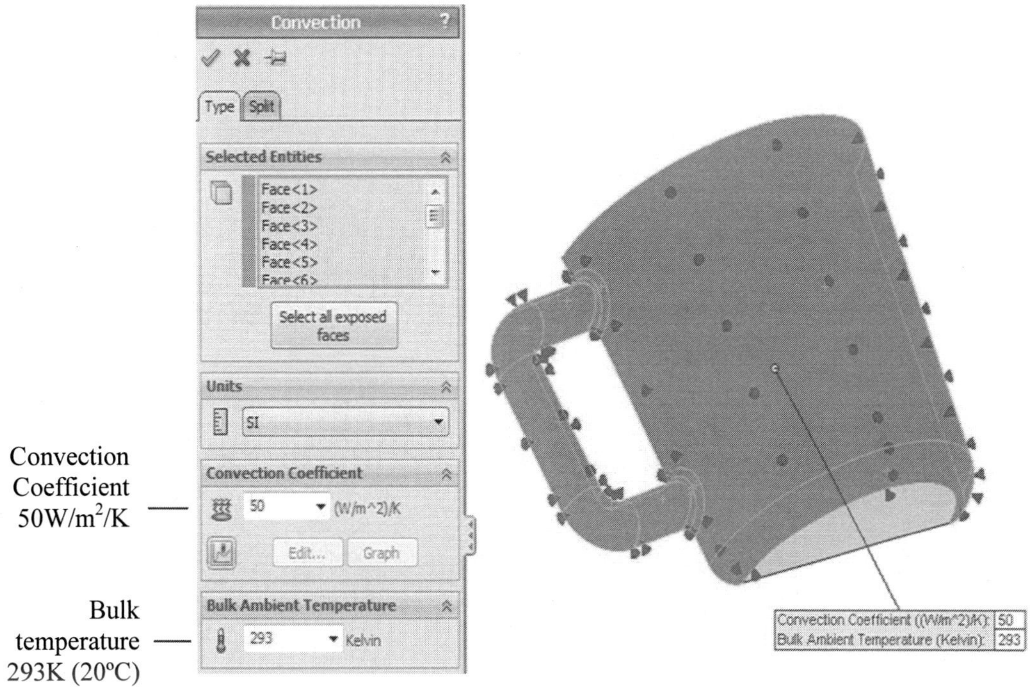

Figure 8-3: Convection boundary conditions on the outside of the mug.

No convection boundary conditions are defined for the bottom face – it is assumed to be insulated. Also, no convection boundary conditions are applied to the faces in the plane of symmetry.

By not defining any convection conditions on the faces in the plane of symmetry, we enforce thermal boundary conditions which require that no heat flows in the direction normal to the plane of symmetry.

Before meshing the model we must remember that in the following thermal analysis, we'll conduct the analysis of thermal stresses. In thermal analysis we'll study temperature results which usually does not require "too much" mesh refinement. It is analogous to the analysis of displacements only (and not stresses) in structural analysis. However, in thermal stress analysis, which is structural analysis, we'll study stresses. The mesh must be identical in thermal and thermal stress analyses and therefore, it must satisfy the more demanding requirements of thermal stress analysis. Define mesh controls (as shown in Figure 8-4) on rounds where stress concentrations are expected.

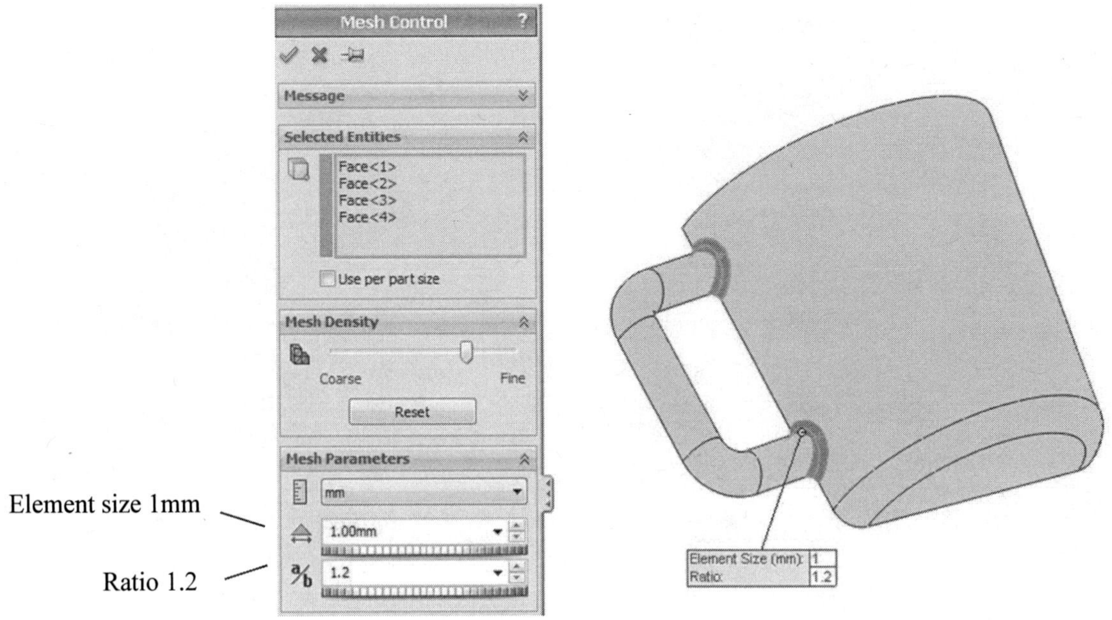

Figure 8-4: Mesh controls on fillets.

1mm element size ensures low turn angle, a 1.2 transition ratio a/b ensures a smooth transition between locally refined mesh and the rest of the model.

Use a global element size of 1.8mm to create a mesh with two elements across the wall thickness. Run the solution of study *01 steady state* and review **Temperature** results (Figure 8-5).

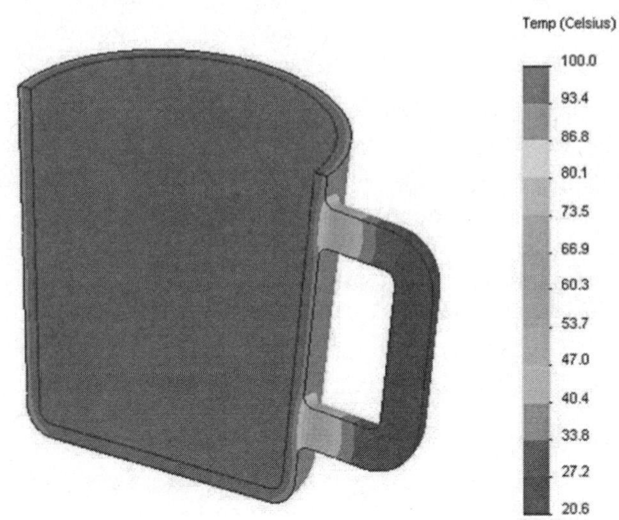

Figure 8-5: Steady state temperature results.

Notice a low temperature gradient across the mug wall.

The temperature results from the steady state thermal analysis conducted in study *01 steady state* are the initial conditions for transient thermal analysis.

Copy study *01 steady state* into *02 transient*. To change from steady state to transient thermal analysis, edit the study properties as shown in Figure 8-6.

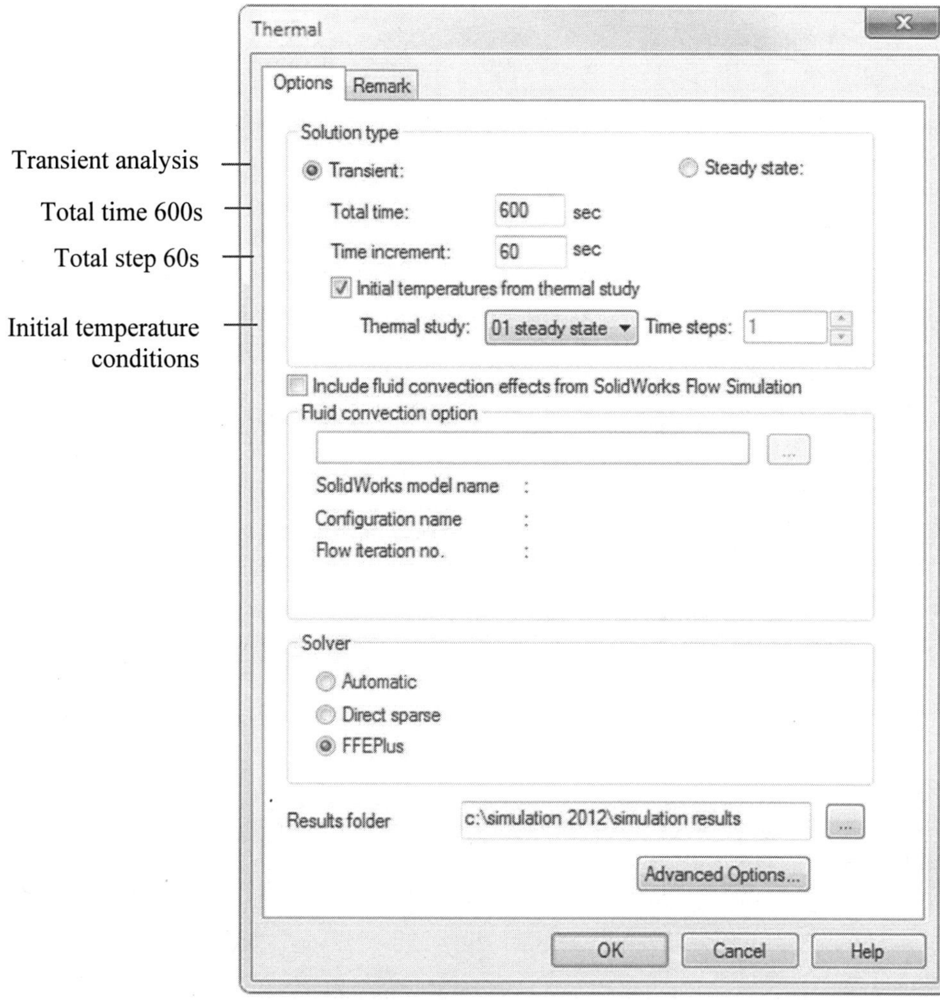

Figure 8-6: Properties of *02 transient* study. The definition includes the duration and time step. Initial temperature conditions are taken from the previously completed steady state thermal study *01 steady state.*

A total time of 600s and a time step of 60s mean that the analysis will be completed in 10 steps.

Delete the prescribed temperature (water has been poured out) and edit convection conditions to include faces where prescribed temperature was defined before (the inside faces are now exposed to air).

Run the transient solution and display a **Temperature** plot (Figure 8-7).

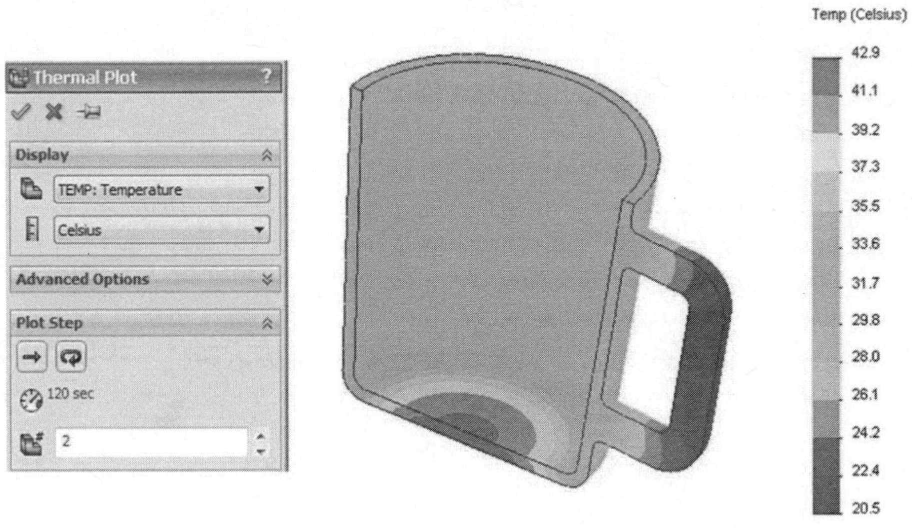

Figure 8-7: Temperature results from time step 2.

Review other steps to see the change of temperature distribution over time.

Probe the temperature plot from any time step to produce temperature time history as shown in Figure 8-8.

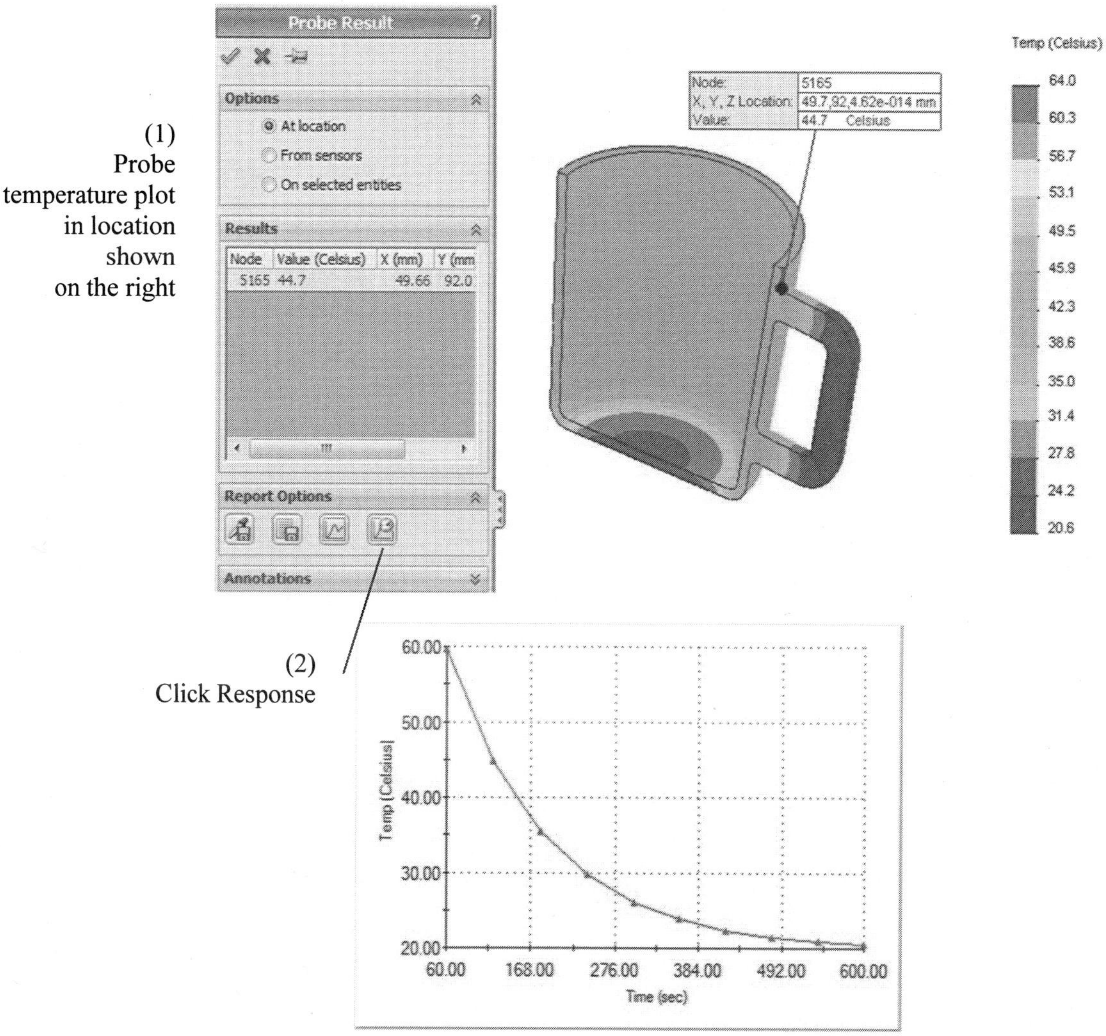

Figure 8-8: Temperature time history from all performed steps 1 through 10.

It can be seen that after 600s the mug cools down almost reaching ambient temperature.

With temperature results from all 10 steps, we may now find out how thermal stresses change over time. Create a static study *03 stress step 1* and define study properties as shown in Figure 8-9.

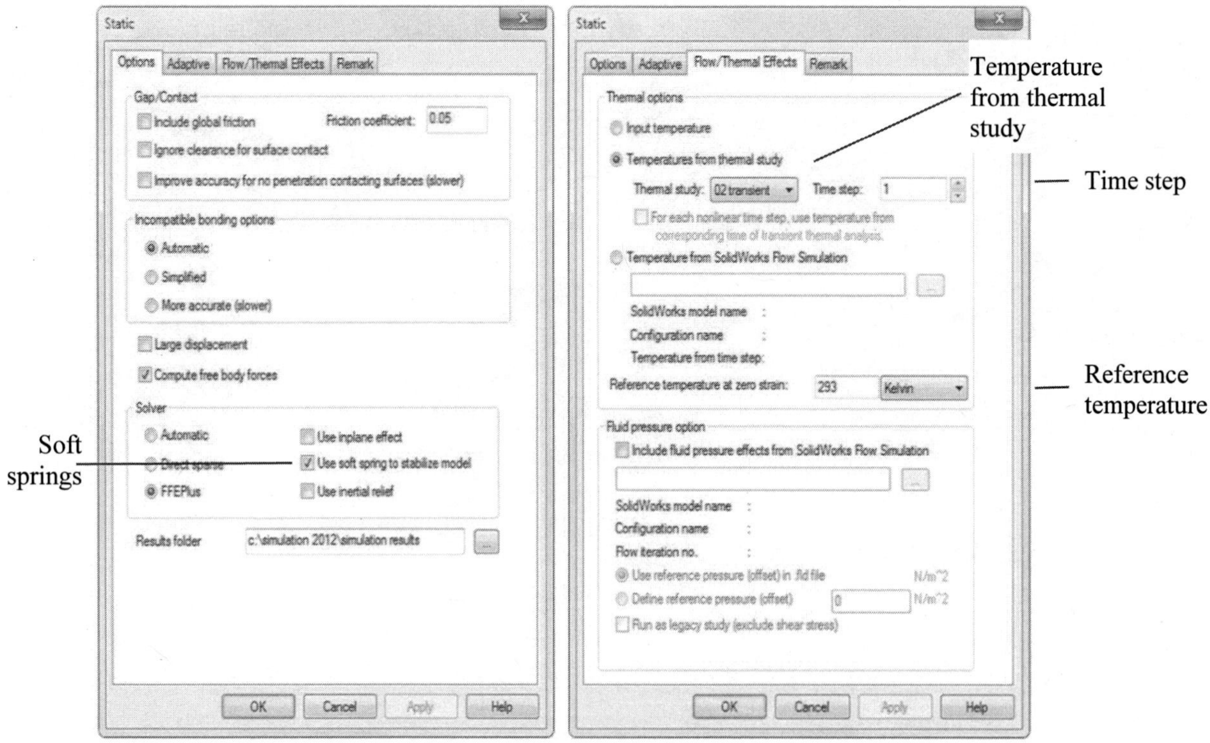

Figure 8-9: Properties of static study used for analysis of thermal stresses.

Select Use soft springs to stabilize the model. The reference temperature at zero strain equals the ambient temperature used in the thermal studies.

While thermal boundary condition require no action (nothing has to be defined on the faces of symmetry), structural boundary conditions must be defined to eliminate out-of-plane motions. Follow Figure 8-10 to define structural symmetry boundary conditions.

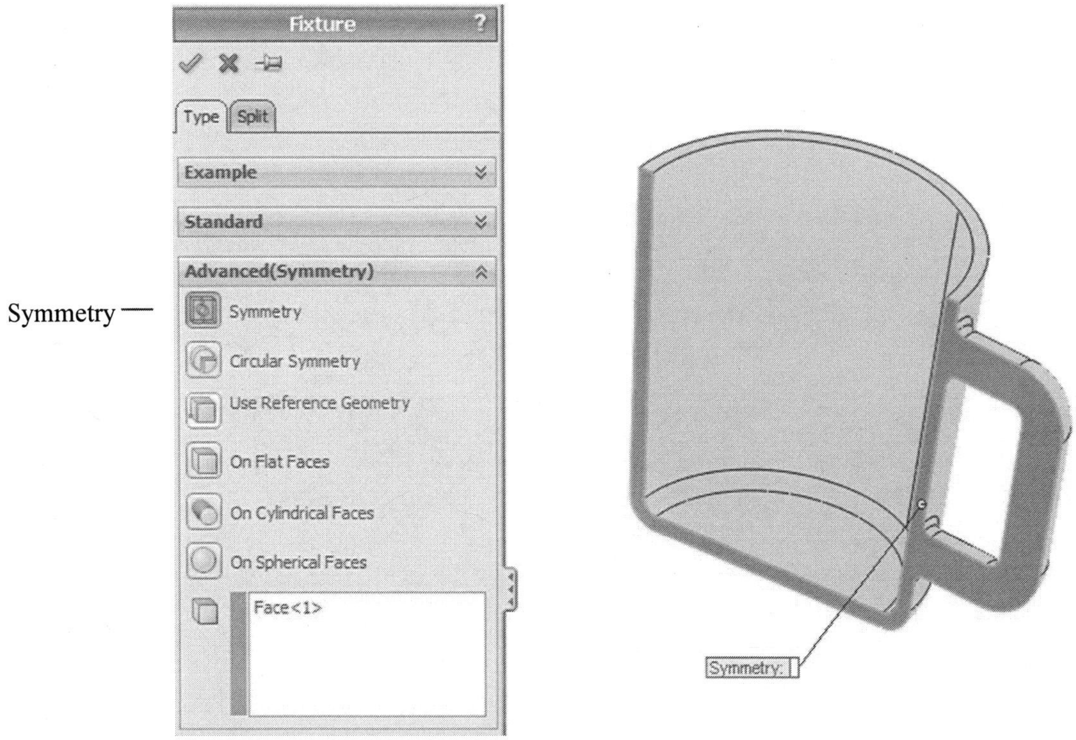

Figure 8-10: Symmetry boundary condition in thermal stress study.

Symmetry boundary conditions suppress translational degrees of freedom of nodes located on the plane of symmetry in the direction normal to the plane.

Symmetry boundary conditions will not restrain the model completely. Under the restraints shown in Figure 8-10, the model is able to slide in two directions along the plane of symmetry and to rotate about the axis perpendicular to the plane of symmetry, meaning that the model has 3 rigid body motions (RBM). We could easily add a **Fixed** restrain somewhere to the model but that would change stress results, remember that we want to see thermal stresses which are caused by uneven temperature distribution throughout the model. This is why we use the soft springs option (Figure 8-9) to eliminate these RBMs.

In a thermal stress analysis, nodal temperatures are imported from the thermal to structural (here static) study and that requires that the meshes in the thermal and structural studies are identical. The best way to make sure the meshes are identical is to copy the mesh from study *02 transient* to study *03 stress step 1.*

Run study *03 stress step 1* and display the stress results. Remember that von Mises stress should not be used for evaluating stress results when brittle material (ceramic porcelain) is analyzed. Instead, use the maximum principal stress, refer to chapter 1 of "**Engineering Analysis with SolidWorks Simulation 2012**" for more information. Repeat the process for more time steps to see how stresses change while the mug is cooling down.

P1 stress results from step1 and step 3 are shown in Figure 8-11.

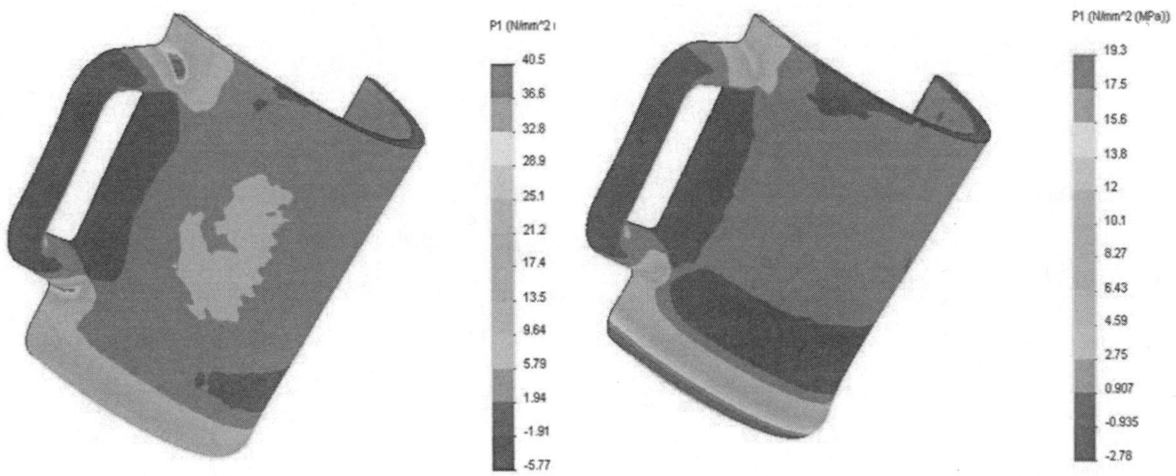

Step 1 Step 3

Figure 8-11: P1 stress results from step 1 and step 3.

Notice the change in location of maximum stress.

Review the stress results from other steps to notice that the highest stress of 41MPa is at the beginning of the cooling process. To calculate the factor of safety, the maximum P1 stress should be compared to the ultimate strength of the ceramic porcelain (173MPa). This comparison gives a factor of safety of 4.2.

To wrap up this exercise, animate displacement results from step 1 to examine the pattern of thermal deformation. Notice that this deformation is caused by thermal effects only. Structural load or restraints have not been used in this analysis.

9: Thermal and thermal buckling analysis of a link

Topics covered

- Buckling caused by thermal effects
- Interpretation of Buckling Load Factor

Project description

A rectangular steel bar is supported by hinges on both ends. Its temperature is raised from an initial temperature of 298K to 500K. We want to know if the bar will buckle.

Procedure

Open part model RECT BAR (Figure 9-1).

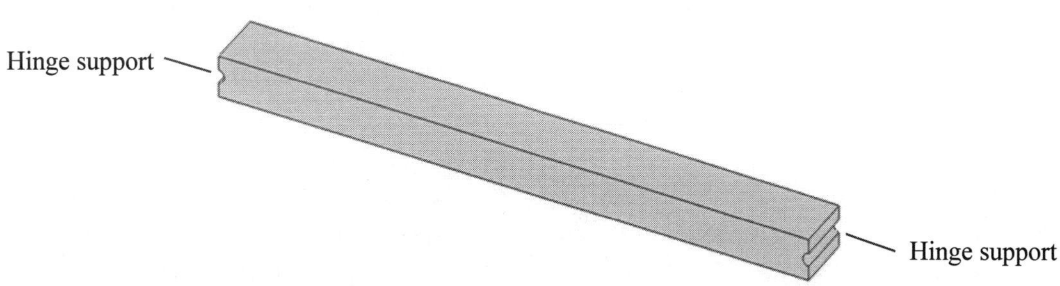

Figure 9-1: Rectangular bar supported by hinges on both ends.

Hinge supports will be applied on both sides to the round notches.

To perform a buckling analysis due to thermal effects we need to know the initial temperature (here 298K) and the temperature distribution at the stage where the possibility of buckling is analyzed. We may proceed in two ways. One way would be to run a thermal analysis to find temperatures needed by buckling analysis. However, the temperature will be a uniform 500K and this can be defined directly in the buckling analysis. There is no need for a pre-requisite thermal analysis. If the temperature were distributed non-uniformly, we would have to find it in a prerequisite thermal analysis.

Create a Buckling study called *01b* and verify that the study properties indicate 298K as the reference temperature at zero strain (Figure 9-2). Thermal options default to **Input temperature** so no action is required.

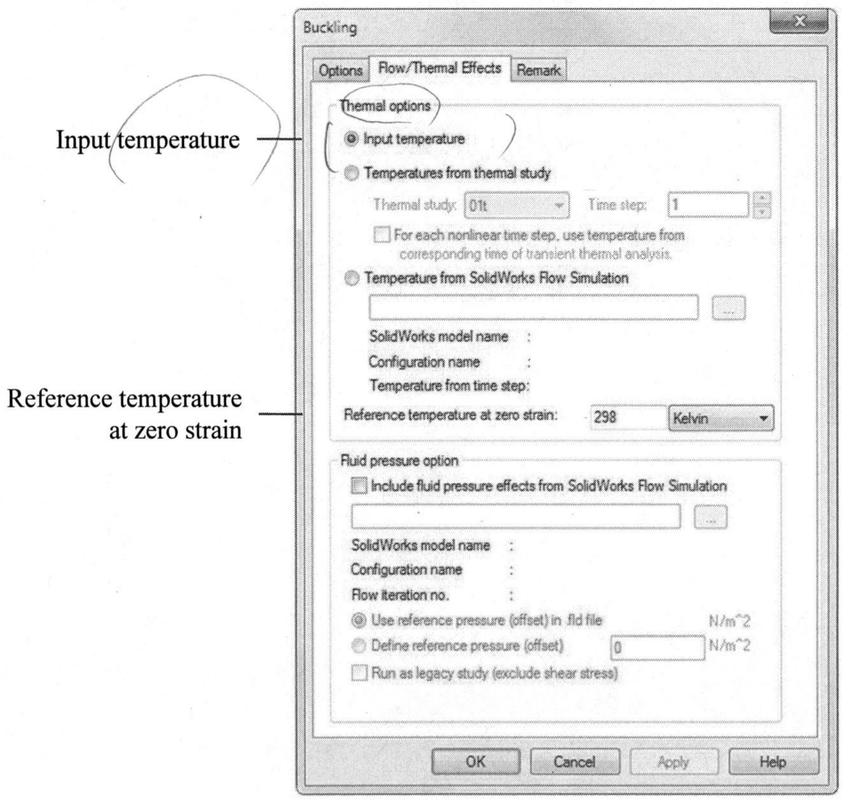

Figure 9-2: Properties of buckling study.

Reference temperature at zero strain is 298K.

Define a **Fixed Hinge** restraint to the round notches on both ends (Figure 9-3).

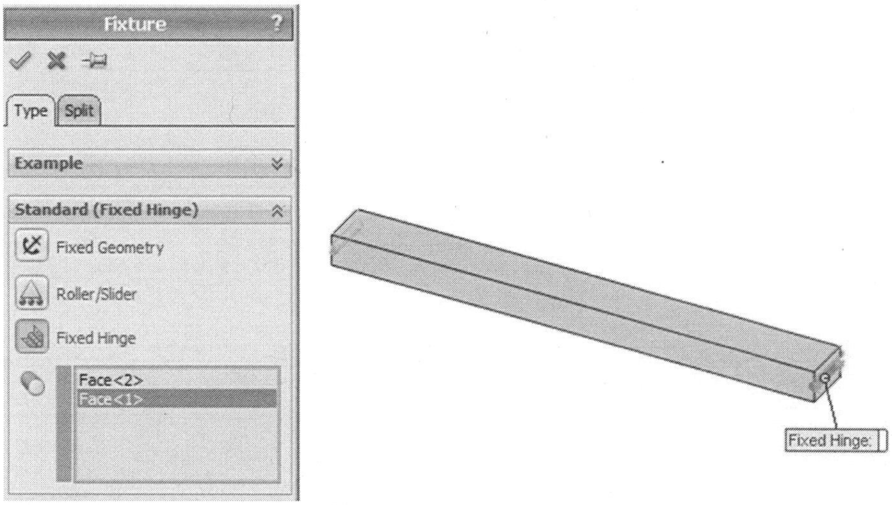

Figure 9-3: Fixed Hinge definition.

Two Fixed Hinge restraints allow for rotations of both ends.

Define a **Temperature** of 500K applied to the solid body as shown in Figure 9-4.

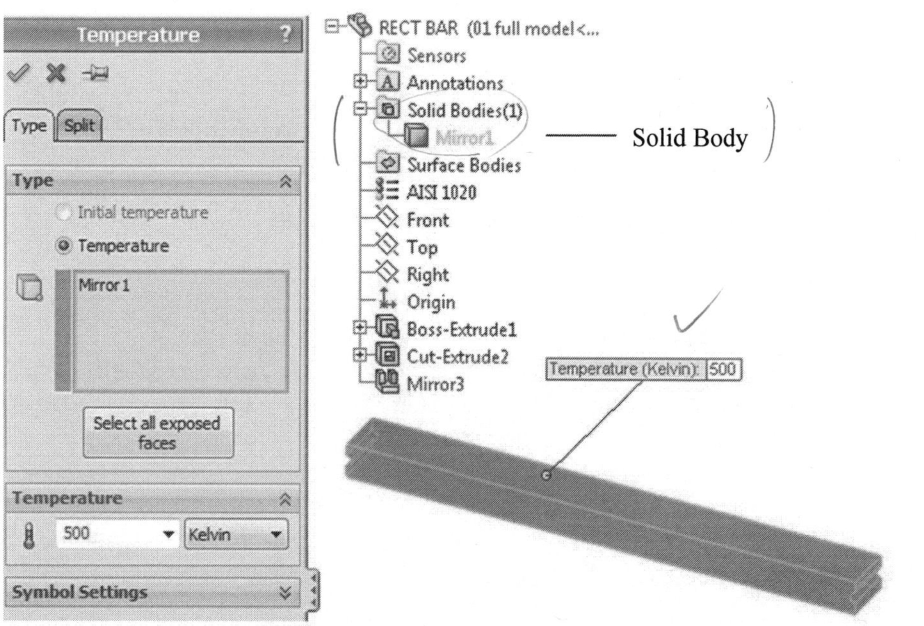

Figure 9-4: Temperature definition.

Select the Solid Body from the fly-out menu.

Run a buckling study using the default element size and display the first buckling mode (Figure 9-5).

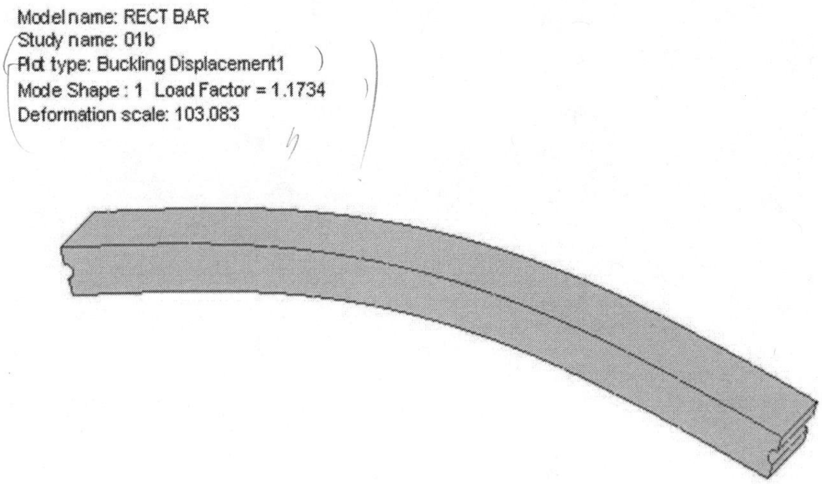

Figure 9-5: The first buckling shape, buckling load factor 1.17.

Colors are deselected.

The first buckling mode has the shape shown in Figure 9-5 and a buckling load factor (BLF) of 1.17. What does a BLF of 1.17 mean? You'll recall that BLF is a ratio between the load causing buckling and the applied load:

$$BLF = \frac{Buckling\ load}{Applied\ load} = 1.17$$

Notice that the only loads on the model are the hinge reactions caused by the fact that thermal expansion is prevented by immovable hinges. A BLF of 1.17 means that the reaction force in hinge supports would have to increase by a factor of 1.17 in order for buckling to take place. It does not refer directly to temperature.

To find these reactions, we need to run a *Static* study. Create static study *01s*, copy the restraints (**Fixed Hinge**), loads (**Temperature**), and mesh from the completed buckling study *01b* and obtain a static solution. Right-click the *Results* folder, select **List result force** and review the reaction forces (Figure 9-6).

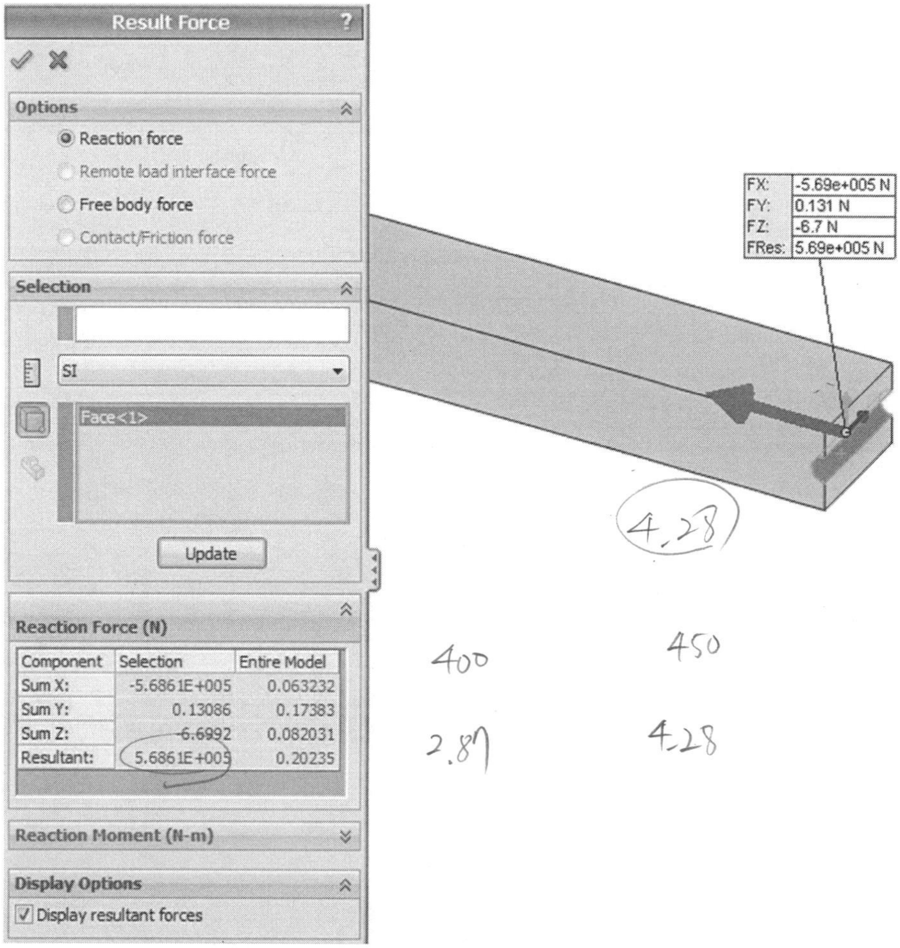

Figure 9-6: Reactions at one end.

Reactions in Y and Z directions are caused by discretization errors.

The reaction in the X direction is the 568600N compressive load caused by the increase of temperature and restrained thermal expansion. This load would have to increase to 568600N × 1.17 = 664560N in order for buckling to take place.

Euler's formula for simply supported beam gives the buckling load 642252N.

$$F_{buckling} = \frac{\pi^2 EI}{l^2} = \frac{\pi^2 \times 200000 \times 52083}{400^2} = 642252N$$

You may want to find a temperature that will cause a hinge reaction of 642252N.

Notes:

10: Radiative power of a black body

Topics covered

- Heat transfer by radiation
- Emissivity
- Black body
- Radiating heat out to space
- Transient thermal analysis
- Heat power
- Heat energy

Project description

A graphite ball has a surface area of $1m^2$. It is surrounded by a vacuum and its initial temperature is 0K. At time t=0s, a source of power activates such that 1000W is generated uniformly in the ball volume. We want to know the steady state temperature of the ball's surface and time required to reach that steady state assuming the ball's surface has the emissive properties of a black body.

The objective of this somewhat abstract problem is to study a single body radiating heat out to space without any interference from other objects. This problem has a very simple analytical solution so we'll be able to compare numerical and analytical results.

Procedure

Open GRAPHITE BALL and create a thermal study called *01 transient*. Use the study properties to define a study as transient (Figure 10-1).

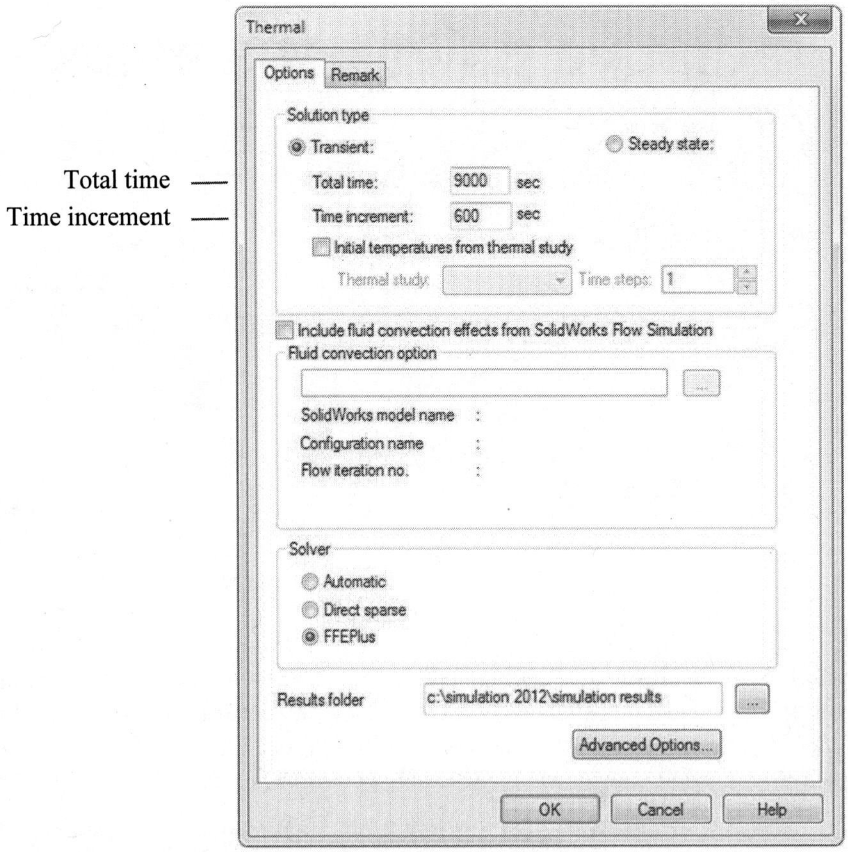

Figure 10-1: Properties of transient thermal study.

Most often some trial runs are required to define a Total time and Time increment.

As always, in a transient thermal analysis, an initial temperature is required. Follow Figure 10-2 to define it as absolute zero.

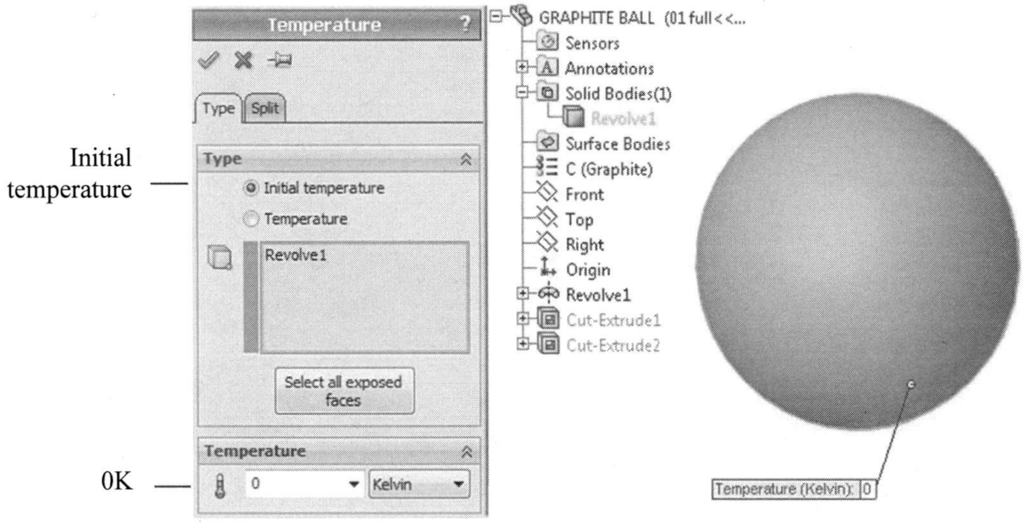

Figure 10-2: Definition of initial temperature.

From the fly-out menu, select the Solid Body to apply the initial temperature to the entire volume. Since there is only one Solid Body in this model, this applies the initial temperature to the entire model.

Figure 10-2 shows the definition of initial temperature to the entire volume of the model. Notice that if the surface is selected instead of the volume, then that surface is given the temperature, the rest of the model is at a default of 0K. Therefore, in this specific example, it would not make a difference to apply the initial temperature to the face or to the volume.

Define **Radiation** boundary conditions to the surface of sphere as shown in Figure 10-3.

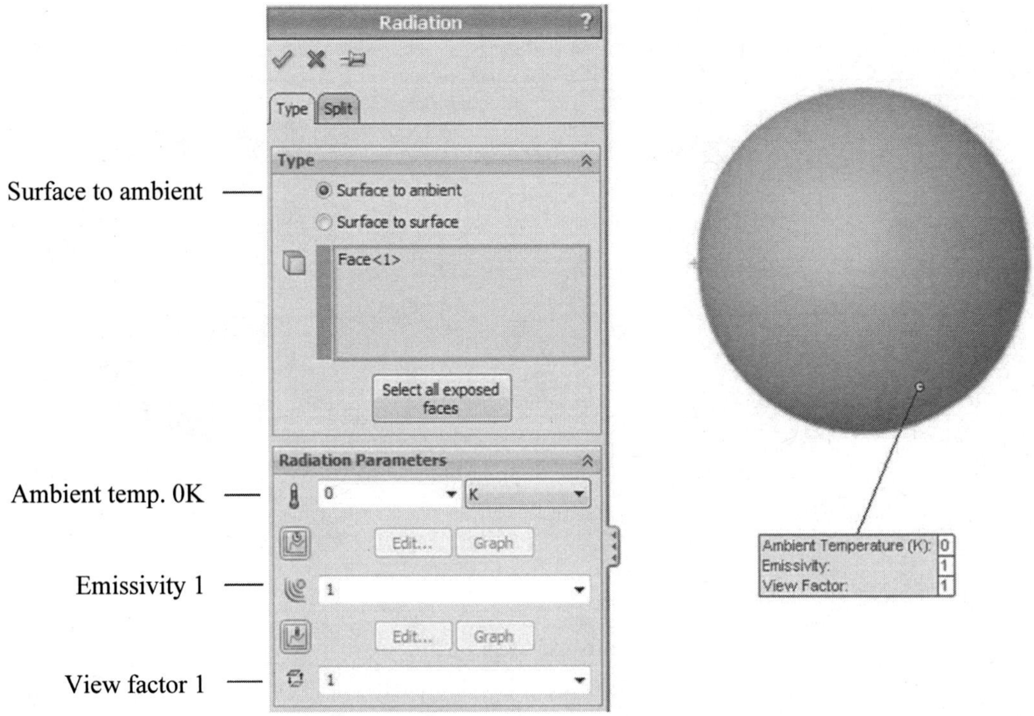

Figure 10-3: Radiation boundary conditions.

Radiation boundary conditions are applied to the face, not to the volume.

An **Emissivity** of 1 means that the ball's face has the emissive properties of a black body. Nothing is better at emitting radiative heat than a black body. A **View Factor** of 1 in combination with a **Surface to ambient** type of radiation boundary condition means that all heat is radiated out to space without interfering with anything.

Define **Heat Power** as shown in Figure 10-4.

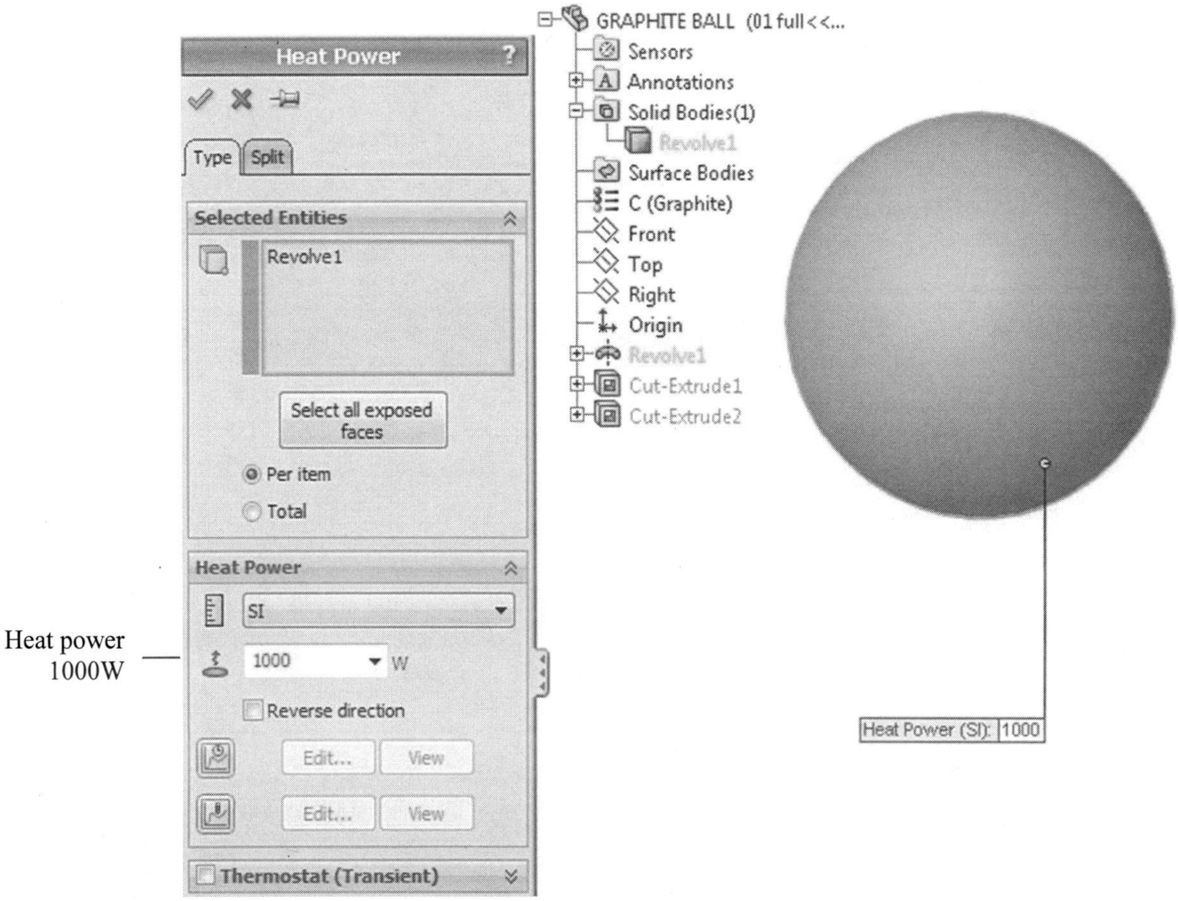

Figure 10-4: Definition of heat power.

From the fly-out menu, select the Solid Body to apply Heat Power to the entire volume of this model.

Mesh the model with a default mesh and run the solution; notice that the solution is completed in 15 steps. Display the **Temperature** results from the last step using a section plot as shown in Figure 10-5.

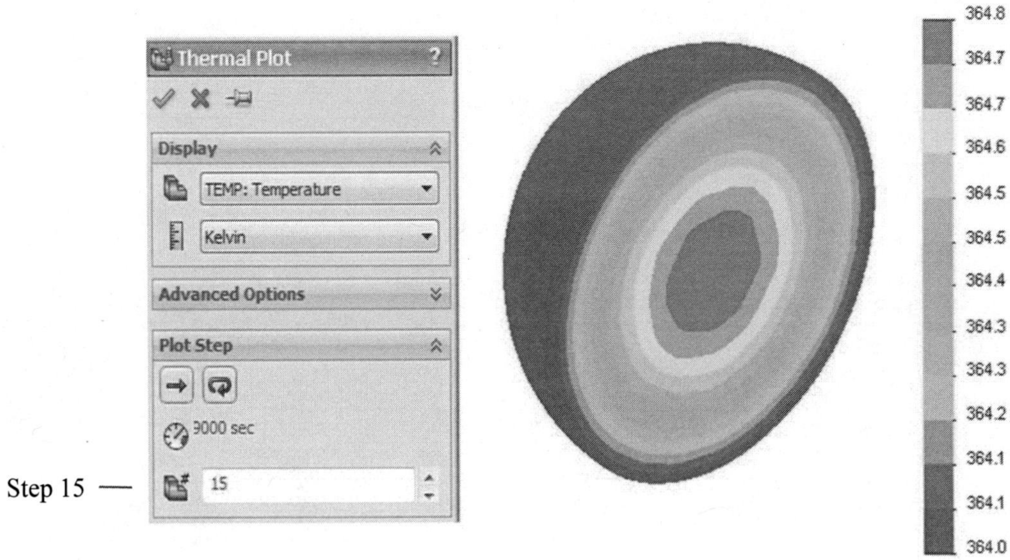

Figure 10-5: Temperature results from step 15.

The section plot indicates a very low temperature gradient (0.8K) in the ball cross section. The color legend changes from 364.0K to 364.8K.

The temperature difference between core (364.8K) and the outside face (364.0K) indicates that the transient heat transfer is still in process but for any practical purpose the gradient 0.8K may be ignored and we may consider this to be the steady state.

To graph a temperature time history, probe any location on the face of the ball. Disable section plot prior to probing and follow the steps in Figure 10-6.

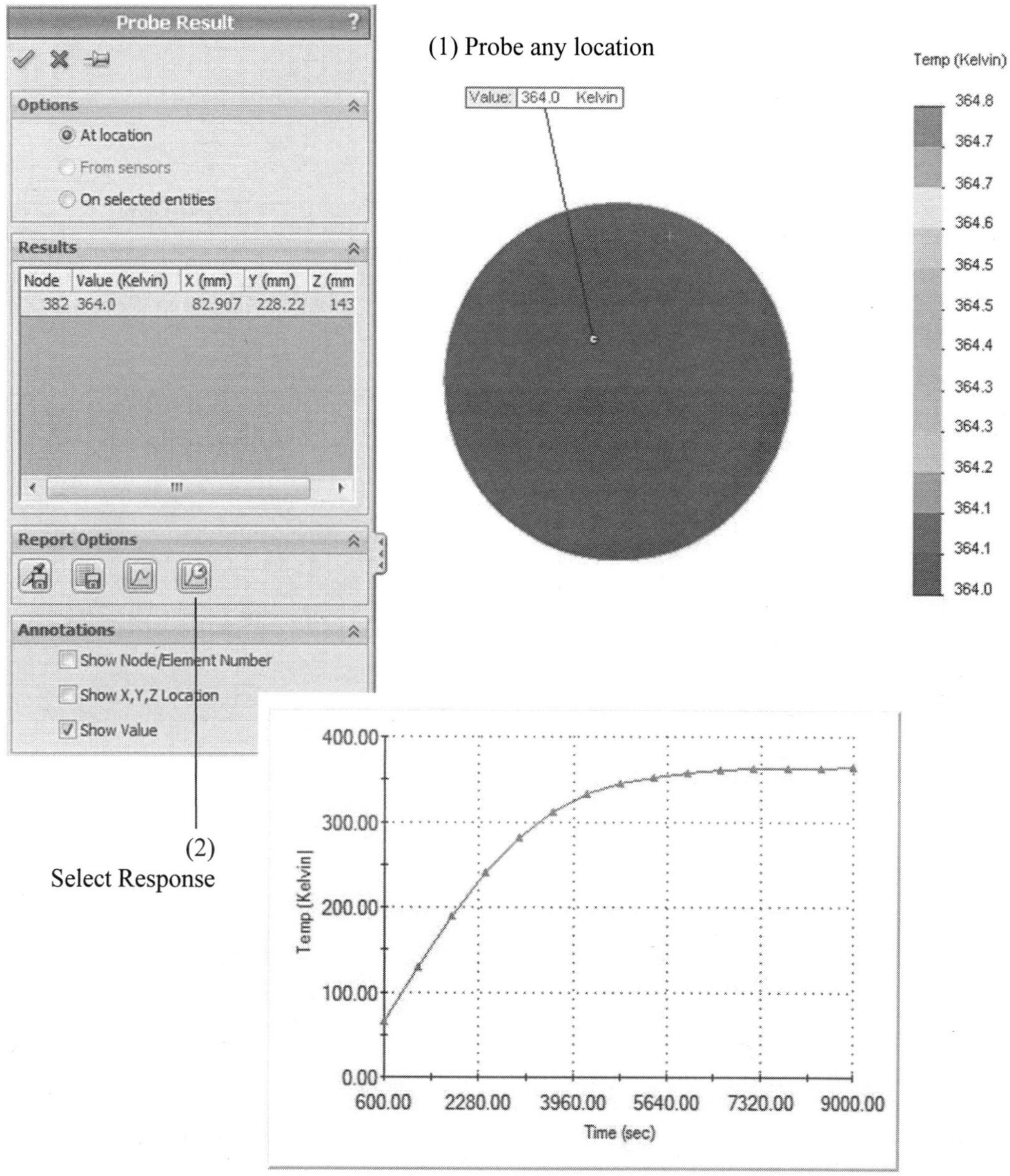

Figure 10-6: The temperature at step 15 (top) and the temperature time history from steps 1-15.

The ball's face temperature is uniform so you may probe any location. You may deselect Show Node/element Number and Show X,Y,Z Location for an uncluttered display of the probed value.

As the graph in Figure 10-6 indicates, the steady state temperature has been practically reached after about 7000s. The temperature shown in Figure 10-6 is therefore the steady state temperature that has established itself as a result of radiative heat flow.

Review the **Heat Power** at step 15 and **Heat Energy** produced during the 9000s (Figure 10-7).

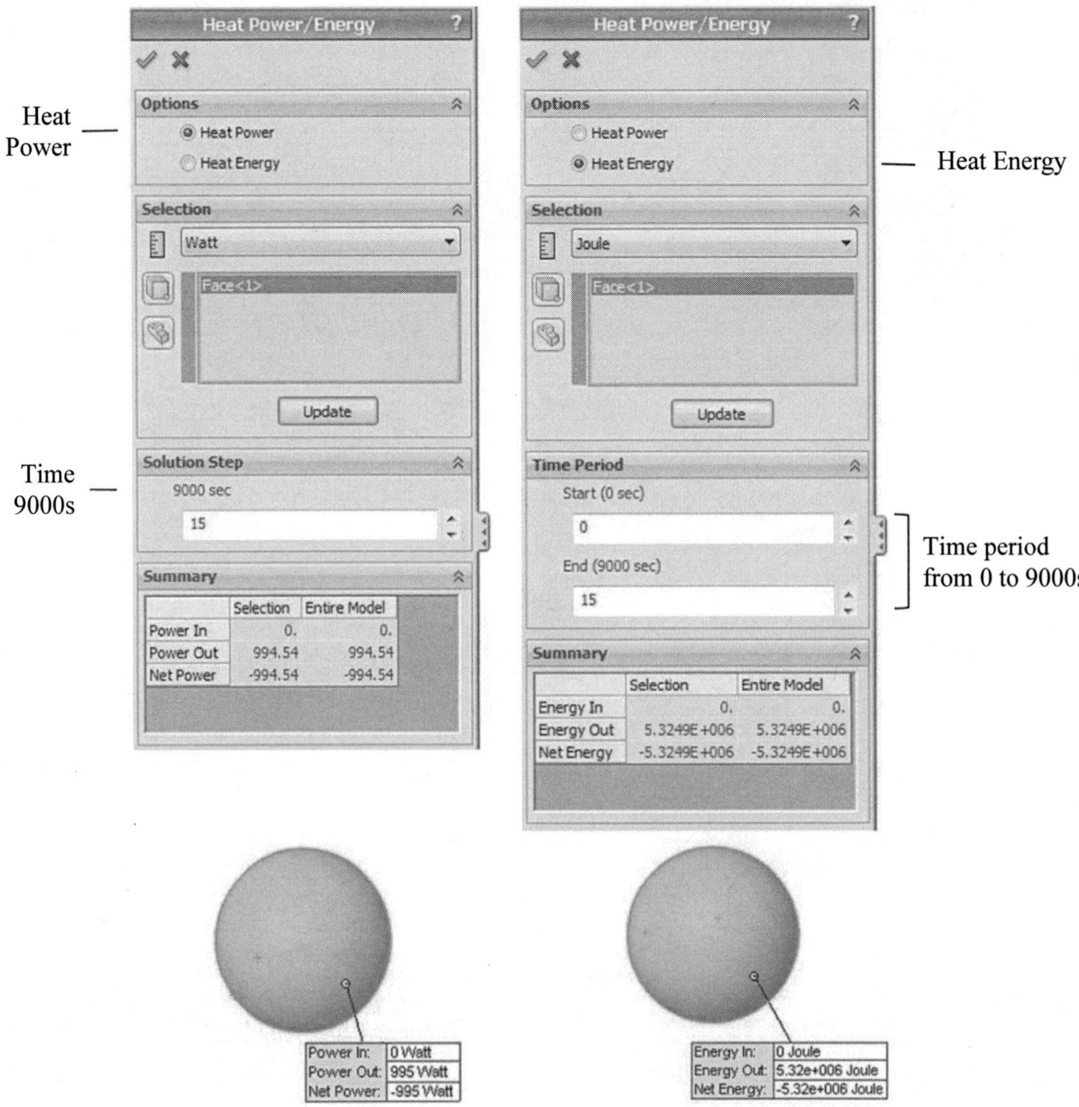

Heat Power emitted by the surface at step 15 (9000s)

Heat Energy that escaped through ball surface during 9000s

Figure 10-7: Heat Power at step 15 and total Heat Energy during 9000s.

After 9000s the face is emitting 995W, the total energy emitted by radiation during 9000s is 5.325MJ.

Use windows as shown in Figure 10-8 to collect information about heat power radiated out at the end of each step. The summary is shown in Figure 10-9.

Step 1: 690W Step 10: 926W Step 15: 995W

Figure 10-8: Energy radiated out by the ball surface during selected steps.

Remember to click Update every time the Solution Step is changed.

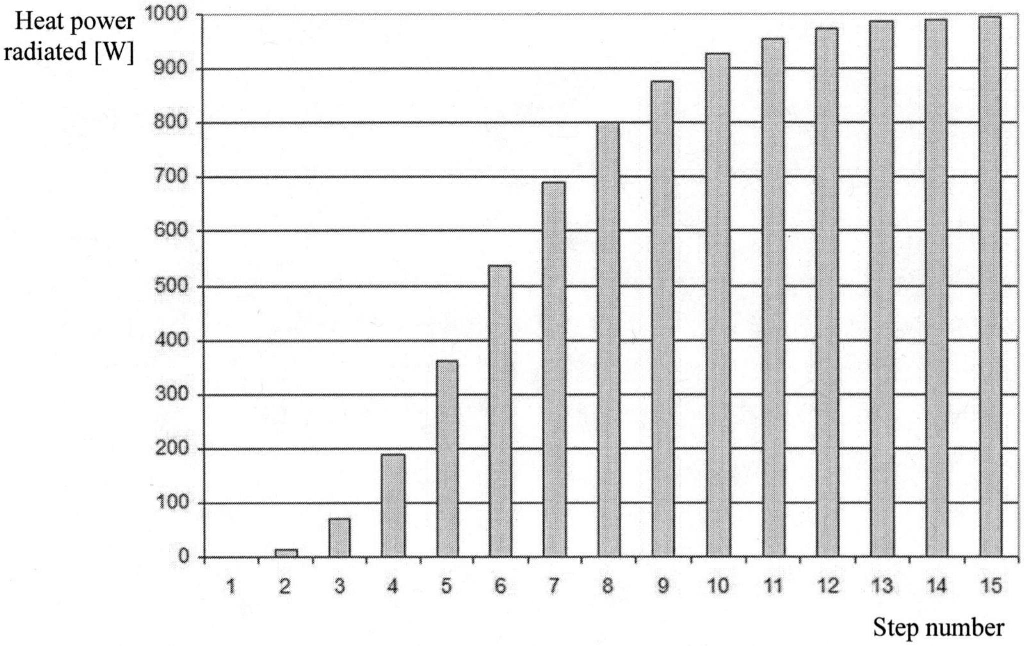

Figure 10-9: Heat power radiated out by the ball surface as function of step number.

Compare this graph with the temperature time history graph in Figure 10-6.

This very simple model geometry makes it easy to compare the results of the numerical simulation with analytical results. Review model and results to notice that:

The emissivity of ball face is $\varepsilon = 1$ (it is a black body)

Stefan-Boltzmann constant $\sigma = 5.67\text{x}10^{-9}$ $\text{W/m}^2/\text{K}^4$ (see chapter 1)

Heat flux $q = 995\text{W}/1\text{m}^2 = 995\text{W/m}^2$ (Figure 10-8)

Using the above, the surface temperature T_S can be found from the Stefan-Boltzman law:

$$q = \varepsilon\sigma T_S^4$$

$$T_S = \left(\frac{q}{\varepsilon\sigma}\right)^{0.25} = \frac{995}{1 \times 5.67 \times 10^{-8}} = 364K$$

This result is the same as the numerical result $T_S = 364\text{K}$ shown in Figure 10-5. If results were truly steady state, we could use a heat flux of 1000W/m^2 from the input data.

We will now review energy balance.

Specific heat of graphite: $c = 44$ J/kg/K (read from material properties)

Mass of graphite ball: 210.64kg (measure this in the SolidWorks model)

Energy used to raise the temperature of the graphite ball from 0K to 364K:

$$E_C = mc\Delta T = 210.64 \times 44 \times 364 = 3374kJ$$

Energy radiated out from the ball's surface (Figure 10-7):

$$E_R = mc\Delta T = 210.64 \times 44 \times 364 = 5325kJ$$

Total energy:

$$E = E_C + E_R = 3374kJ + 5325kJ = 8699kJ$$

This result is within 4% of the total energy calculated as:

$$E = P \times t = 1000W \times 9000s = 9000kJ,$$

where P is heat power and t is the duration of the analyzed process.

Notes:

11: Radiation of a hemisphere

Topics covered

- Heat transfer by radiation
- Emissivity
- Radiating heat out to space
- View factors
- Heat power

Project description

A nickel hemisphere is heated in its volume with 800W. It is insulated on the outside faces while the concave face exchanges heat by radiation with a large enclosure at 30°C. The surface emissivity is 0.4. The hemisphere is in vacuum. We'll calculate the steady state temperature of the hemisphere.

Procedure

Open model HEMISPHERE and create a thermal study called *01 steady state* (Figure 11-1).

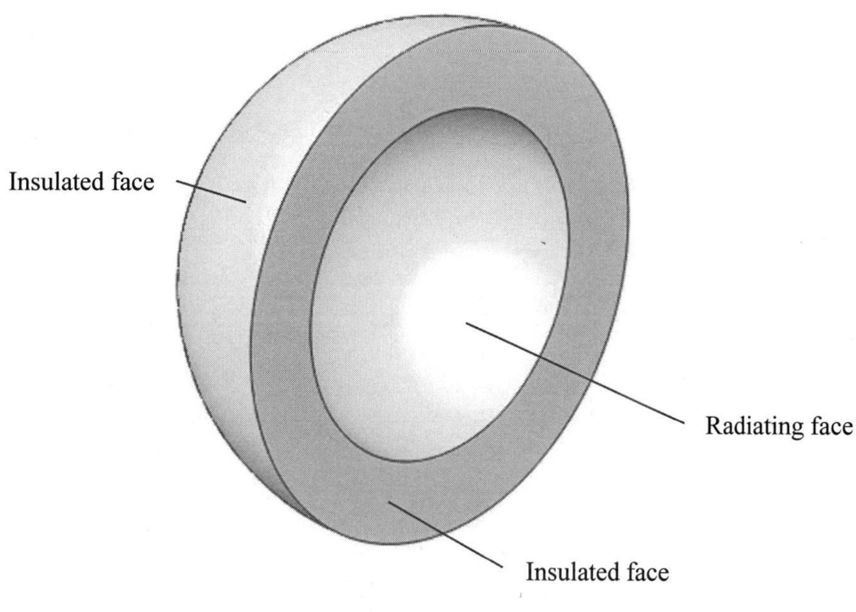

Figure 11-1: Hemisphere model.

The concave face radiates heat out to open space characterized by an ambient temperature of 30°C. The other two faces are insulated. Heat transfer takes place only through the concave face.

Define **Heat Power** as shown in Figure 11-2.

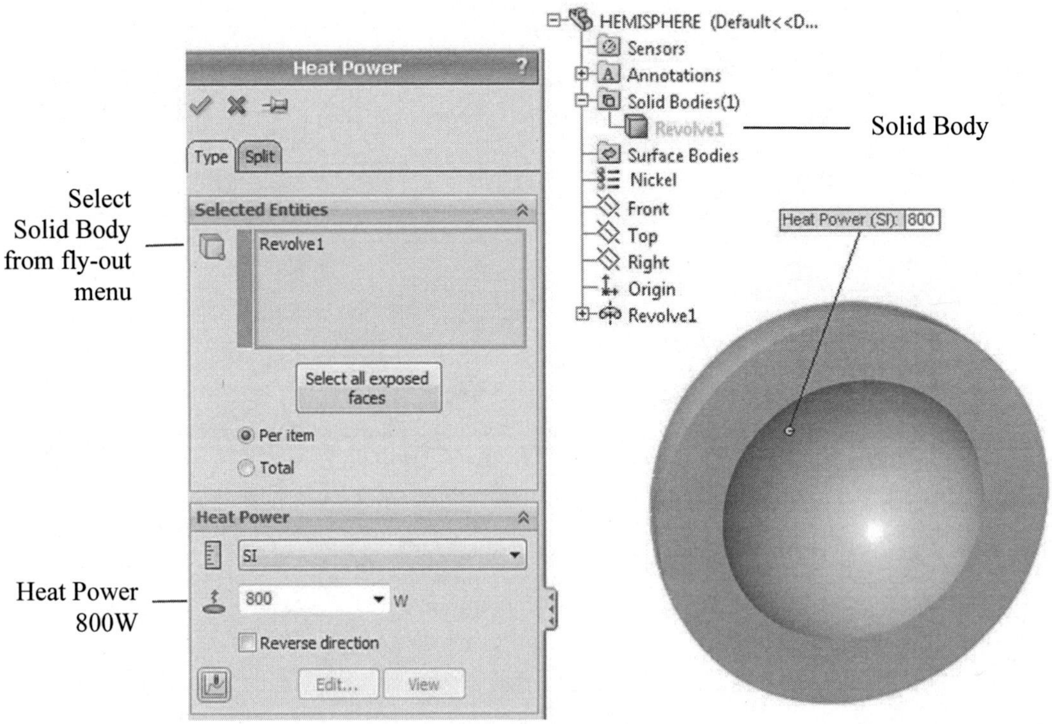

Figure 11-2: Heat Power is generated in the entire volume of the model.

Select Solid Body Revolve1 from the fly- out menu.

Define **Radiation** boundary conditions as shown in Figure 11-3.

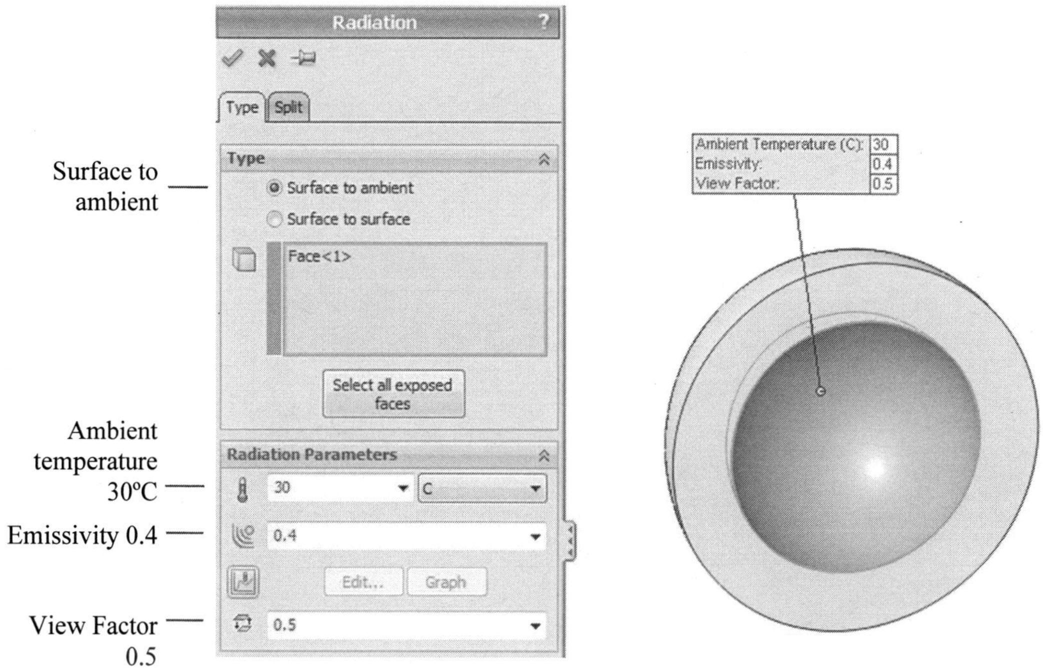

Figure 11-3: Radiation boundary conditions.

Radiation boundary conditions are defined for the concave face.

You may conceptualize **Ambient temperature** as the temperature of a large enclosure in which the HEMISPHERE is located (Figure 1-7 (2)). **Emissivity** is a measure of how well the face emits radiation in comparison to a black body which has emissivity equal to 1. **View Factor** is a measure of what portion of radiation is radiated out directly to space. If radiation boundary conditions are **Surface to ambient** with a **View Factor** equal to 1, all power is radiated out directly to space as was the case with GRAPHITE BALL in chapter 10. The **View Factor** of 0.5 used in the HEMISPHERE accounts for the fact that this concave face can "see itself"; some heat radiated out hits this surface again before being finally radiated out to space.

Mesh the model using a **Curvature based mesh** (Figure 11-4).

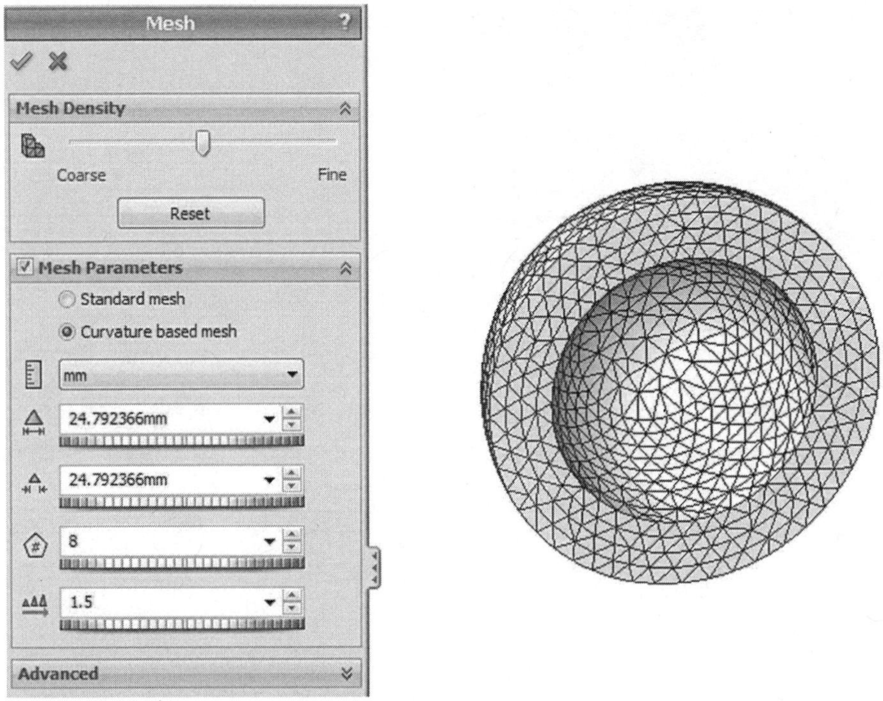

Figure 11-4: Mesh parameters are all on defaults.

A curvature based mesh is a natural choice for this type of geometry.

Obtain a solution and show a **Temperature** plot (Figure 11-5).

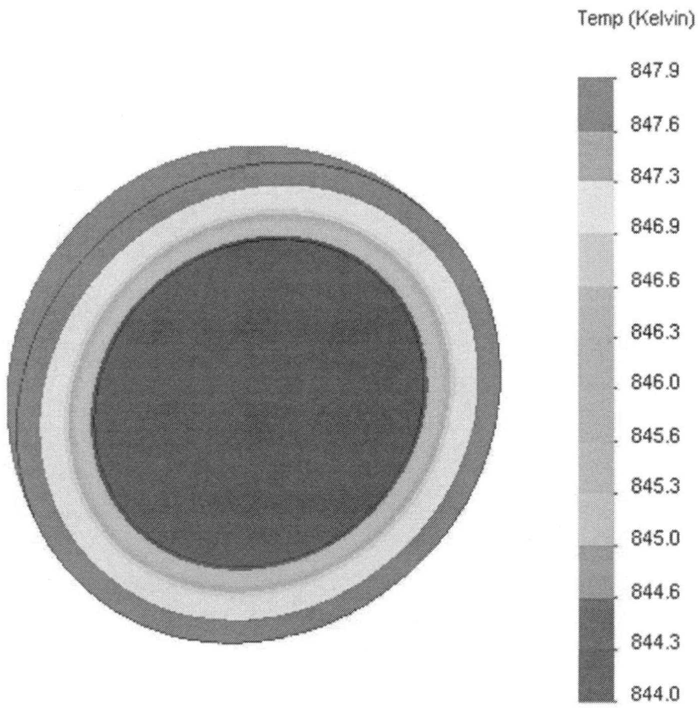

Figure 11-5: Temperature result plot.

In radiation problems temperature should be expressed in Kelvins.

Notice the practically uniform temperature distribution in the model due to the high thermal conductivity of nickel.

Follow steps in Figure 11-6 to review **Heat Power** results and verify that all power generated in the volume to HEMISPHERE is radiated out by the concave face where the radiation boundary conditions have been defined.

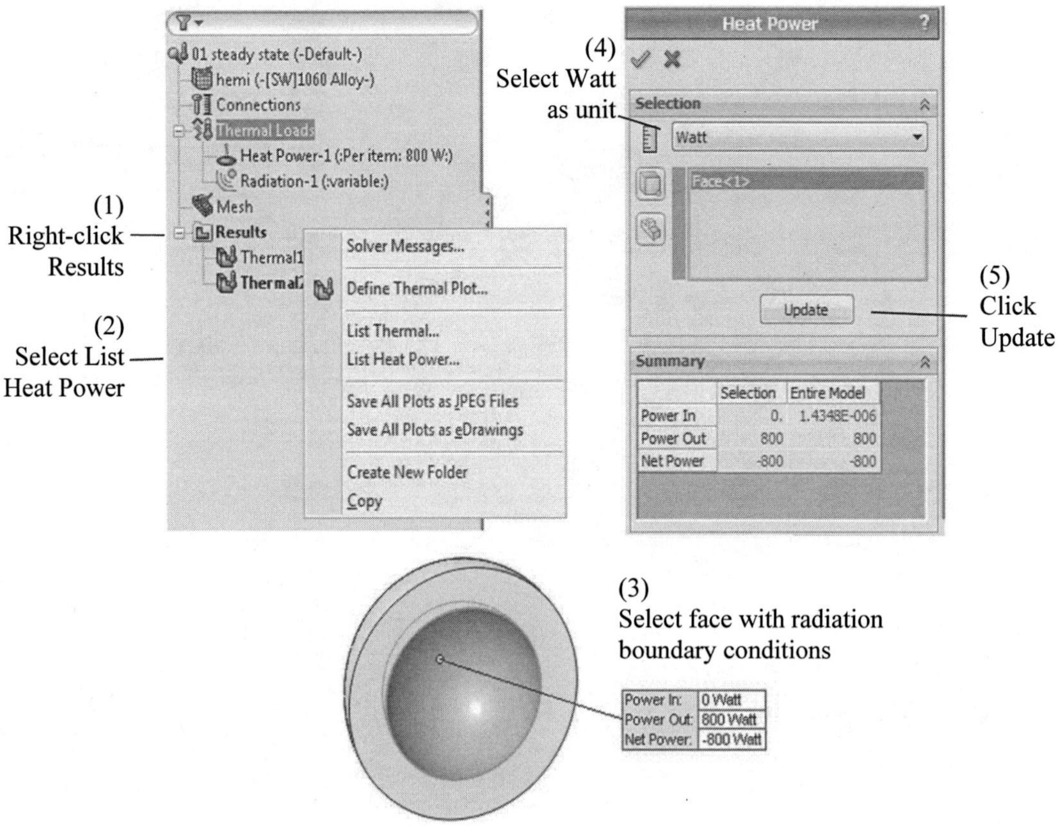

Figure 11-6: Heat Power radiated out is 800W.

The generated heat leaves the HEMISPHERE through the face where the radiation boundary conditions have been defined.

12: Radiation between two bodies

Topics covered

- Heat transfer by radiation
- Emissivity
- Radiating heat out to space
- View factors
- Heat power
- Closed system
- Open system

Project description

Heat power is generated in the volume of one solid body and is radiated out to the second body which dissipates it by convection. This example may have little relevance to any practical problem but it allows studying different options in radiation heat transfer available in **SolidWorks Simulation**.

Procedure

Open assembly model BLOCKS (Figure 12-1) and create a thermal study *01 surface to surface closed system.*

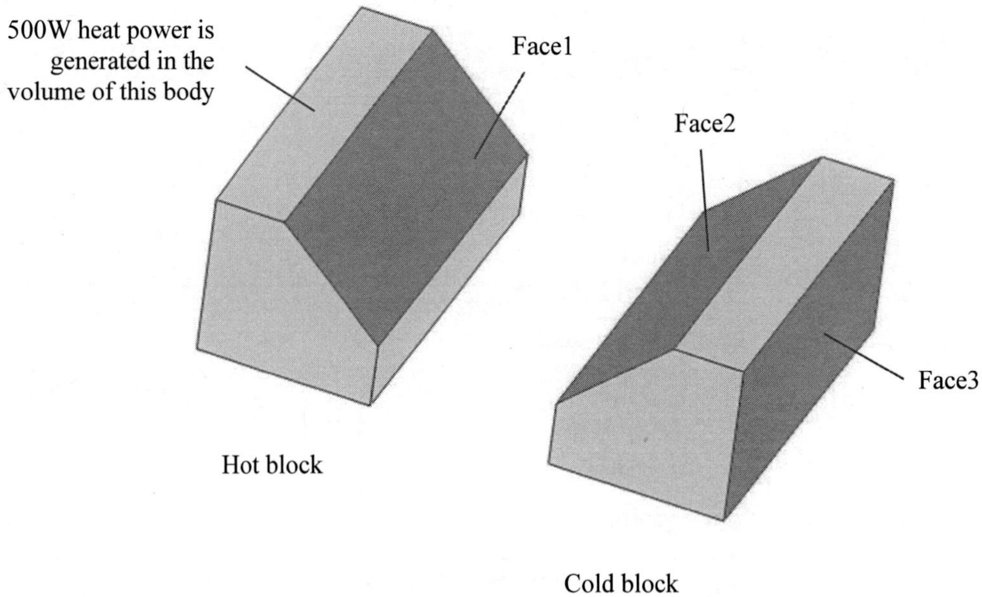

Figure 12-1: BLOCKS assembly consists of two identical solid bodies.

There are two mechanisms responsible for heat transfer in this model: radiation and convection. Face 1 and Face 2 exchange heat by radiation. Face 3 dissipates heat by convection.

Notice that heat transfer between detached bodies can only be exchanged by radiation.

Apply **Heat Power** as shown in Figure 12-2.

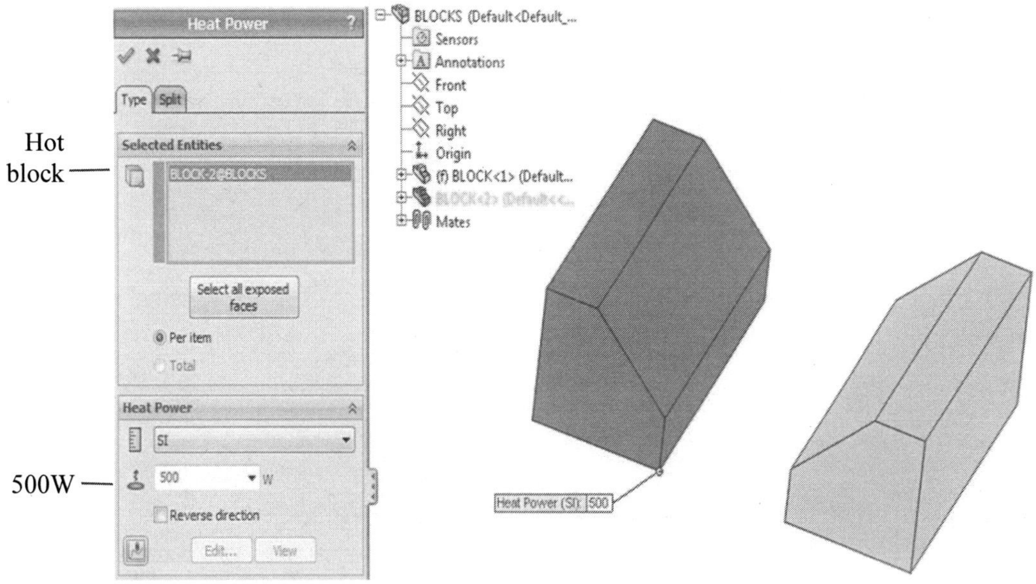

Figure 12-2: 500W Heat Power is applied to the left block.

Select the block from the fly-out menu.

Apply **Radiation** boundary conditions as shown in Figure 12-3.

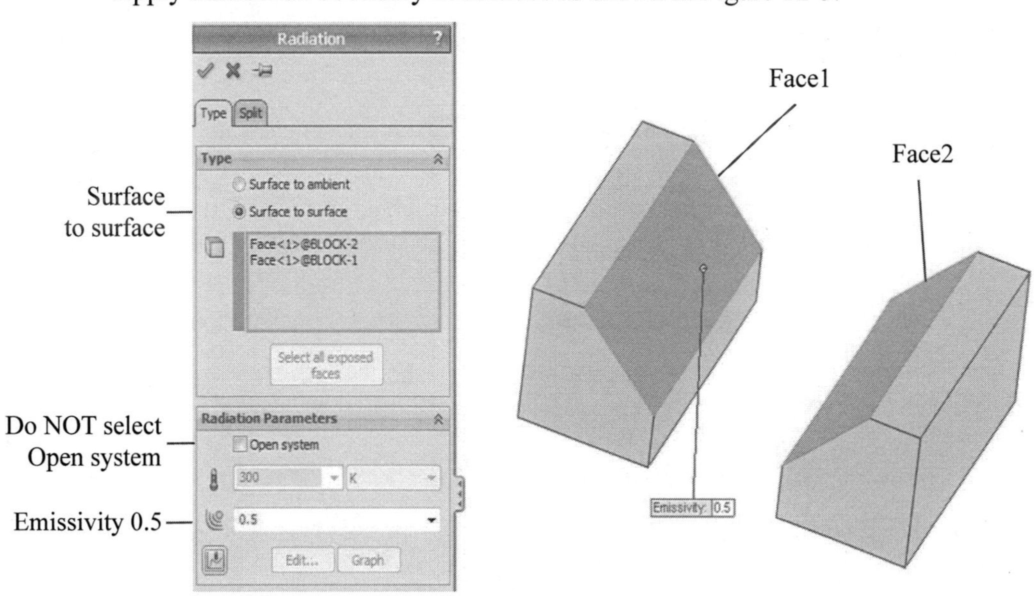

Figure 12-3: Radiation boundary conditions.

Heat is exchanged between the selected Face1 and Face2.

It is important to comment on the **Radiation** boundary conditions defined in Figure 12-3. Without selecting **Open system** we assume that all heat radiated out of face 1 travels without any loss to face 2. This is of course unrealistic but the objective of this exercise is to demonstrate differences between **Radiation** boundary conditions in open and closed systems.

So far we have established a mechanism of heat flow by radiation between two bodies. Now we have to define how heat exits the system. Define **Convection** boundary conditions as shown in Figure 12-4.

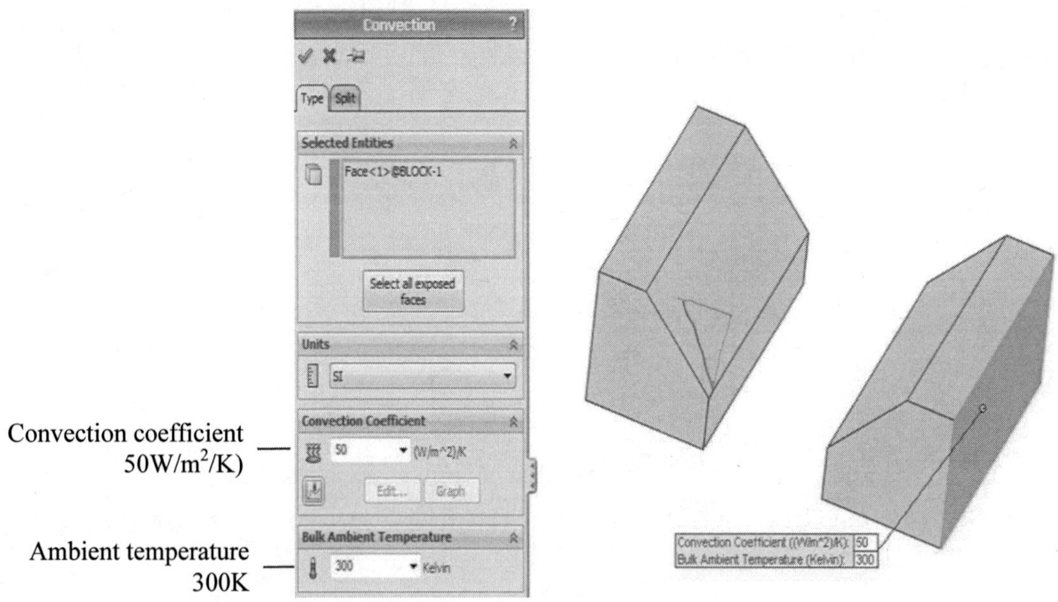

Figure 12-4: Convection boundary conditions.

The selected face exchanges heat with fluid.

The face where the **Convection** boundary condition is defined must be in contact with a fluid to be able to exchange heat by convection. The faces with **Radiation** boundary conditions are exposed to a vacuum but no heat is radiated out to space because **Open system** is deselected; all other faces are insulated, meaning that no heat exchange takes place there.

Mesh the model with a default mesh and run the solution. Review the **Temperature** plot as shown in Figure 12-5.

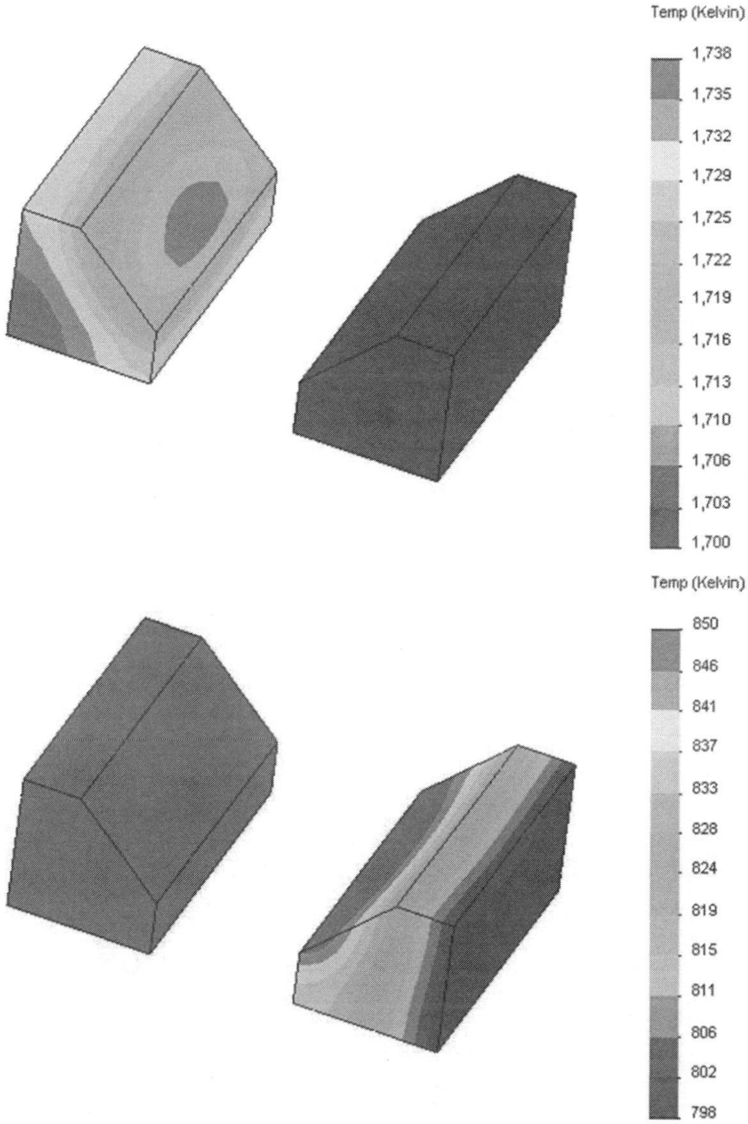

Temperature range 1700-1738K

Temperature range 798-850K

<u>Figure 12-5: Temperature results.</u>

Two plots with different temperature ranges are used to show temperature distribution in the hot and cold blocks.

Use Chart options to define temperature ranges.

Temperature results are presented in Figure 12-5 using two plots with different temperature ranges: 1700-1738K to show temperature distribution in the block radiating out heat and 798-850K to show temperature distributions in the block receiving heat by radiation.

Review **Heat Flux** results using a vector plot as shown in Figure 12-6.

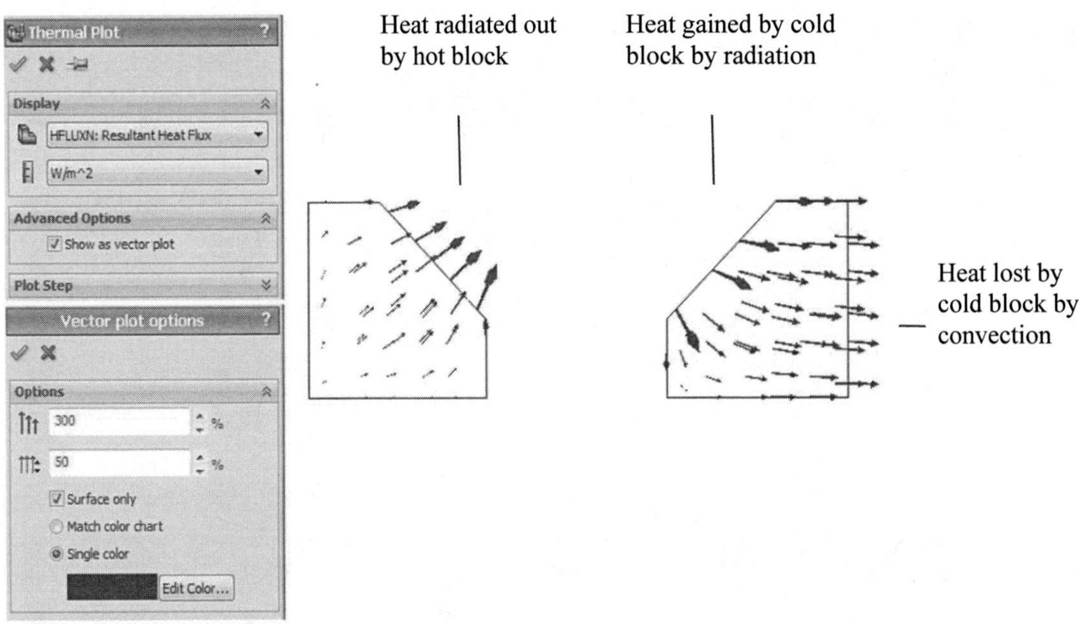

Figure 12-6: Heat Flux results.

The vector plot offers a convenient way to analyze the path of heat flow.

To verify that the entire heat generated in the hot block indeed travels through a vacuum to the cold block, we may probe **Heat Power** on any of the three faces that participate in heat exchange as shown in Figure 12-7.

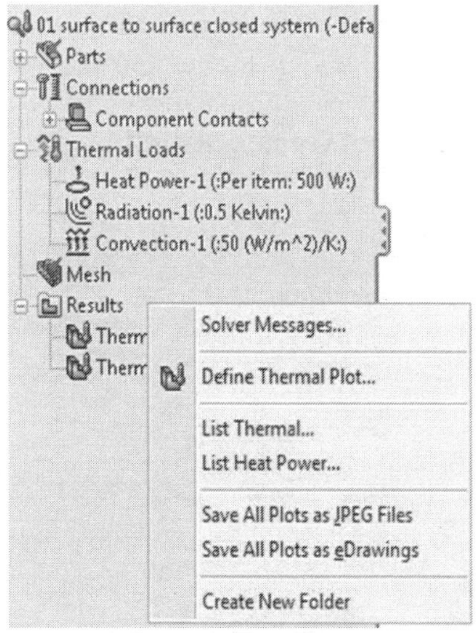

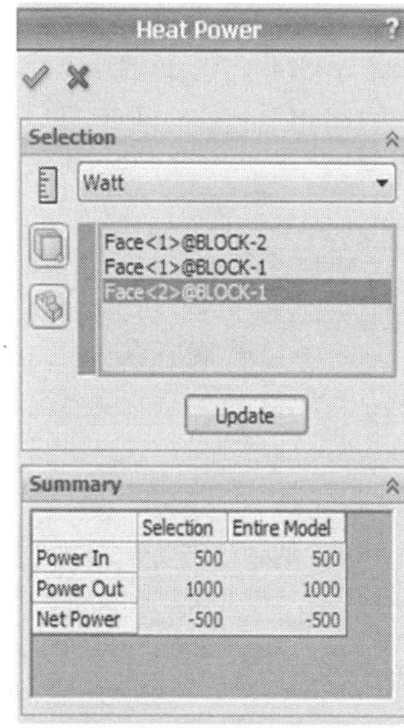

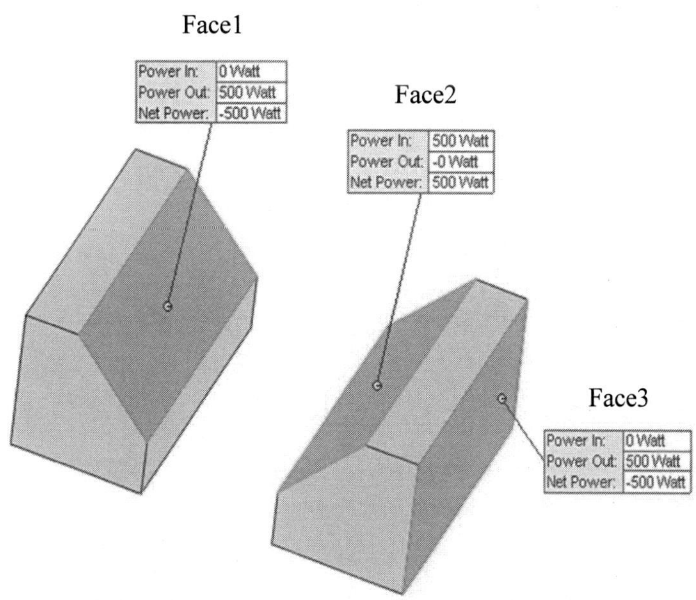

Figure 12-7: Heat Power results.

Heat Power is probed on all faces where thermal boundary conditions have been defined.

As the sign of **Net Power** indicates, Face1 and Face3 loose heat, Face2 gains heat. Compare this with Figure 12-6.

This completes the analysis carried under the assumption of a closed system. Now copy the study *01 surface to surface closed system* into study *02 surface to surface closed system*. The difference between these two studies is that the radiation boundary condition now specifies **Open system** (Figure 12-8).

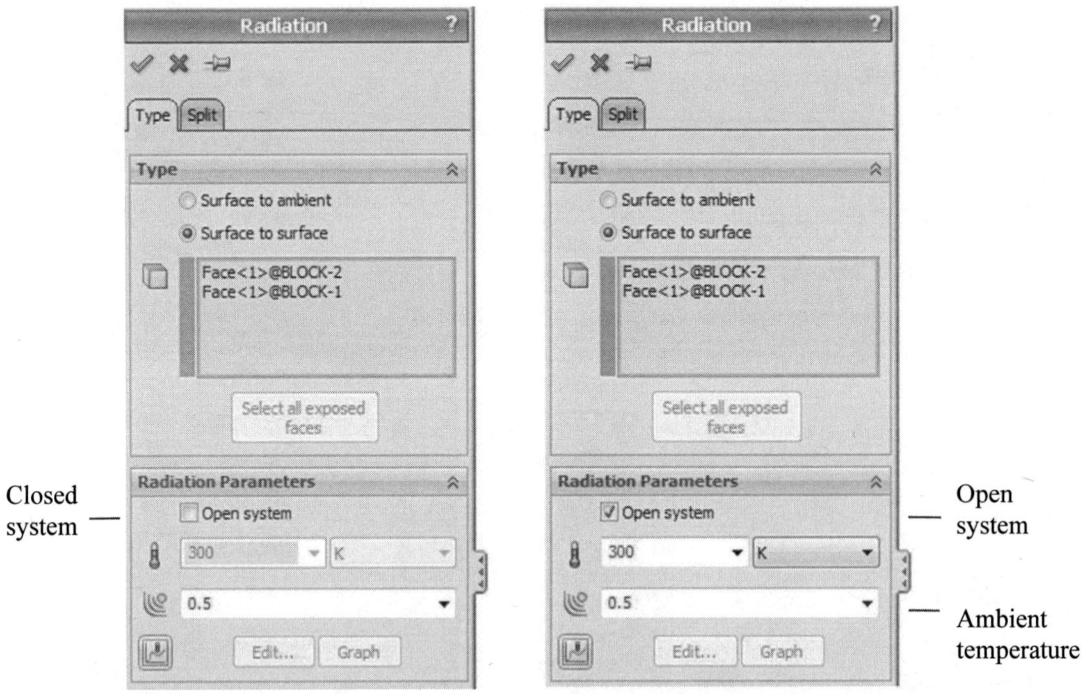

Study *01 surface to surface closed system* Study *02 surface to surface open system*

Figure 12-8: Radiation boundary conditions in two studies.

Open system allows the heat to be radiated out to space.

Notice that while specifying **Open system** we also have to define **Ambient Temperature** because heat is now radiated out to space. **Ambient temperature** is the temperature of a distant enclosure inside in which the two blocks are located as shown in Figure 1-7 (2).

Temperature and **Heat Flux** results in **Open system** are shown in Figures 12-9 and 12-10.

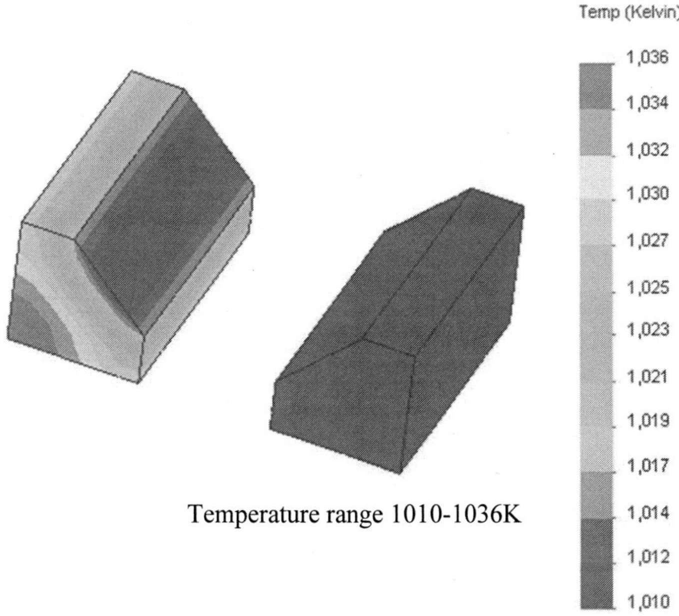

Temperature range 1010-1036K

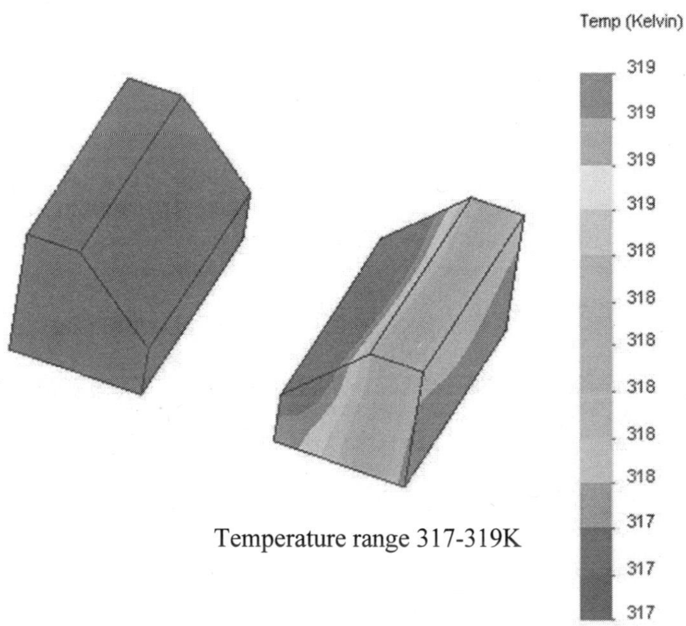

Temperature range 317-319K

Figure 12-9: Temperature results in Open system.

Two plots with different temperature ranges are used to show temperature distribution in the hot and cold blocks.

.

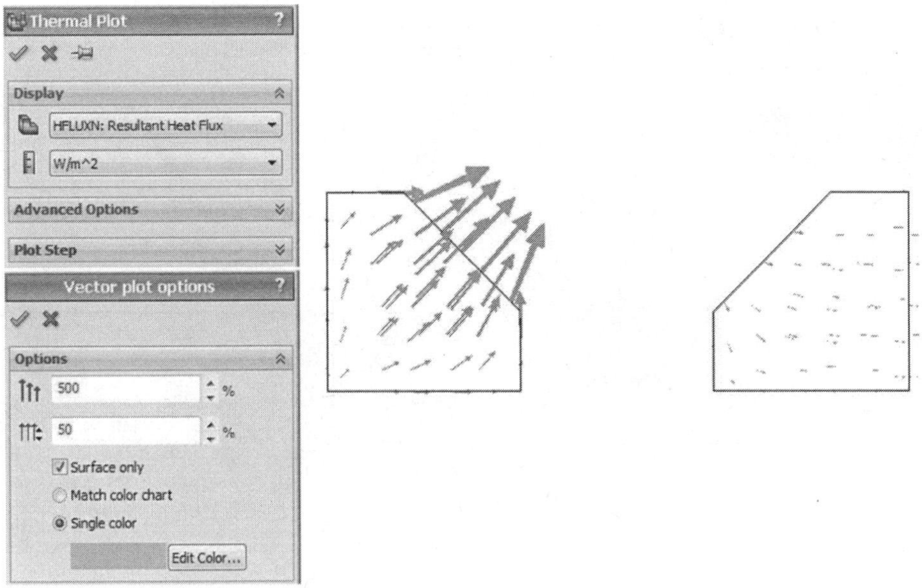

Figure 12-10: Heat Flux results in Open system.

Heat Flux vectors are barely visible in Cold block because very little heat "makes it" to the Cold block. Most of it is lost to the surrounding space.

Follow the same steps as shown in Figure 12-7 to probe **Heat Power** and find out how much heat is transferred from the hot block to the cold block and how much is radiated out to space (Figure 12-11).

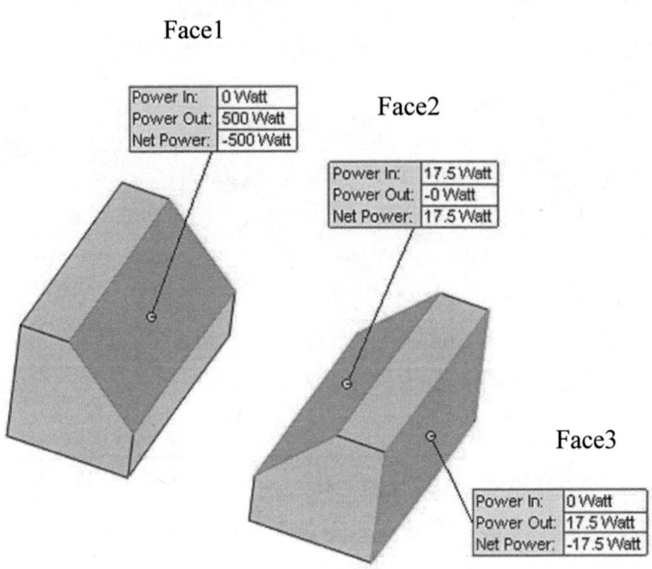

Figure 12-11: Heat Power results in an Open system.

Only 17.5W makes it from Face1 to Face2.

As Figure 12-11 shows, 500W-17.5W=482.5W is radiated out to space. The 17.5W of heat that reaches the Cold block travels by conduction through the Cold block to the face where the **Convection** boundary condition is defined. Upon reaching it, it is dissipated by convection to the surrounding fluid.

To illustrate an important difference between the study with **Closed system** and **Open system**, delete or suppress the **Convection** boundary condition in study *01 surface to surface closed system* and try running it. This results in an error (Figure 12-12) because in a closed system, in the absence of **Convection**, a mechanism of heat transfer does not exist.

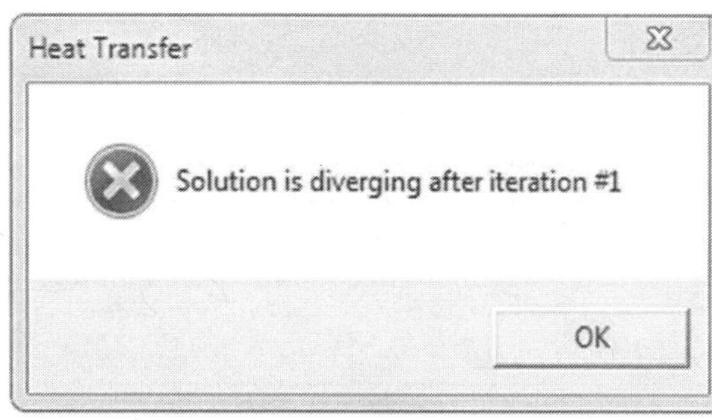

Figure 12-12: An error message when the solution is attempted with a Closed system and no Convection boundary conditions.

This error message is produced by an Iterative solver. A Direct Sparse solver enters into an infinite loop.

If you try the same using an **Open system**, the solution will be completed. This is because Face1 and Face2 can now exchange heat not only between themselves, but also can radiate it out to space. Therefore, heat may now exit from the hot block through Face1, to the cold block through Face2. Heat can also escape to space from either face (Figure 12-13).

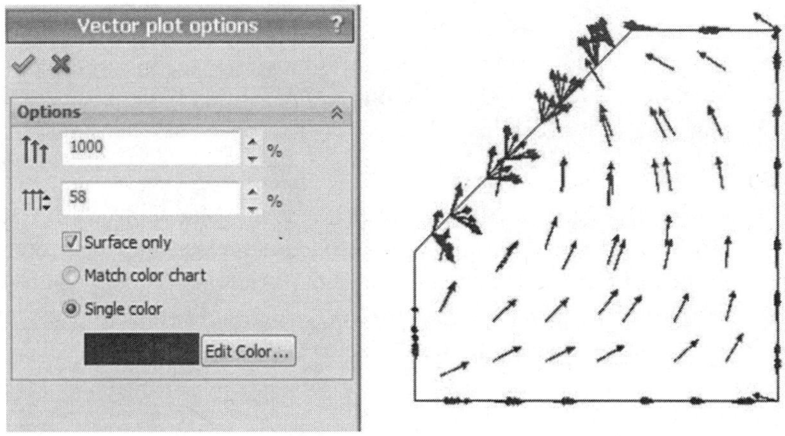

<u>Figure 12-13: In the absence of convection in the Open system, heat enters and exits the Cold block through Face2.</u>

The Hot block is hidden in SolidWorks.

13: NAFEMS Benchmarks

Topics covered

- Importance of benchmarks
- One dimensional heat transfer with radiation
- One dimensional transient heat transfer
- Two dimensional heat transfer with convection

Project description

Benchmarks are "standard" tests which can be applied to any Finite Element system. They are intended for users who are interested in the performance of specific codes. The classic set of benchmarks was first published in 1986 by the National Agency for Finite Element Methods and Standards (NAFEMS – see chapter 16). NAFEMS benchmarks were designed to be a little more "searching" than those typically published by software developers since these naturally intended to demonstrate the favorable performance of a system rather than deficiencies. While those tests were critical, they were not designed in such a way that any competent commercial system would not be able to provide satisfactory results.

In this chapter we will test the performance of **SolidWorks Simulation** in three NAFEMS thermal benchmarks with known analytical solutions. Performance will be evaluated by comparing **SolidWorks Simulation** results with targets (expected results) as specified in each test.

Very simple geometries used in these tests lend themselves to more than one representation. Therefore, these exercises will also serve as a review of finite element modeling techniques available in thermal analysis with **SolidWorks Simulation**.

Procedure

The thermal T2 tests code performance in steady state thermal analysis. A 1D bar has a constant prescribed temperature of 1000K applied to end A, and radiation to an ambient temperature of 300K to end B. There are no other boundary conditions present, meaning that the bar is insulated and there is no heat generated anywhere; the cross section is uniform (Figure 13-1).

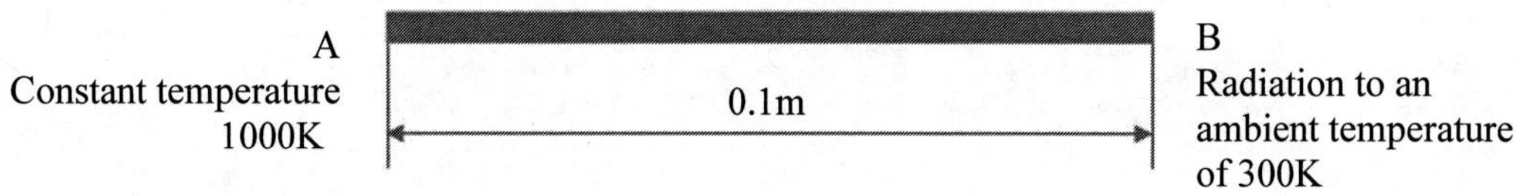

Figure 13-1: Geometry and boundary conditions of test T2.

Since this is a 1D model, only length needs to be specified.

Benchmark test T2 specifies material properties as follows:

Conductivity = 55.6W/m/K

Specific heat = 460J/kg/K

Density = 7850kg/m^3

Emissivity at boundary B = 0.98

Notice that specific heat and density are not required for steady state thermal analysis.

The target in test T2 is temperature at end B. To pass the test, an FEA program should find this temperature to be equal to 927K.

This very simple geometry can be modeled in a number of ways, either as a 3D or 2D problem. 1D elements are not available in **SolidWorks Simulation**. Therefore, our choice is between 3D and 2D representations.

Should we decide to model this as a 3D problem, any prismatic bar with a uniform cross section along the length could be used (Figure 13-2).

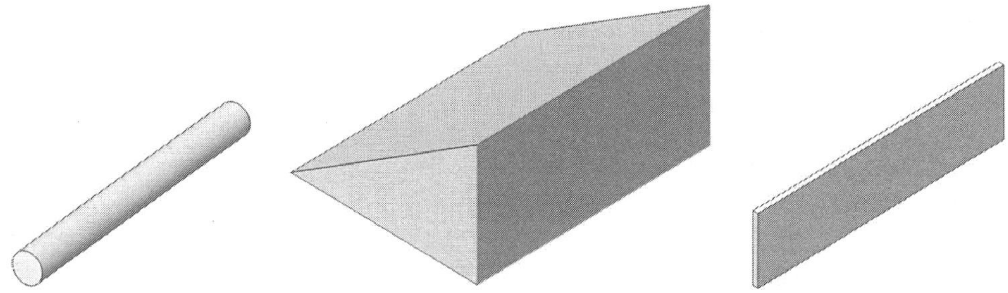

Figure 13-2: Examples of CAD geometry that could be used in a T2 test if 3D models were desired.

The shape and the area of the cross section are irrelevant in this 1D problem. Any of the above bars can be used as long as it has a length of 0.1m.

Should we decide to model this as a 2D problem, there is again more than one way to accomplish it. First, a bar with a round cross section could be used to create a 2D axisymmetric model. Second, a bar with a rectangular cross section could be used to create a 2D extruded model (Figure 13-3). Alternatively, a surface geometry could be prepared in **SolidWorks** and treated as an axisymmetric or extruded model in a 2D study.

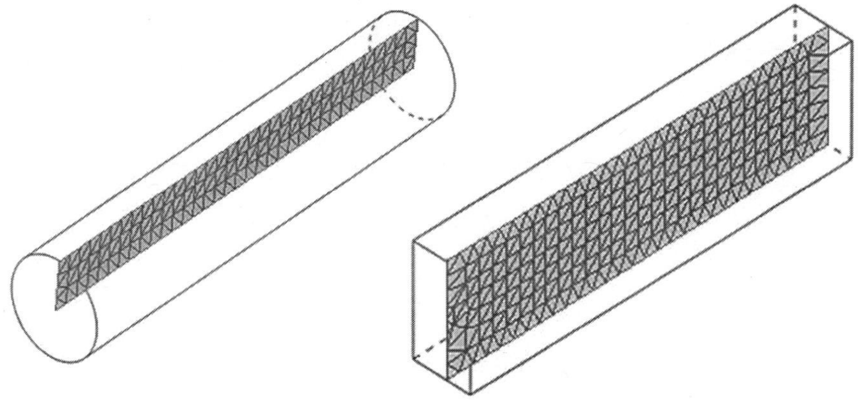

Figure 13-3: Examples of CAD geometry that could be used in a T2 test if 2D models were desired.

Large finite elements are shown for clarity of this illustration. We'll use much smaller elements for analysis.

For the T2 test, we will use a round bar and treat the problem as 3D. In test T3 which uses identical 1D geometry, we will use a square bar treating this problem as 2D extruded.

Open part model T2, create a steady state thermal study and apply thermal boundary conditions as shown in Figure 13-4 and Figure 13-5.

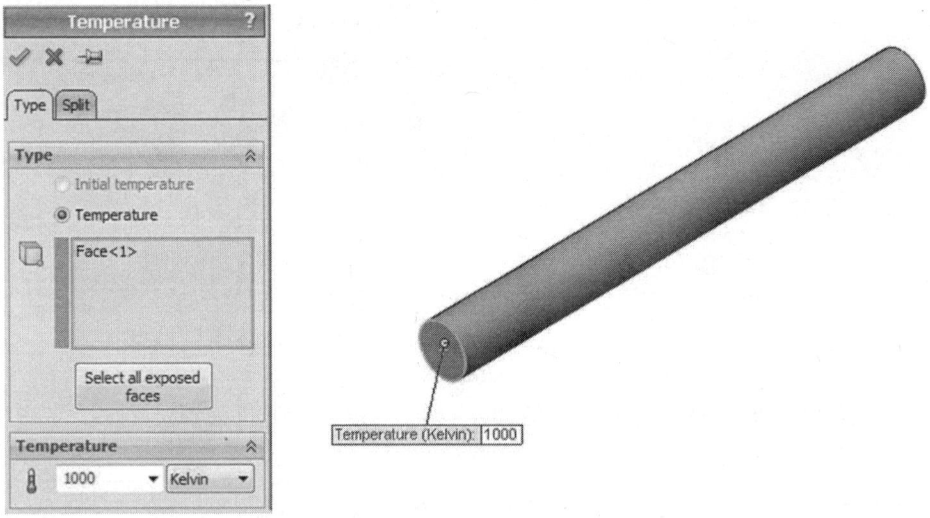

Figure 13-4: The boundary condition on side A is a prescribed temperature of 1000K.

A prescribed temperature is applied to side A.

Create a custom material with properties specified in benchmark test T2 and apply it to the model. To define a custom material, refer to Figure 7-11.

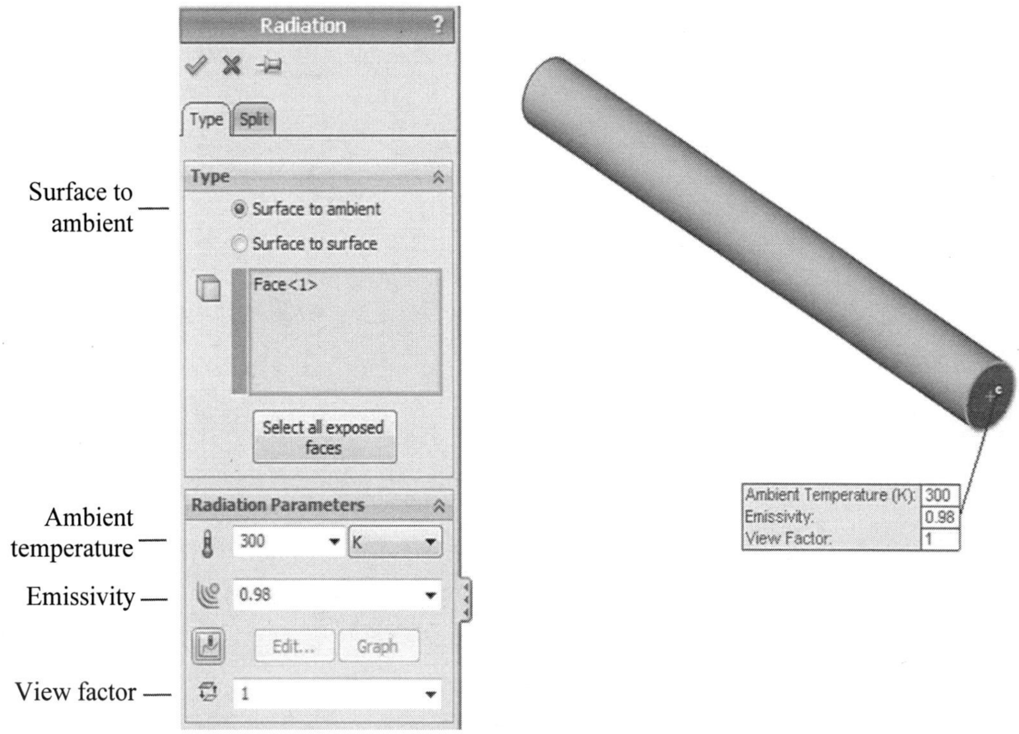

Figure 13-5: The boundary condition on side B is a Radiation Surface to ambient.

A radiation boundary condition is applied to side B.

An **Ambient temperature** of 300K is the temperature of a distant enclosure which receives heat radiated out from side B. An **Emissivity** of 0.98 is a material property. This is very close to the emissivity of black body so the material is very good at radiating out heat. To understand the meaning of a **View factor** of 1, take into consideration that **Surface to ambient** radiation is specified and that there is only one face in the model. A **View factor** equal to 1 means that the heat is radiated directly; the heat radiated out does not "bounce-off" the face again.

Mesh the model with a default mesh and obtain a solution. Show the **Temperature** plot and probe it as shown in Figure 13-6.

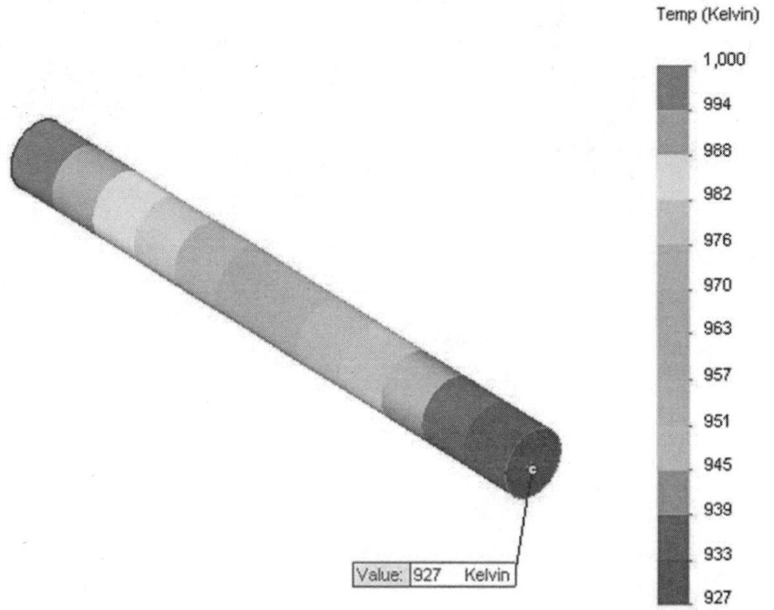

Figure 13-6: Probing shows the temperature on the side where the radiation boundary condition has been defined.

The probed temperature is 927K.

Probing shows a temperature of 927K as specified in the benchmark target. This demonstrates the correct performance of **Simulation** in this radiation problem. Try running the same problem with a view factor of less than 1, which makes it more difficult to radiate the heat out. The temperature will then be higher than 927K.

Benchmark test T3 requires a transient thermal analysis.

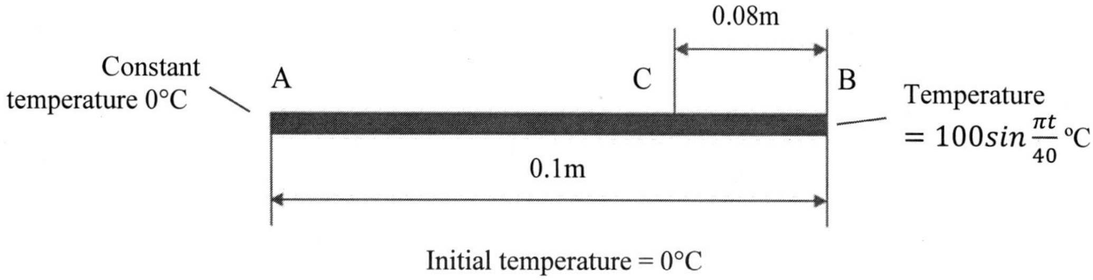

Figure 13-7: Geometry and boundary conditions of test T3.

The initial temperature is 0°C. The geometry is identical to test T2.

Benchmark test T3 specifies material properties as follows:

Conductivity = 35.0W/m/K

Specific heat = 440.5J/kg/K

Density = 7200kg/m^3

Notice that the temperature on side B is a function of time so this is a transient thermal problem; therefore specific heat and density are required.

The target in test T3 is a temperature at point C at time t=32s. To pass this benchmark test, the FEA program should find this temperature to be 36.6°C.

Open part model T3 and defined a thermal study using 2D simplification (Figure 13-8).

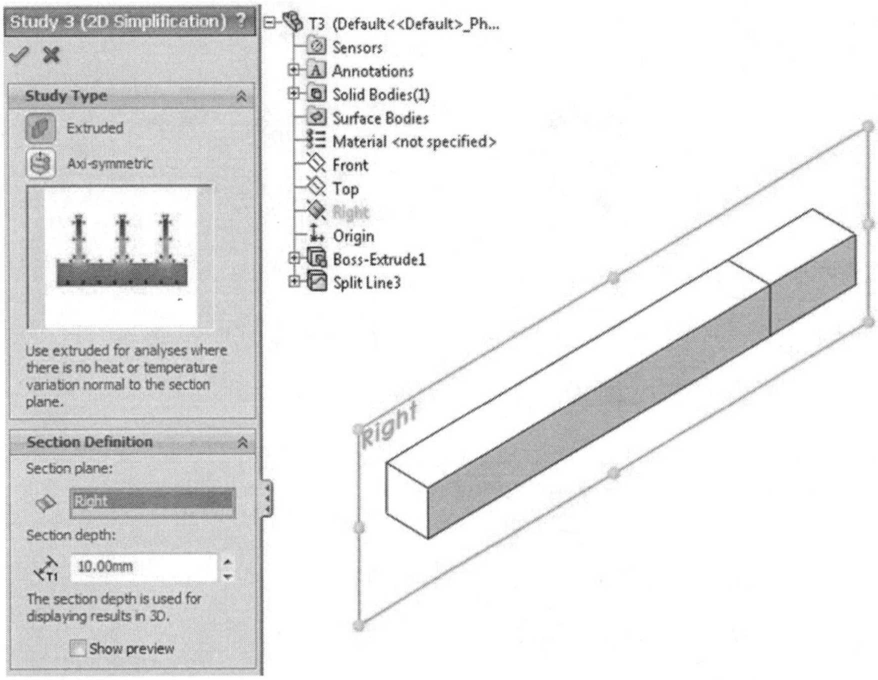

Figure 13-8: The 2D Simplification uses an Extruded 2D representation.

Show preview is deselected to show solid geometry instead of the 2D section. Any thickness may be entered. The split line is where temperature results will be probed.

Define study properties as shown in Figure 13-9.

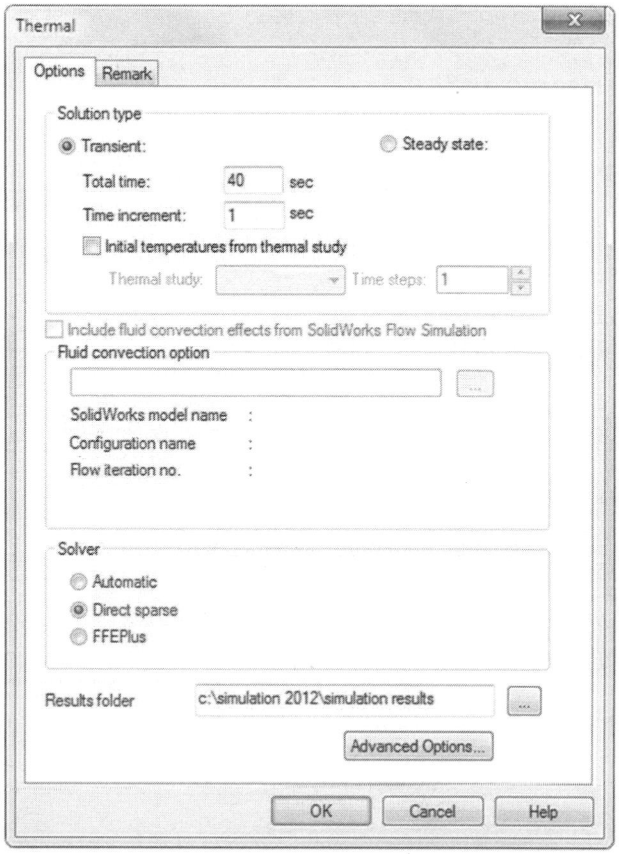

Figure 13-9: Properties of the transient thermal study.

The transient thermal study will be conducted in 40 steps with time increment of 1s.

Apply an **Initial Temperature** to faces as shown in Figure 13-10 and a **Prescribed Temperature** to side A as shown in Figure 13-11.

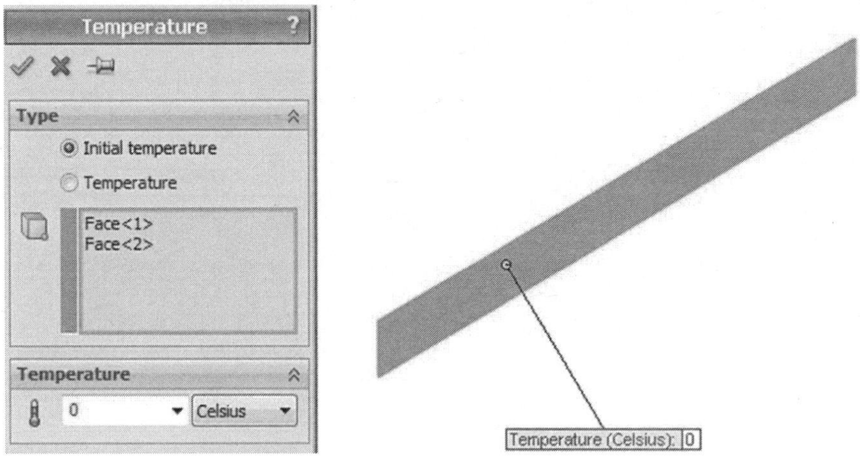

Figure 13-10: Definition of an initial temperature.

Initial temperature is applied to two faces; there are two faces in the 2D model because of the split line.

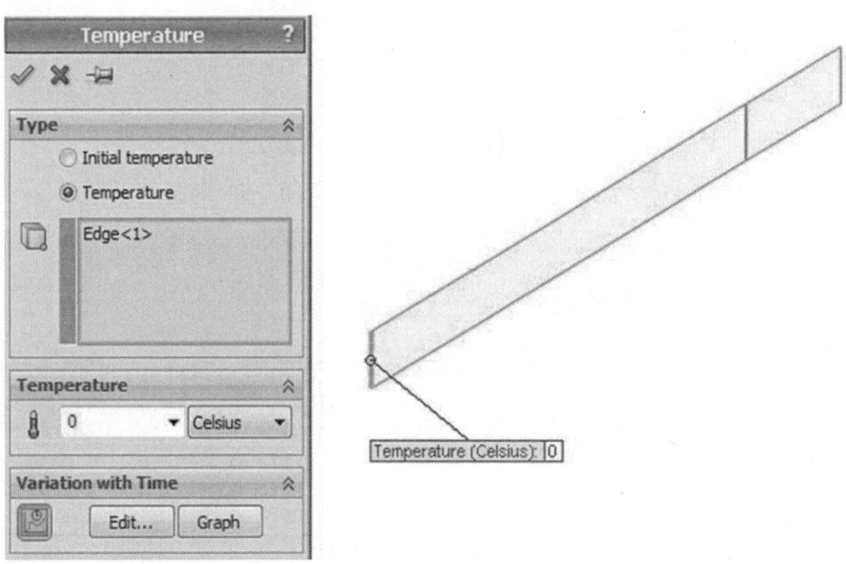

Figure 13-11: Definition of a prescribed temperature on side A.

Temperature is applied to the edge which represents the face in the 2D model.

Follow the steps in Figure 13-12 to define a time dependent temperature on side B.

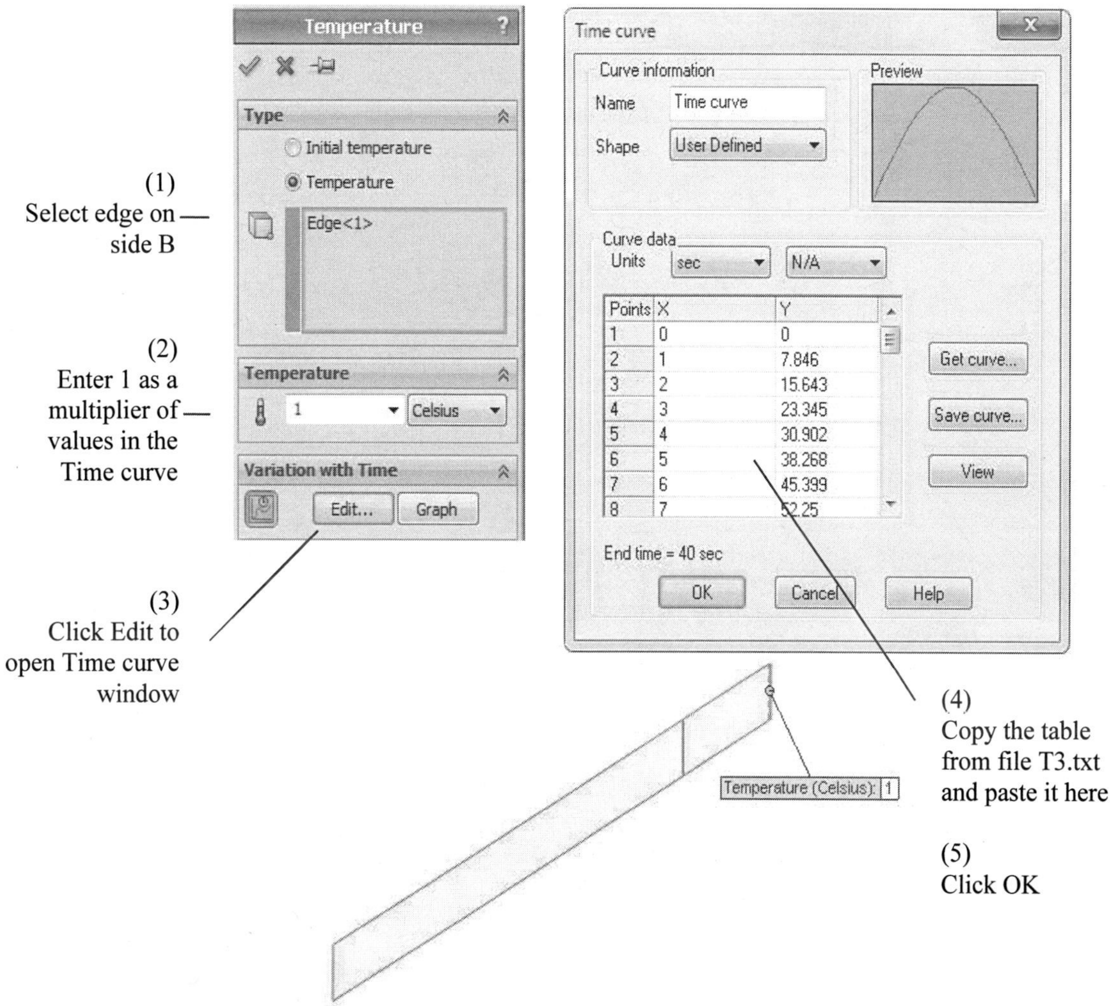

Figure 13-12: Definition of the time dependent temperature on side B.

The time dependency is illustrated by a curve shown in the Preview image.

The table in file T3.txt has been created in Excel by tabulating the equation shown Figure 13-7.

Create and apply a new material to the geometry (conductivity = 35.0W/m/K, specific heat = 440.5J/kg/K, density = 7200kg/m^3). Mesh the model with the default element size and obtain a solution. To check the target probe **Temperature** plot as shown in Figure 13-13.

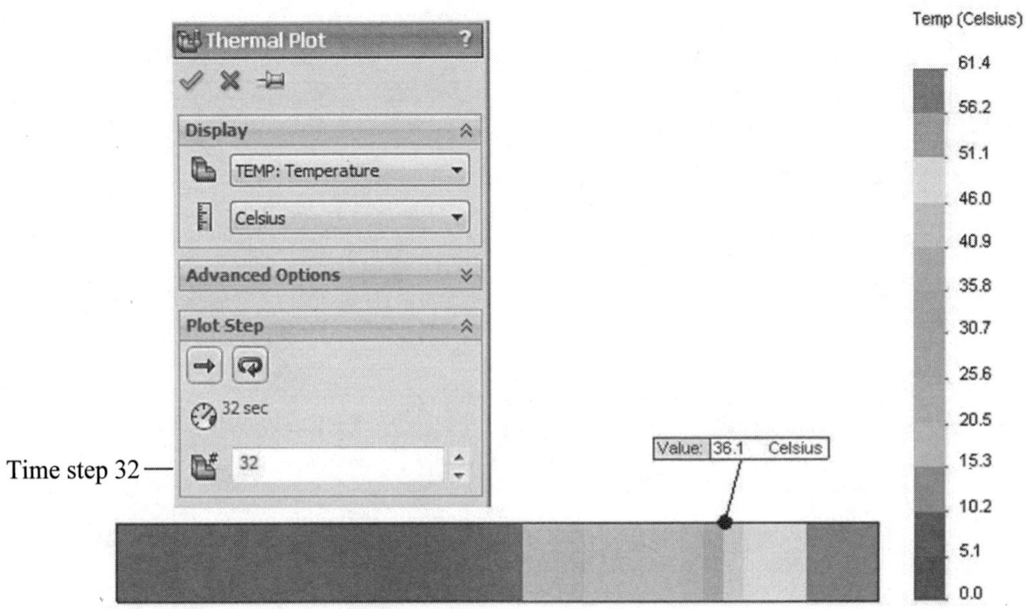

Figure 13-13: Probing temperature plot in location C.

Make sure the plot is for time 32s and probing is where split line separates the two faces.

Probing shows a **Simulation** temperature result of 36.1°C, very close to the benchmark test T3 target of 36.6°C.

Benchmark test T4 is about conductive heat transfer induced by prescribed temperatures and convection to an ambient temperature (Figure 13-14).

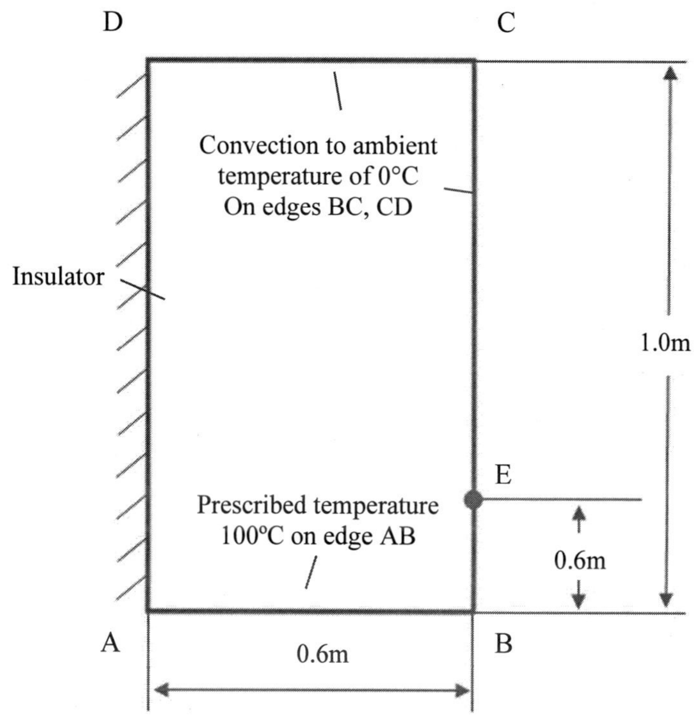

Figure 13-14: Geometry and boundary conditions of test T4.

This is a 2D problem, the thickness is uniform.

Benchmark test T4 specifies a material conductivity and convection properties as follows:

Conductivity = 52.0W/m/K

Convection = 750W/m^2/K

The target in test T4 is temperature at point E. To pass the test, the FEA program should find this temperature to be 18.3°C.

Test T4 is a 2D problem which is represented as a surface in **SolidWorks**. Open model *T4* and create a thermal study using 2D Simplification as shown in Figure 13-15.

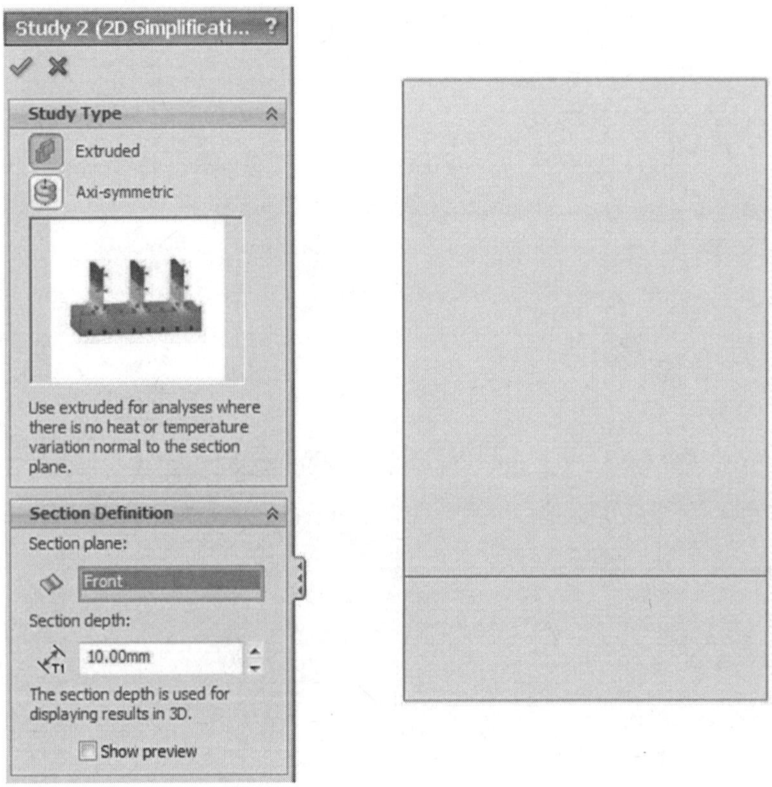

Figure 13-15: 2D Simplification uses Extruded 2D representation.

This is a 2D extruded problem, the thickness is uniform; any thickness may be entered.

Apply a prescribed temperature and convection boundary conditions as shown in Figure 13-16 and Figure 13-17.

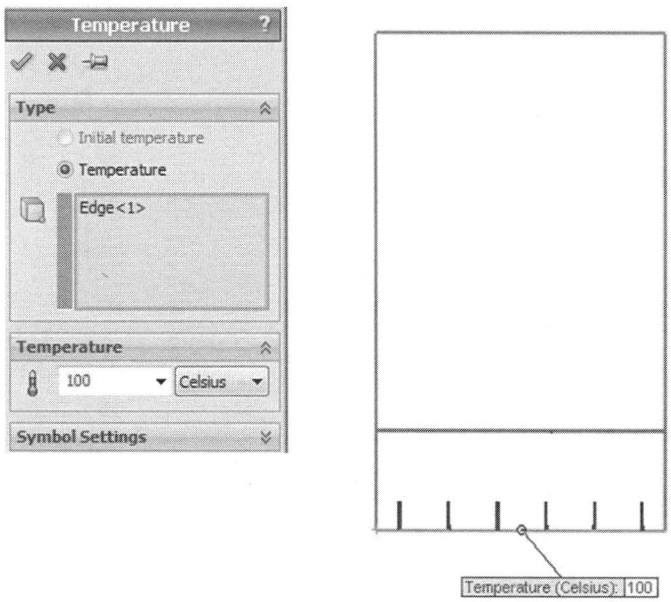

Figure 13-16: Definition of prescribed temperature in test T4.

Apply a temperature of 100°C to the lower edge. Prescribed temperature symbols are shown.

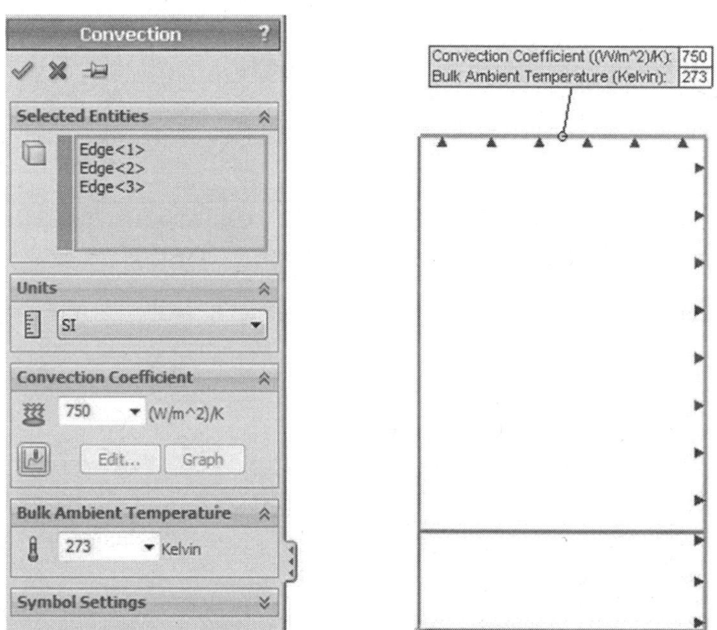

Figure 13-17: Definition of convection boundary condition in test T4.

Apply a convection of 750W/m^2/K and an ambient temperature of 273K to the top and right edges. Convection symbols are shown.

Create and apply a new material with conductivity equal to 52.0W/m/K and convection equal to 750W/m^2/K. Mesh the model with a default mesh and obtain a solution. Probe the **Temperature** plot at point E as shown in Figure 13-18.

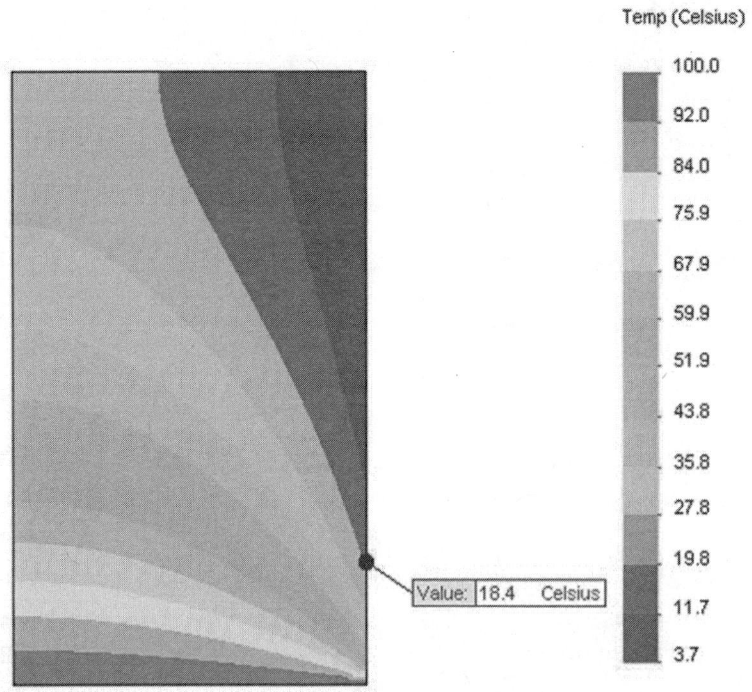

Figure 13-18: Probing temperature results in test T4.

Probe at the intersection of the vertical edge with the horizontal split line.

Probing shows a temperature 18.4°C, very close to the target value of 18.3°C.

14: Summary and miscellaneous topics

Topics covered

- Summary of exercises in chapters 1-13
- Nonlinear transient problems
- Closing remarks

As shown in the flowchart in Figure 14-1, thermal analysis may be linear or nonlinear, steady state or time dependent.

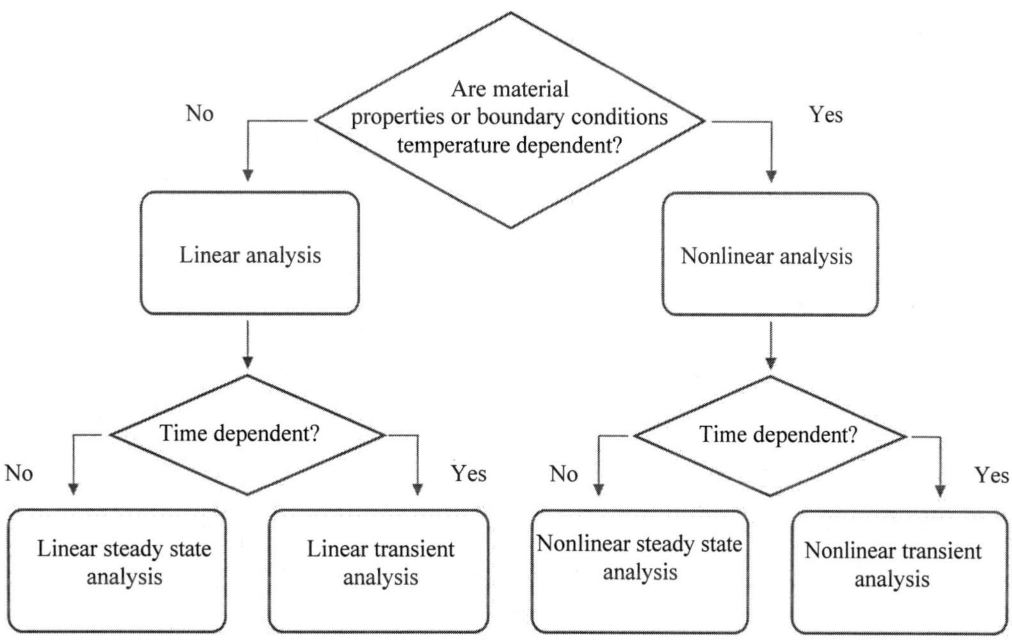

Figure 14-1: Classification of thermal analysis with regard to time dependency and nonlinearity.

This is a repetition of Figure 1-12.

In linear analyses, the conductivity matrix does not change during the solution process, in nonlinear analyses it must be modified. In steady state analyses, the boundary conditions do not change during the solution process, in time dependent (transient) analyses, boundary conditions change.

The table in Figure 14-2 classifies examples discussed in chapters 1-13 in terms of nonlinearity and time dependency.

Chapter	Model	Linear steady state analysis	Linear transient analysis	Nonlinear steady state analysis	Nonlinear transient analysis
1	BRACKET TH	yes			
1	HEAT SINK 01	yes			
1	DOUBLE SYM	yes			
1	AXI SYM	yes			
2	HOLLOW PLATE TH	yes			
3	L BRACKET TH	yes			
4	STEEL ROD	yes			
4	TWO RODS	yes			
5	HEATING DUCTS	yes			
6	HEATING DUCTS	yes			
7	HOT PLATE	yes	yes		
8	MUG	yes	yes		
9	RECT BAR	yes			
10	GRAPHITE BALL			yes	
11	HEMISPHERE			yes	
12	BLOCKS			yes	
13	T2			yes	
13	T3		yes		
13	T4	yes			
14					

Figure 14-2: Classification of exercises with regard to time dependency and nonlinearity.

When "yes" appears both in steady state and transient analysis, it means that more than one study was conducted.

All radiation problems are nonlinear because a radiation boundary condition is a function of temperature. The fact that this is temperature to the fourth power makes radiation problems strongly nonlinear. However, none of the exercises discussed so far presented a transient and nonlinear problem.

What would make a transient, nonlinear problem? This could be any radiation problem with at least one time dependent boundary condition. This could be also any transient problem with, for example, a temperature dependent material property. We will analyze both problems starting with a radiation problem which can be seen as a continuation of radiation topics presented in chapters 10 through 12.

Open assembly model SPACE HEATER. The model consists of an aluminum Reflector and a glass Bulb. Faces that exchange heat by radiation are indicated in Figure 14-3, Front view. The rim, and back face are assumed to be insulated. A split line on the back face (Figure 14-3, Back view) defines the position of the temperature probe. A fillet at the base of stem is also assumed to be insulated; it won't have any boundary conditions defined. This is done to simplify calculations of view factors and this omission won't have much of an effect because of the small surface area of the fillet.

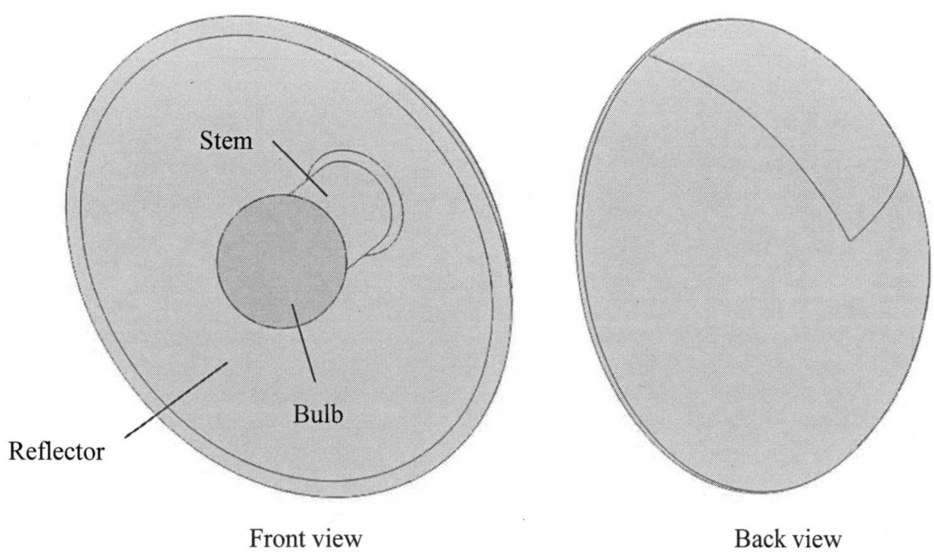

Figure 14-3: SPACE HEATER assembly.

Review this model in a section view to see that the Bulb is hollow.

Radiation is the only mechanism of removing heat from this model. Conduction is present but heat traveling by conduction through the Bulb and Reflector is also removed by radiation. Create a **Steady State** thermal study called *01 steady state*. Define **Heat Power** and **Radiation** conditions as shown in Figures 14-4, 14-5, and 14-6.

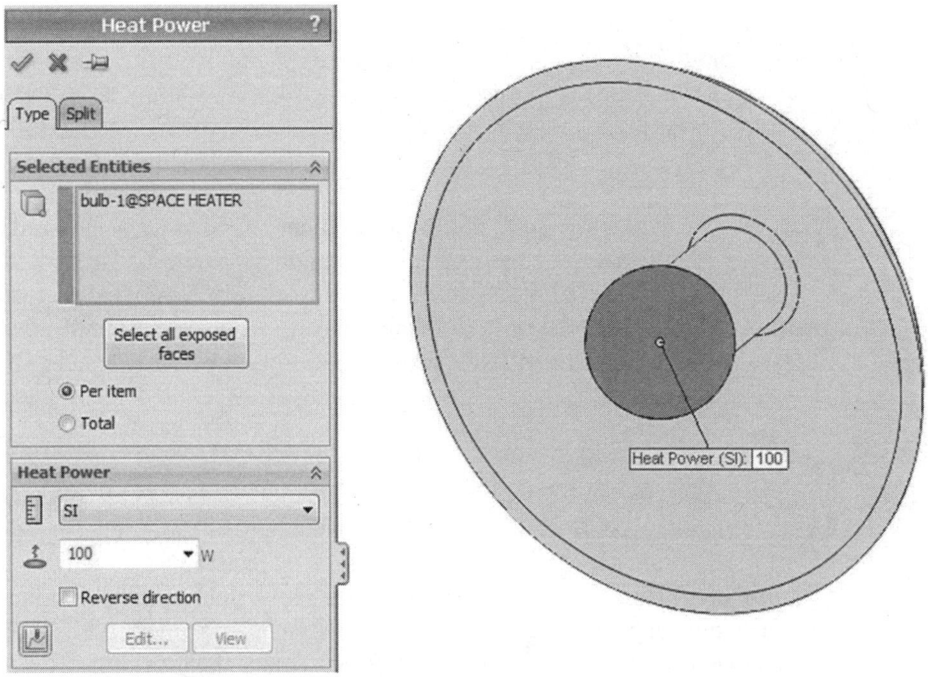

Figure 14-4: Heat power definition.

Apply 100W to the entire Bulb; select it from the fly-out menu.

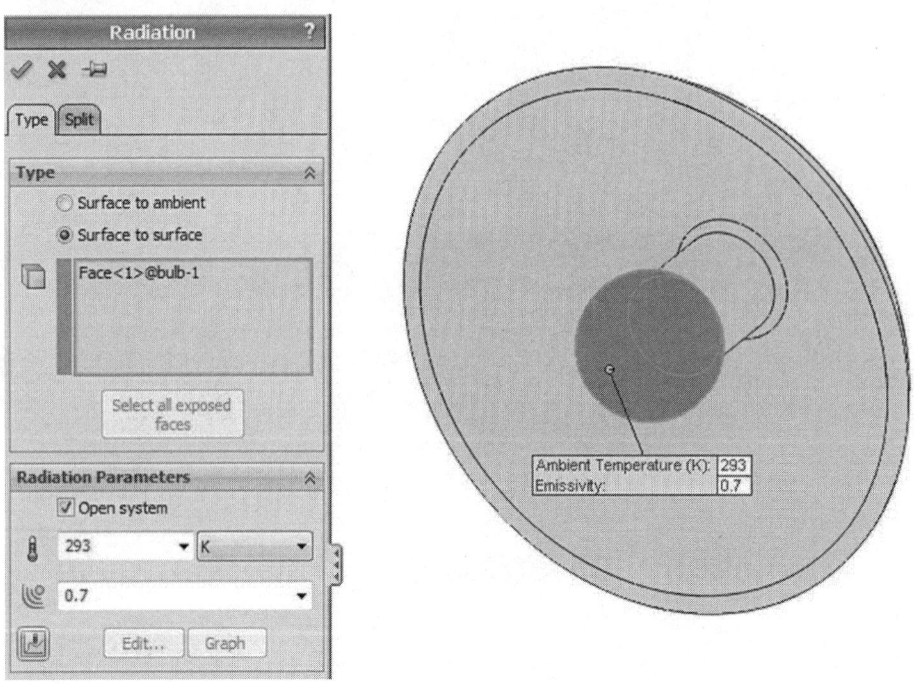

Figure 14-5: Radiation definition on the Bulb surface.

Open system means that some heat is radiated out to space and not to the Reflector. The ambient temperature is 293K, and emissivity of Bulb surface material is 0.7.

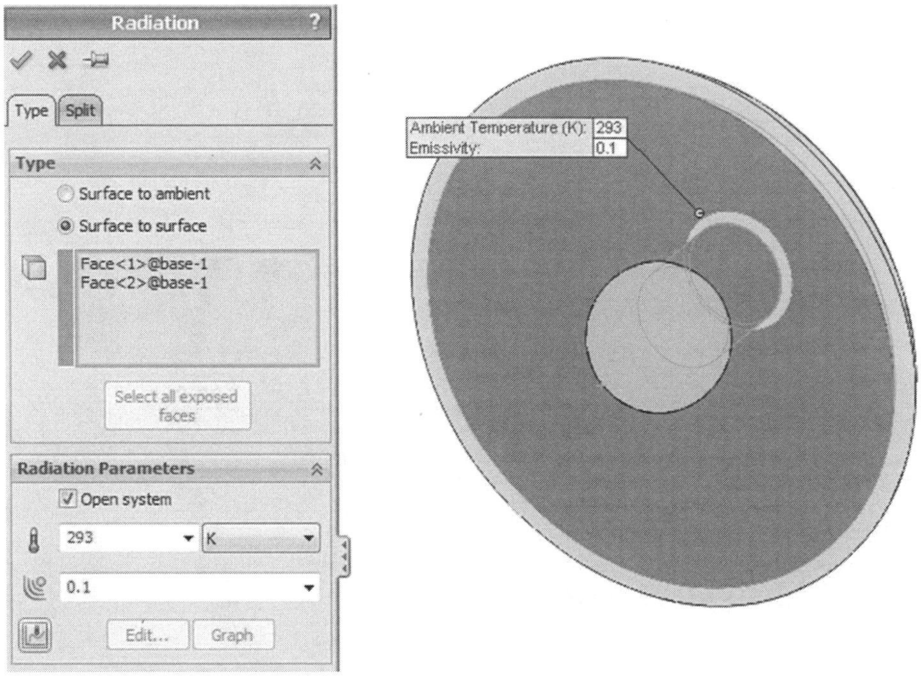

Figure 14-6: Radiation definition on Reflector surface and stem.

Open system means that some heat is radiated out to space and not all to the Bulb. Ambient temperature is 293K, and emissivity of these faces is 0.1. Note that the Reflector is designed to reflect radiation, which is why the value of the emissivity coefficient is low.

Mesh the assembly with the default element size, which produces a mesh barely acceptable for temperature analysis. Analysis of heat flux would definitely need a more refined mesh especially at the area of the fillet. Run the solution and review the steady state temperature as shown in Figure 14-7.

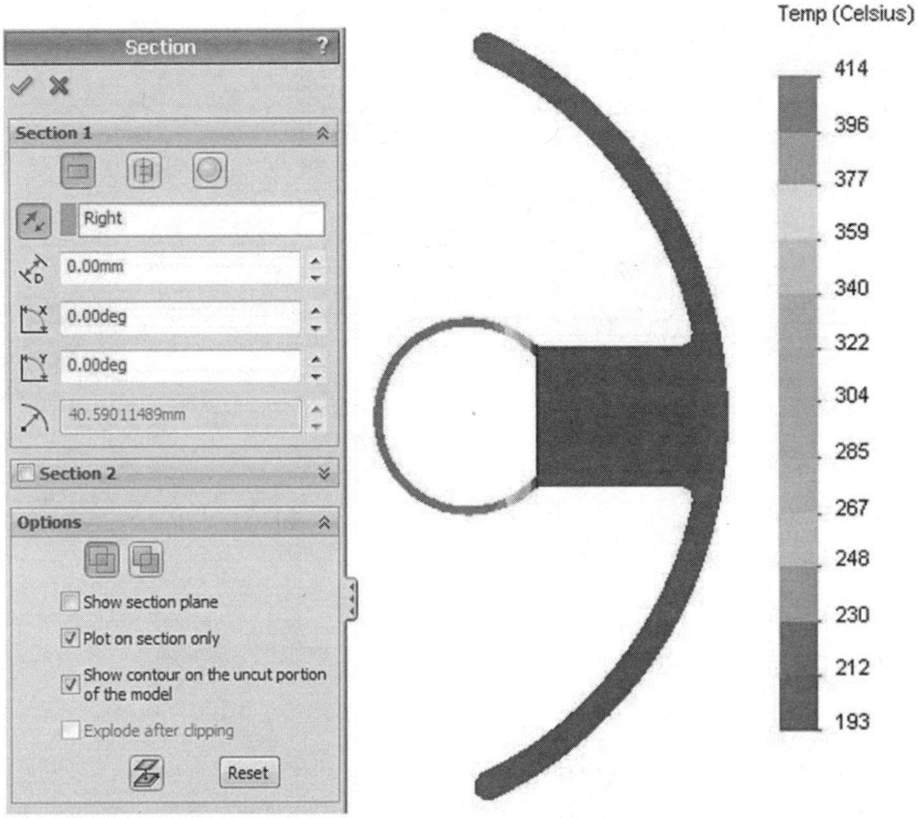

Figure 14-7: Steady state temperature results.

This section plot uses settings shown in the Section window.

Even though the geometry has axial symmetry, the radiation problem can't be simplified to a 2D axisymmetric model. This is because finding **View Factors** requires 3D geometry.

Notice that we have just solved nonlinear, steady state problem. We will now make it into a transient problem. Copy study *01 steady state* into *02 transient*. Define properties of the transient study as shown in Figure 14-8.

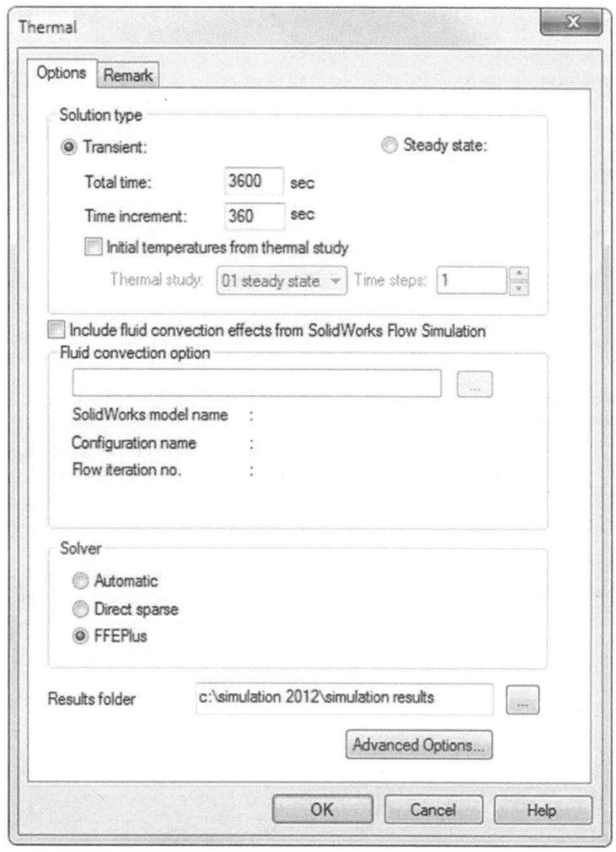

Figure 14-8: Properties of the transient thermal study.

The duration of analysis is 1 hour covered in 10 steps at 6min intervals. This analysis will take 6 times longer than the previous steady state analysis.

Remember that transient thermal analysis requires an **Initial Temperature**. Define it as 298K for the entire assembly (Figure 14-9).

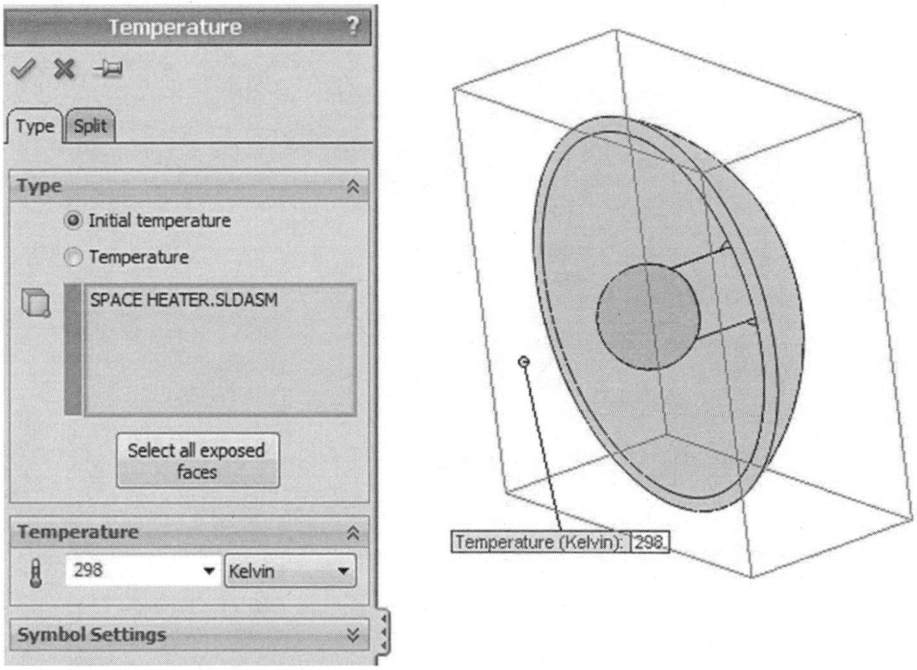

Figure 14-9: Definition of Initial Temperature for the assembly.

Select the assembly from the fly-out menu. Notice that the temperature callout refers to the origin of the assembly.

Run study *02 transient* and display the **Temperature** plot from any time step. Probe the temperature of the Bulb and Reflector then display these temperatures as function of time; follow the steps in Figure 14-10.

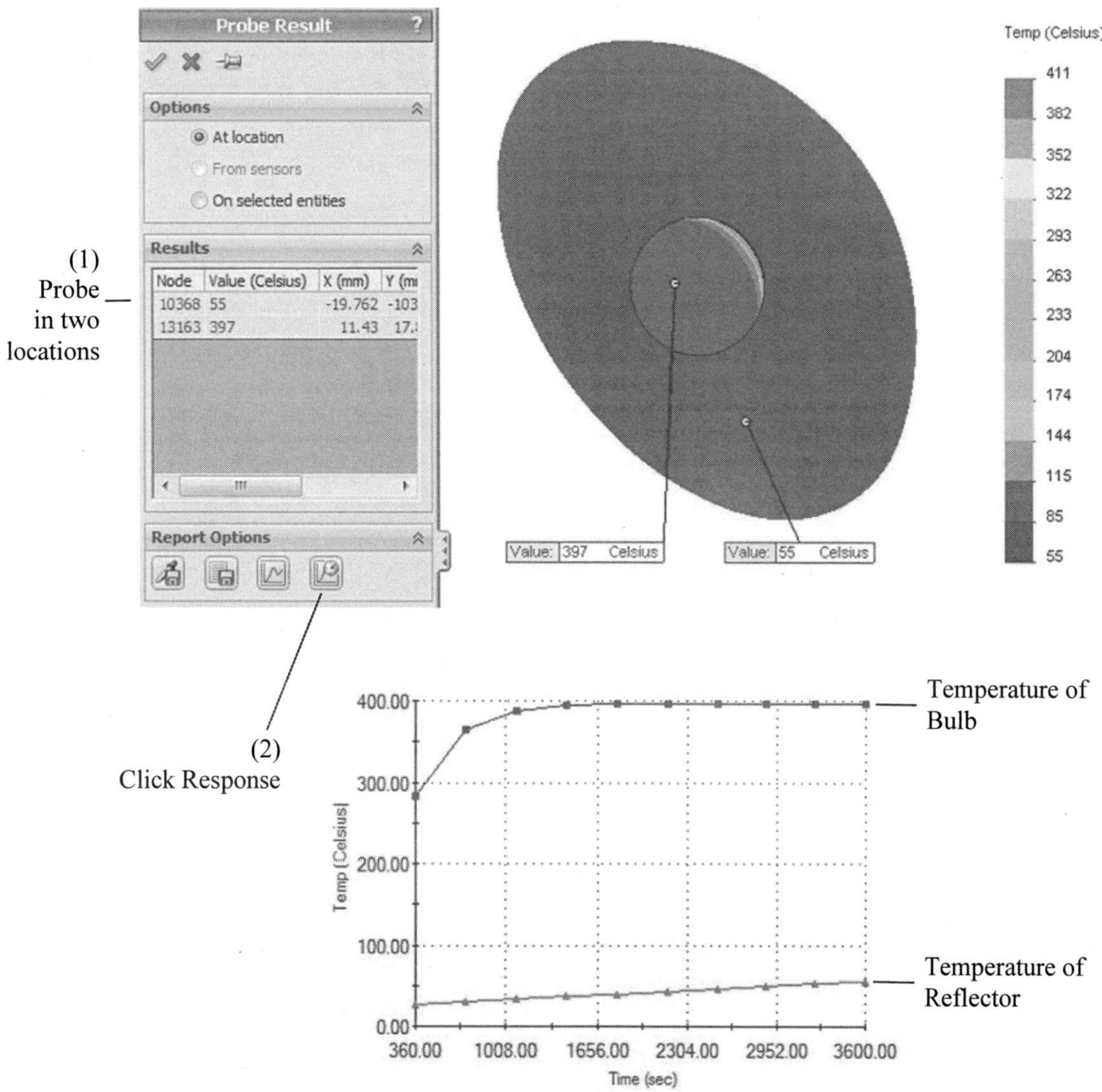

Figure 14-10: Temperature of the assembly for the last step and Response graph showing temperatures in the probed location as function of time.

The temperature of the front side of the Bulb and of the Reflector are very uniform, you may probe just about anywhere.

Results indicate that the Bulb reaches steady state temperature after about 1500s. The duration of analysis was too short for the Reflector to reach the steady state temperature.

In the next model the source of nonlinear behavior is a material property. Open part model RADIATOR AXISYM. Our goal is to study temperature fluctuation on the ribs when a time variable temperature is applied to the end face of the stem. Create a thermal study with **2D Simplification** using axial symmetry (Figure 14-11).

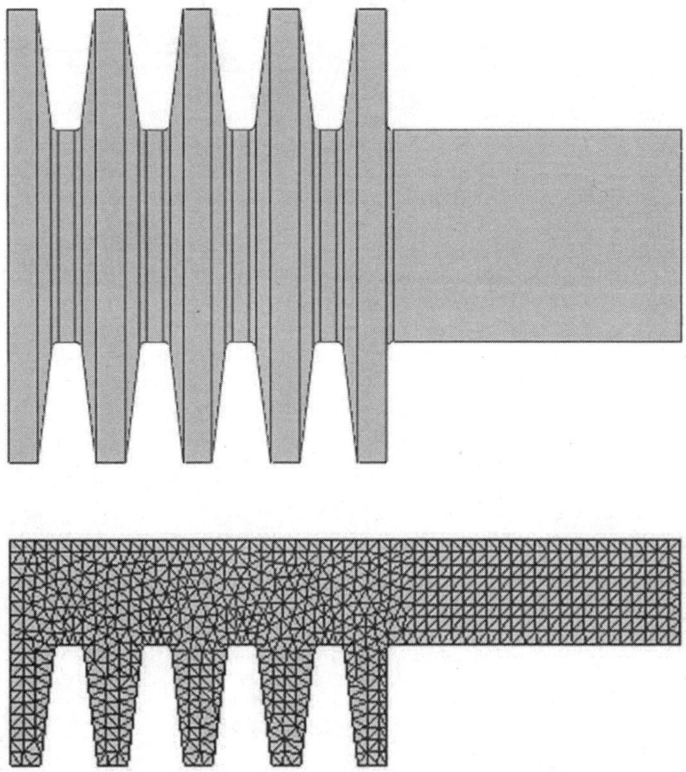

3D CAD model

2D axisymmetric Simulation model

Figure 14-11: The 3D model can be represented in 2D as half of the radial cross.

Using 2D elements, we can use a fine mesh with no need for any mesh control. Shown above is a mesh that used the default element size. The mesh is acceptable for temperature analysis but may require refinement for heat flux analysis.

To create material with temperature dependent conductivity, first copy the material 1060 Alloy into **Custom Materials** in the **Thermal** folder, then follow the steps in Figure 14-12.

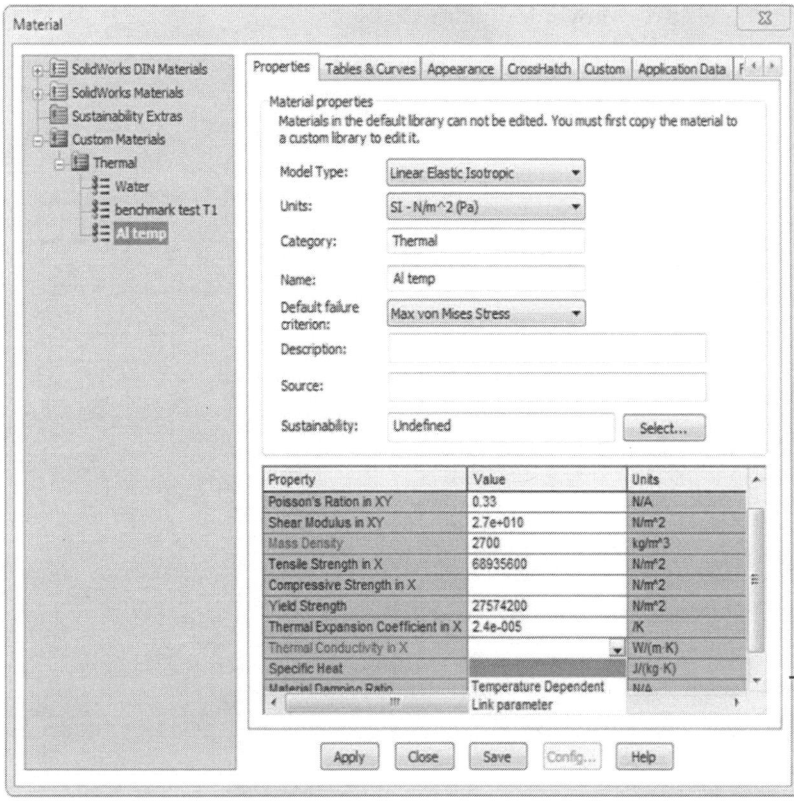

(1)
Copy material AL1060 into Thermal folder in Custom materials

(2)
Use drop down arrow in Thermal Conductivity line to select Temperature Dependent

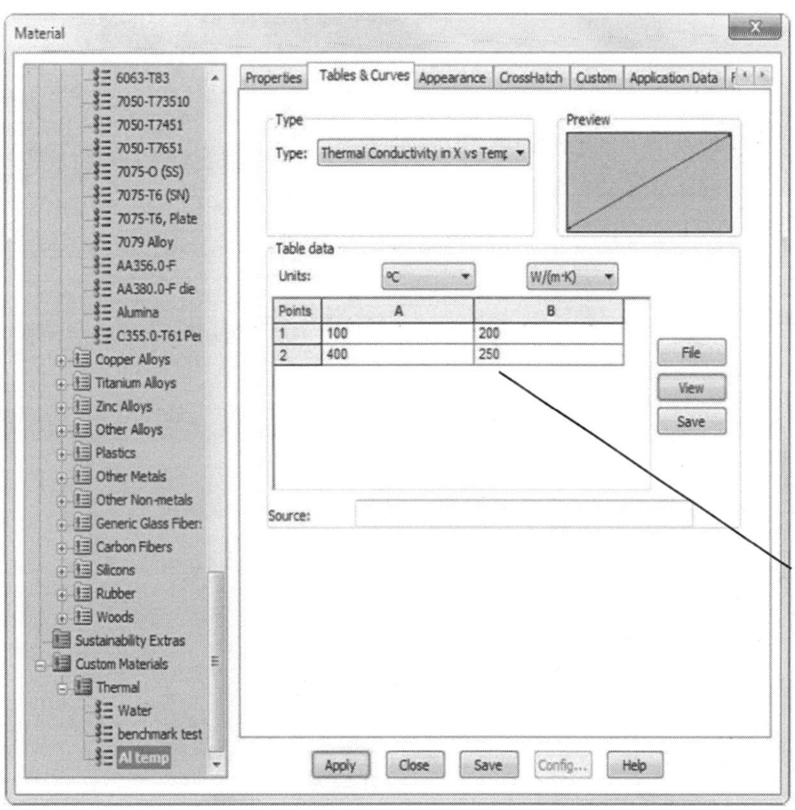

(3)
Set units to °C and W/m/K;
Enter coordinates of two points as shown

Figure 14-12: Definition of custom material with temperature dependent conductivity.

Define study properties as shown in Figure 14-13.

Figure 14-13: Definition of properties of the transient study.

The total duration is 560s; the time increment is 4s. The analysis will be conducted in 140 steps.

Define an Initial Temperature of 0°C as shown in Figure 14-14.

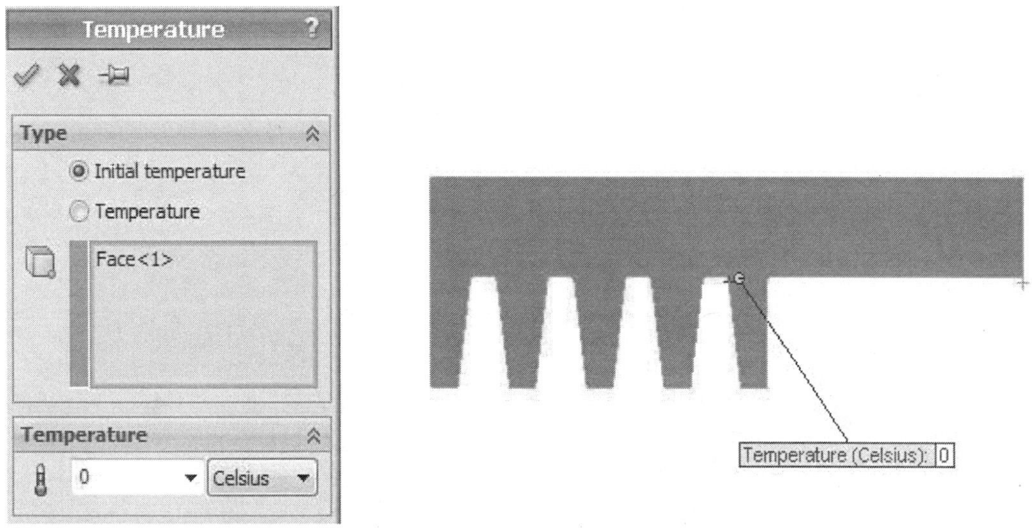

Figure 14-14: An initial temperature of 0°C is applied to the face that represents the 2D model.

An initial temperature would not be required in a steady state analysis.

Define the time dependent temperature to the right end. The time dependency follows the equation:

$t = 100sin\frac{\pi t}{20} + 100$ °C.

You can use Excel to prepare a table with 1s steps for $0 \leq t \leq 560s$.

or copy table from file RADIATOR.TX

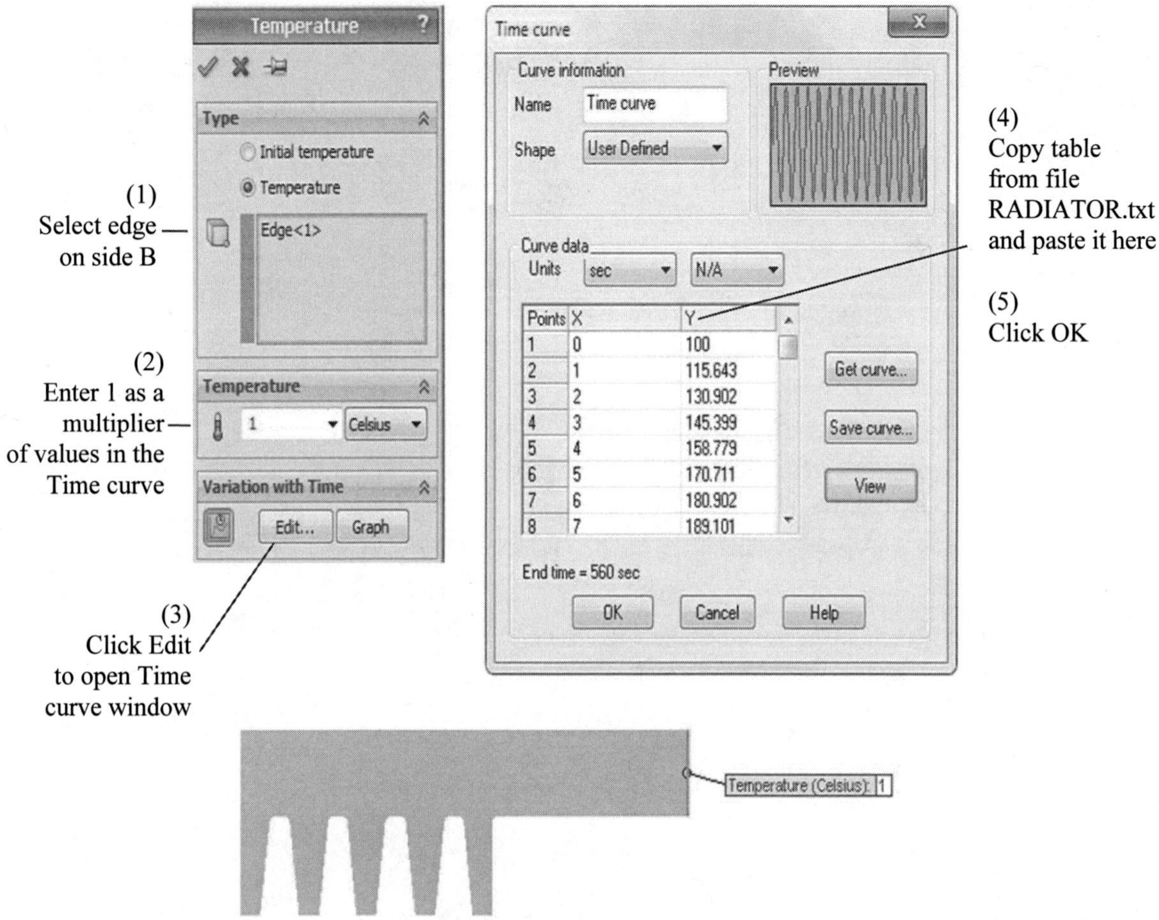

Figure 14-15: Definition of time dependent temperature.

These steps are similar those in Figure 13-12.

Mesh the model with the default mesh (Figure 14-11) and obtain a solution. Display the **Temperature** plot from any step and probe results in two locations as shown in Figure 14-16.

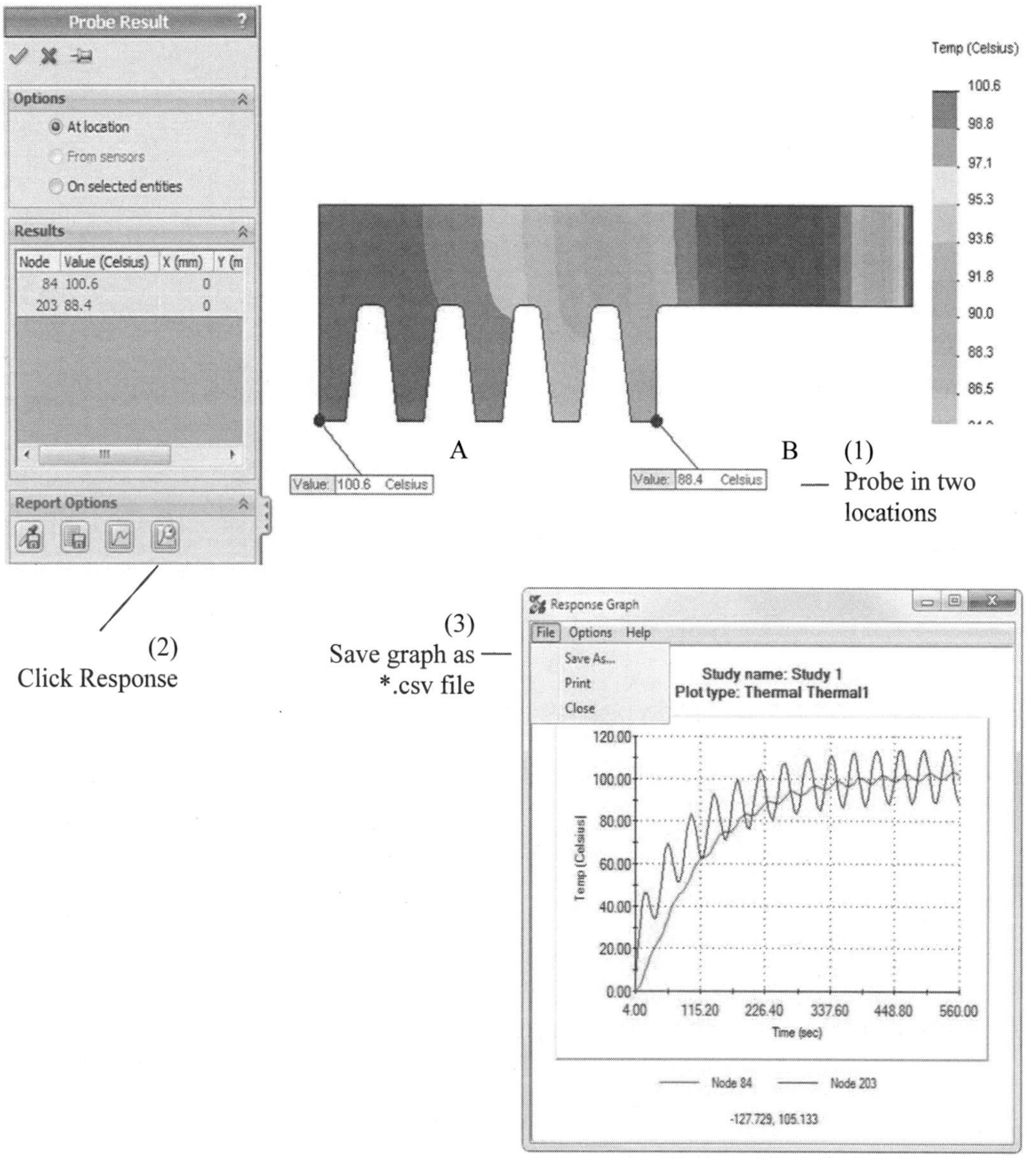

<u>Figure 14-16: Probe temperature results in two locations as shown.</u>

*Save the graph as a *.csv file.*

The results are easier to present using Excel which offers better graphing tools than those in **SolidWorks Simulation**. The temperature in the two probed locations is shown as a function of time in Figure 14-17.

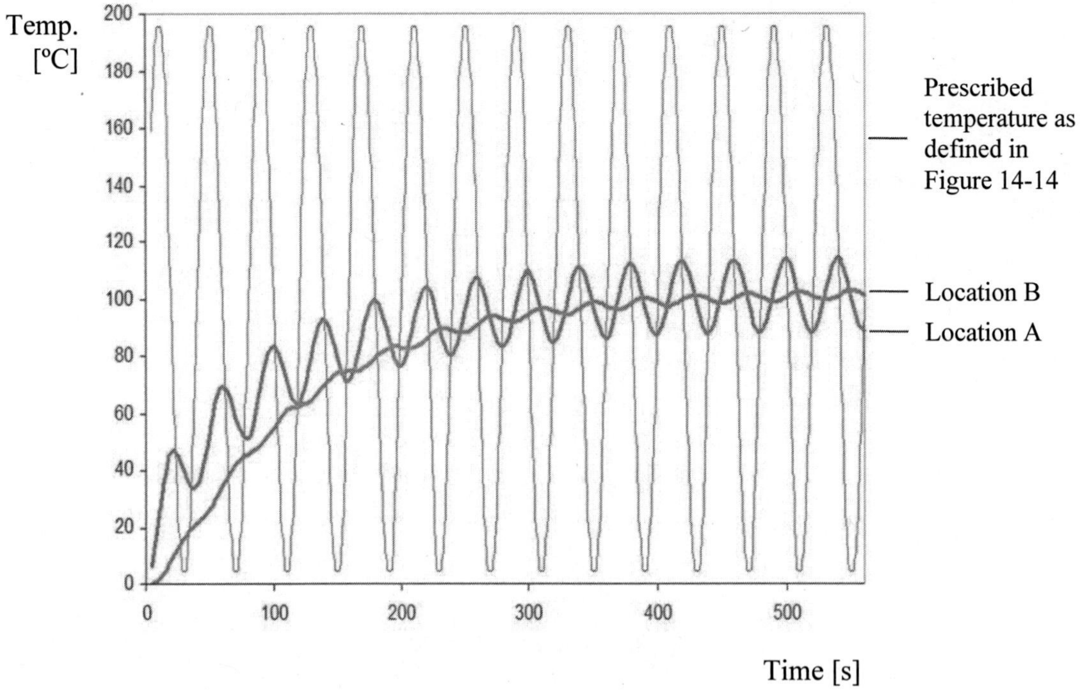

Figure 14-17: Probed temperature results in locations A and B.

This graph also shows the prescribed temperature oscillating between 0° and 200°C.

As we can see in Figure 14-17, temperature oscillations diminish as we move further away from where the oscillating prescribed temperature is applied. This is the effect of thermal inertia.

Notice that the RADIATOR AXISYM problem is transient and nonlinear. It solves fast thanks to the 2D representation that greatly reduces the numerical effort. Benefits of the 2D representation are particularly high when transient and/or nonlinear problems are solved.

Chapters 1 through 14 presented a variety of heat transfer and related structural problems. Our focus was on the understanding of the physical phenomena while avoiding excessively complex models which would make solution time unnecessarily long. You will notice that the same principles and modeling techniques apply to models of any complexity.

Notes:

15: Glossary of terms

The following glossary provides short descriptions of selected terms used in this book.

Conduction
Conduction is a mode of heat transfer in which the heat energy is transferred on a molecular scale with no movement of macroscopic particles. Fourier's Law characterizes heat flow by conduction. The coefficient of thermal conduction characterizes heat transfer in solid bodies.

Conductivity
Conductivity characterizes heat flow per unit area in the normal direction in a solid body which takes place as a result of a temperature difference.

Convection
Convection is a mode of heat transfer between a solid face and a fluid. The movement of macroscopic particles transfers the heat energy. The convection coefficient characterizes convection between a solid body and its surrounding fluid.

Emissivity
Emissivity is the ratio of the total energy emitted by a surface to the total energy emitted by a black surface at the same temperature.

Heat
Heat is a form of energy of a system when temperature difference exists between a system and its surroundings.

Heat flux
Heat flux is the rate of heat transfer per unit area.

Heat transfer
The transfer of heat energy from one system to another.

Linear analysis
An analysis is linear when none of the parameters characterizing boundary conditions, material properties and loads is temperature dependent.

Nonlinear analysis
An analysis is nonlinear when at least one of the parameters characterizing boundary conditions, material properties or loads is temperature dependent.

Radiation
Radiation heat transfer occurs by means of electromagnetic waves. The heat energy can be transferred in vacuum. The Stefan-Boltzmann law characterizes radiative heat transfer.

Specific heat
Specific heat is the energy required to raise the temperature of a unit of mass through a one degree Celsius (or Kelvin) temperature rise.

Steady state analysis
In steady state analysis none of the parameters characterizing boundary conditions, material properties or loads is time dependent.

Temperature
Temperature is a measure of heat energy. It can be measured in K (Kelvin), °C (Celsius), and °F (Fahrenheit). Notice that the degree symbol ° is not used with K.

Thermal expansion
Thermal expansion is the tendency of matter to change in a volume in response to a change in temperature. It is described by a coefficient of thermal expansion.

Thermal stress
Thermal stress is stress induced in a structure as a result of non-uniform temperature distribution in the structure.

Transient analysis
An analysis is transient if at least one of the parameters characterizing boundary conditions, material properties or load is time dependent.

View factor
View factor is a ratio of the energy reaching the second surface to the energy emitted by the first surface. If only one surface is involved and it is radiating all of its heat out, the view factor accounts for the fact that some radiation hits the same surface again before being finally radiated out to space.

16: References

This textbook, "Thermal Analysis with SolidWorks Simulation 2012", builds on an understanding of structural analysis with the Finite Element Method and assumes familiarity with structural and introductory thermal analysis to the extent of the textbook listed in (1).

To review fundamentals of Heat Transfer and fundamentals on the Finite Element Method, readers are referred to the following literature listed here in the order of relevance.

1. Kurowski P. "Engineering Analysis with SolidWorks Simulation 2012", Schroff Development Corporation 2012
2. NAFEMS Background to Benchmarks, NAFEMS 1993
3. How to undertake Finite Element Based Thermal Analysis NAFEMS 2002
4. Incropera F., Dewitt D., Bergman T., Lavine A. "Fundamentals of Heat and Mass Transfer", John Wiley & Sons, Inc., 2006
5. Logan D. "A First Course in the Finite Element Method", Brooks/Cole 2007

The full list of NAFEMS publications can be found at www.nafems.org. Another internet site with a number of FEA related publications is presented by Design Generator Inc. Publications related to FEA fundamentals, training, and implementation can be found at: www.designgenerator.com/publications.htm

Notes:

17: List of exercises

Chapter	Part	Assembly
1	BRACKET TH, HEAT SINK 01, DOUBLE SYM, AXI SYM	
2	HOLLOW PLATE TH	
3	L BRACKET TH	
4	STEEL ROD	TWO RODS
5		HEATING DUCTS
6		HEATING DUCTS
7		HOT PLATE
8	MUG	
9	RECT BAR	
10	GRAPHITE BALL	
11	HEMISPHERE	
12		BLOCKS
13	T2, T3,T4	
14	RADIATOR AXISYM	SPACE HEATER